Critical Essays on
Joyce Carol Oates

Critical Essays on Joyce Carol Oates

Linda W. Wagner

G. K. Hall & Co. • Boston, Massachusetts

Library of Congress Cataloging in Publication Data
Main entry under title:

Critical essays on Joyce Carol Oates.

  (Critical essays on American literature)
  Includes bibliographical references and index.
    1. Oates, Joyce Carol, 1938–   —Criticism and
interpretation—Addresses, essays, lectures.
I. Wagner, Linda Welshimer. II. Series.
PS3565.A8Z63   813′.5′4   79-17232
ISBN 0-8161-8224-8

This publication is printed on permanent/durable acid-free paper
MANUFACTURED IN THE UNITED STATES OF AMERICA

CRITICAL ESSAYS ON AMERICAN LITERATURE

This series seeks to provide its readers with the best reprinted criticism available along with, in various volumes, original essays, interviews, bibliographies, letters, manuscript sections, and other materials published for the first time. In accord with these standards, Linda W. Wagner's volume on Joyce Carol Oates reprints important reviews and essays as well as substantial new scholarship. We are honored that Joyce Carol Oates has written the preface for this book. In addition, this volume contains new criticism by Irving Malin, Ellen Friedman, Eileen T. Bender, Peter Stevens, and G. F. Waller. As the first collection of criticism on this writer, this book will make a permanent and important contribution to American literary scholarship.

JAMES NAGEL, GENERAL EDITOR

Northeastern University

CONTENTS

PREFACE

Once a literary work is published it passes forever out of the private and protective world of the writer's imagination, and out of his or her possession. It cannot be reclaimed. It belongs to anyone who happens to come across it, to anyone who happens to have a thought or an emotion or an utterance about it: its merit may be, curiously, that it provokes in *another* person a response that moves beyond the personal and into the problematic dimension of art. For literary criticism, serious criticism, is of course an art-form—one of the most difficult of art-forms.

Should a writer read reviews of his work?—should he read critical essays? Is it possible to learn from others' opinions, others' views? The history of "informed" response to our outstanding writers has been an unhappy one. Faulkner, Henry James, James Joyce, D. H. Lawrence, Herman Melville, Virginia Woolf: all had to suffer objurgation and mockery as well as simple incomprehension. And not only at the hands of professional (i.e. hack) reviewers, for Virginia Woolf appeared to be incapable of reading James Joyce, and Eliot tirelessly insisted that Lawrence's work had no merit, and Lawrence disliked Joyce, and Joyce and Proust saw nothing remarkable in each other's work; and, as his work increased in complexity and scope, Henry James had to suffer increased hostility. That Faulkner's novels should be greeted with perfunctory uncomprehending jeers in *The New Yorker* is highly discouraging, but perhaps instructive. *What*, precisely, is it possible for the writer himself to learn from written response to his work? In our time, I firmly believe, the level of reviewing and critical writing in general has risen substantially—it is an excellent time for writers and critics both—yet the problem remains. A work of art created with any degree of seriousness, over a protracted period of time, reflects, in various rippling quivering layers, the selves that constituted the writer during the period of composition. To write that work one had to be that person, or persons; to see that one ought to have written it differently—with more, or with less, clarity; with more, or with less, humor, or sympathy, or malice, or intelligence, or inventiveness, or self-consciousness—one would have to be another person. At the point at which we *see* ourselves we are no longer the selves we *see*.

Mirrors reflecting mirrors reflecting mirrors—and each subtly distorting that hazy field we call "reality!" Reading reviews and criticism is, then, for the writer, always distracting. But then they are not really written for the writer's eye. One has the uneasy sense that he is violating someone else's privacy—inadvertently reading someone else's mail—letters in which *his* name appears, in an ongoing and systematically developed argument that seems to be about him, yet necessarily excludes him. What is the morality of reading about oneself, when reviews and essays are so clearly written with another audience in

xi

mind? One owes it to one's literary friends, I have often thought, to give them space and freedom and privacy to say whatever they wish: *not*, that is, to read them. And the uncomprehending and dismissive and occasionally malicious notices are too discouraging. Many a writer, confronted with an angry attack, wonders if he had better stop writing—for the original point, that of giving something to the world, a true "gift" of sorts, offered with a necessary humility, seems to have been lost. Artists in our society, it has been observed, draw the kind of vituperative abuse that used to be reserved for ax murderers and corrupt politicians; but since the nature of their "crime" is unclear, they can never hope for acquittal.

Since writing is a highly deliberate craft, one which demands painstaking experimental work, the writer tends to spend most of his time (even while daydreaming) sifting through various aesthetic possibilities. Novelists are the most pragmatic of people. *How* to attain a specific end will quickly come to seem more important (because it involves ingenuity and labor) than *what* the end is. James Joyce's critics have written thousands of pages of critical commentary on his use of the *Odyssey*, but Joyce might have used another classical work instead, or he might have used *Faust*: he needed a structure, as a general might need a bridge to get his troops across a river, and once the end is attained, the means are irrelevant. Moralists like to chide artists for caring more about their art than about morality; but an artist is, by definition, one who grows to care more about the interior workings of his art than about its external appearance, simply because he spends all his time on the interior workings, is fascinated, maddened, defeated, delighted, intimidated, or frustrated by them—no matter that "theme," "subject matter," "plot," or even "message" will strike others as more significant.

Moralizing, visionary, and skeptical impulses contend in most writers, pulling a work in one direction, and then in another. In theory a novel *is* this way, or that way: it celebrates the family, or attacks the family; it praises love, or mocks love; it is "about" the hunt for the White Whale, or "about" an American named Newman in Europe; it moves toward tragedy, or comedy, or satire, or. . . . In theory. But in reality, in the existential unfolding fact of the work, it is always something else, something indefinable. That the writer labors to *discover* the secret essence of the novel is perhaps the writer's most baffling secret, about which he cannot speak, any more than we are capable of speaking about the unconscious—the unconscious being precisely that which is never experienced by consciousness. (For dreams return to us only as memories, and "memories" are phenomena of consciousness.)

For the writer it is the scaffolding that made his work possible, which was of course removed when the work was completed, that may have been, in fact, the secret (and ceaselessly exciting) reason for the work's creation. Or he may have ached to employ, for decades, a certain stretch of sandy soil by a railroad track, where yarrow, blackeyed-Susan, and Queen Anne's lace grew . . . or he may have wanted to describe an abandoned country cemetery . . . or a wide windy desolate Detroit street . . . or perhaps it was a fragment of conversation, imperfectly overheard . . . or an intuition of such vivid, heartstopping authority that it seemed to have come from a source beyond himself. Perhaps, on the other hand, quite coolly, he wanted to decide for himself the "problem" of evil—what better way than to construct a novel elaborate and ingenious enough to dramatize every conceivable point of view?

But once the work is completed these initial ideas—these impulses—fade. They are absorbed into the texture of the work and cannot be extracted from it. No reader would guess at them; no critic would care about them; and the writer himself, as time passes, will gradually forget.

Apart from the paraphernalia of professional reviewing and criticism, apart from the dizzying phenomenon of mirrors reflecting mirrors, one *does* hope, however quixotically, for the ideal reader. To have that ideal reader—or two, or three—or a half-dozen—seems to make the effort worthwhile. And I count myself remarkably blessed that I have these ideal readers, as a number of contributions to this collection suggest.

JOYCE CAROL OATES
January, 1979

Joyce Carol Oates
Chronology of Books

1963   *By the North Gate* (stories)

1964   *With Shuddering Fall*

1966   *Upon the Sweeping Flood* (stories)

1967   *A Garden of Earthly Delights*

1968   *Expensive People*   *Women in Love* (poems)

1969   *them*   *Anonymous Sins* (poems)

1970   *The Wheel of Love and Other Stories*   *Love and Its Derangements* (poems)

1971   *Wonderland*

1972   *Marriages and Infidelities* (stories)   *The Edge of Impossibility: Tragic Forms in Literature*
                                                 ed., *Scenes from American Life: Contemporary Short Fiction*

1973   *Do With Me What You Will*   *Angel Fire* (poems)
                                      Dreaming America and Other Poems

1974   *The Hungry Ghosts: Seven Allusive Comedies*   *New Heaven, New Earth: The Visionary Experience in Literature*
        The Goddess and Other Women   *Miracle Play*
        Where Are You Going? Where Have You Been? Stories of Young America

1975   *The Assassins: A Book of Hours*   *Fabulous Beasts* (poems)
        The Seduction and Other Stories
        The Poisoned Kiss and Other Stories from the Portuguese, by "Fernandes."

1976   *Childwold*
        Crossing the Border (stories)
        The Triumph of the Spider Monkey

1977   *Night-side* (stories)   *Season of Peril* (poems)

1978   *[The] Son of the Morning*   *Women Whose Lives Are Food, Men Whose Lives Are Money* (poems)
        Collected Short Stories: All the Good People I've Left Behind

INTRODUCTION

Joyce Carol Oates:
The Changing Shapes of Her Realities*

I. THE WORK

The appearance of Joyce Carol Oates on the mid-sixties literary scene has been termed "phenomenal" by more critics than one. After the publication of *By the North Gate* in 1963 and *With Shuddering Fall* in 1964, collections of stories, poetry, novels, plays, and books of literary criticism have been published almost without interruption—several volumes to the year—with a regularity that showed Oates' terrific dedication to her work. There was never any question of her being possessed by a competitive spirit, of being frenetic or frugal in using old material—she was, rather, the serious writer intent on telling stories, an artist in the Dostoevsky-Balzac-Faulkner mode who believed in the writer's responsibility to draw a culture and its people, to present its discrete components so that readers might gradually come to understand some of the mystery that life at its most complex includes. " 'I have a laughably Balzacian ambition to get the whole world into a book,' "[1] she confessed in 1972; and, in 1978, she added a stronger moral element to that ambition:

> A writer's job, ideally, is to act as the conscience of his race. People frequently misunderstand serious art because it is often violent and unattractive. I wish the world were a prettier place, but I wouldn't be honest as a writer if I ignored the actual conditions around me.[2]

In 1979, Joyce Carol Oates has retained that wide ambition (to be both moral conscience and Balzacian observer), along with that early reputation as phenomenon. She has now published thirty-five books, at only slightly past forty herself. She has been Professor of English at the University of Windsor for a decade, having taught before that at the University of Detroit (from Lockport, New York, she was educated at Syracuse University and the University of Wisconsin). She is one of America's most productive and diligent writer-teachers, whose energies go consistently into new directions for her work, and into describing those directions in countless reviews and essays about other writing. Her interest in craft, sometimes obscured by the apparent ease with which she writes, surfaces frequently when she discusses literature; her enthusiasm for the contemporary is evident when she says, in 1978, "it *is* a good time to be an imaginative writer. Most writers today are free of the necessity of telling a story

*Reprinted with permission in part from *The Great Lakes Review*, 5 (Winter 1979).

in a conventional manner; now we are able to use fantasy and surrealism and even mythic and fairy-tale elements in our art."

To view Oates' fiction in retrospect is to be surprised that what seemed to be basically "realistic" fiction has so many variations, and shows such range of experimentation, such wealth of literary antecedent. But whether she writes a comic *Expensive People*, an impressionistic *Childwold*, or that strangely heightened realism of *them* and the short stories, her interest is less in technical innovation than it is in trying the border between the real and the illusory, in testing the space in which those two seemingly separate entities converge. As she once wrote, "Most literature deals either consciously or unconsciously with the problem of reality: it asks what is real in the world, which values are real. . . ."[4]

Oates' conviction—made increasingly clear in the progression of her fiction—is that people in the modern world generally pretend to be tied to the factual, the largely physical details of living (accordingly, reassuringly, she will give numerous details about a dimestore cosmetic counter or a physician's crowded dining table). But although we focus on these tangible props, our understanding of them does not necessarily help us apprehend the larger forces behind them. Oates has repeatedly been called a "realist" because her technique often does suggest that method; but for the most part, her accumulation of fact is an irony—locating and describing the easily discernible is precisely what will *not* work in any full confrontation with reality. Much of her fiction operates from that premise: the countless details of Jules' life in *them* finally do not explain his behavior during the 1967 riots, just as Elena's history in *Do With Me What You Will* does little to explicate her acts. The fascination for Oates as writer lies in acknowledging that her readers' interest will center on character rather than on milieu ("All literature deals with contests of will"[5]), and then working within a method which seems to emphasize the latter.

If Oates is never a simple realist, neither is she the traditional character-oriented story teller. Her insistence on the importance of character remains oblique to usual protestations of that sort. Since one of the comforts of art is that it allows the artist to create order, to impose a personal moral standard on chaotic surroundings, most writers use character to reflect those personal standards. Agamemnon receives a heinous punishment for what most readers could distinguish as his tragic flaw of pride; Tess of the D'Urbervilles, like Jay Gatsby, suffers because of the moral hypocrisy of the culture: in these cases we reflect the authors' judgments about their characters. The point is that there *are* acknowledged, and shared, judgments. Because life operates thus and so, predictable things—just or not—happen. Injustices can confirm the system as clearly as justice, and more dramatically.

In Oates' fiction, for all its emphasis on fact and all its reliance on powerful character, the assumption that the artist is in control is clearly absent. Artist-as-judge has become artist-as-recorder. Her readers have sometimes expressed dismay that such unpleasant things happen to characters, while Oates as author appears to have little opinion about these reprehensible situations—little opinion, little sympathy, little outrage. What kind of moral judgment underlies

Oates' fiction? So different is her approach to the use of character-to-instruct that many readers feel uncomfortable interpreting her fiction. Despite the rhetoric modern writers gave to being objective, the difference between Oates and Hemingway proves how seldom that 1920's "objectivity" was truly impartial. Hemingway consistently judged his characters; much of his narrative was spent reporting to the reader which characters' behavior met his code. Oates seldom reports; she tends to judge implicitly. Content to observe people in their usually mundane worlds, she presents them in their touching inarticulateness; most important, she ascribes little if any "meaning" to their suffering. Recognizing the mysteries of life—especially at this commonplace and often silent level—is Oates' accomplishment; translating that mute suffering so that readers are moved by it even when they do not fully understand it is her aim. As she explained in a 1974 interview, "the main thing about me is that I am enormously interested in other people, other lives. . . . I am fascinated by people I meet . . . and I hope my interest in them isn't vampiristic, because I don't want to take life from them but only to honor the life in them, to give some permanent form to their personalities. It seems to me that there are so many people who are inarticulate but who suffer and doubt and love, nobly, who need to be immortalized or at least explained."[6]

Oates' fascination with character has, in effect, created her prolegomenon, for her world view is one that recognizes the primacy of emotion over reason, that emphasizes the reality of human passion. As she asks in the preface to *The Edge of Impossibility*, "what are we except passion, and how are we to survive when this passion breaks its dikes and flows out into nature? . . . Art is built around violence, around death; at its base is fear."[7] The force, the intensity of passion, is an index of a character's being able to transcend the trivial. All these details in Oates' fiction insist, more clearly than any philosophical treatise could, that the mundane will only starve us; that coherent pattern is not, in itself, adequate. Her admiration for writers such as Chekhov, Yeats, and the absurdist playwrights stems from the fact that they resist "systematic definitions"; they "remain true to their subject—life—by refusing to reduce their art to a single emotion and idea."[8]

As Oates matured as a writer, and as she moved from the generally realistic method of her earliest fiction, she came to value most those writers who were not afraid to plumb the human mysteries, to run that "course between unknowable extremities, the antimonies of day and night, life and death." In her study of D. H. Lawrence as well as in her essays on Yeats, her emphasis falls consistently on their audacity, their attempt to deal with all "the richness of pain and chaos."[9] She writes admiringly, "Yeats' works are filled with violence. It is the flooding of the ego by the fury of the veins, a sudden and irrevocable alliance with nature's chaos."[10] In this fusion of passions, some spark of the unknowable catches the observers' attention (and the act of "observation" shares in that emotional fusion; it is never so detached, clinical, as the word out of context might suggest).

Her 1973 collection of short fiction, *Scenes from American Life*, presents a paradigm of Oates' personal movement from the ostensibly objective and factual to the strange, mysterious, fantastic—or, at least, inexplicable. As she explains in her preface,

> this anthology begins with stories that appear—like our most innocuous dreams—to be "realistic," "normal." It concludes with strange stories that call attention to themselves as artificial constructions, daring us to believe in them. The gradual movement from one to the other, from lies that seem quite plausible to lies that exhibit themselves proudly as lies, is not meant to suggest any development, any progress from simple to complex—and certainly it is not meant to suggest any degeneration, any fashionable decadence![11]

Whatever the technique—and her anthology emphasizes that great range of technique and approach of which the contemporary reader has long been aware—at base "there are the same kinds of human emotions, someone's vivid psychic experience. . . . Emotions flow from one personality to another, altering someone's conception of the world: this is the moment of art, the magical experience of art. It is a revelation."[12]

Oates' own stylistic changes, and her approaches to what have remained remarkably consistent themes, depend in large part on that kind of progression—from dealing with "lies that seem quite plausible" to "lies that exhibit themselves proudly as lies"; from the painfully serious to the near-comic or grotesque; from the halting pace of detailed realism to the flurry of surreal speed. The progression is not, of course, rigid; hints of Oates' later styles occurred in her first writings (sections of *Son of the Morning*, 1978, share many qualities with passages in *A Garden of Earthly Delights*, for example). The connotation of "progression" to suggest a linear course is somewhat misleading: Oates' later fiction moves instead toward an unfolding, an opening; its movement is circular rather than linear, hoping to lead in and down as well as out, aiming toward revealing those emotions common to every person—reader, character, author.

Throughout Oates' fiction, the emotion that recurs most often is a numbing disbelief. Clara in *A Garden of Earthly Delights* "wondered how she would live out the rest of her life"[13] as Lowry left her. She is sixteen. "I never expected happiness. I was trying to survive" one heroine says as she marries a man even less suitable than her first husband had been. And "The Lady with the Pet Dog" confesses, "I'm not unhappy, back there. I'm nothing. There's nothing to me." In a moment of introspection she too asks, "How will I live out the rest of my life?"[14] Very few of Oates' characters ever glimpse any idea of individual potential.

Most of them look for fulfillment in romantic love, although in Oates' fiction, genuine love is rare. It remains illusive, even though mentor figures deify it: "A man must love and must be loved or he himself cannot be healed, cannot heal others."[15] Oates' plots are often based on the search for love; perhaps that is one reason she writes frequently about teenagers, though her characters of every age and marital state are usually in quest of some idealized romance. This pervasive use of the love relationship suggests the real vacuum in the lives (and imaginations) of her characters. For example, the single-mindedness of the fifteen-year-old Connie in "Where Are You Going, Where Have You

Been?" underscores the assumptions of the title—women and girls are possessions to be watched, valuable chiefly for their physical properties (beauty, chastity). In Oates' cryptic accumulation of detail, she conveys not only literal meanings but also attitudes toward the women described:

> Her name was Connie. She was fifteen and she had a quick, nervous giggling habit of craning her neck to glance into mirrors or checking other people's faces to make sure her own was all right. Her mother, who noticed everything and knew everything and who hadn't much reason any longer to look at her own face, always scolded Connie about it. "Stop gawking at yourself. Who are you? You think you're so pretty?" she would say. Connie would raise her eyebrows at these familiar old complaints and look right through her mother, into a shadowy vision of herself as she was right at that moment: she knew she was pretty and that was everything. Her mother had been pretty once too, if you could believe those old snapshots in the album, but now her looks were gone and that was why she was always after Connie.[16]

Choosing the term "psychological realism," Oates achieves her seemingly objective tone here at least partly by writing in third person. No matter how many factual details she gives about a character, the point of view distances the reader, as in this scene from *A Garden of Earthly Delights* when Swan, Clara's illegitimate son, makes his pledge to protect his mother,

> So Swan understood. Revere was going to be his father, but his real father was someone else. He felt that suddenly. He and his mother had a secret no one could make them tell. He would die with that secret. He would protect his mother from anyone who threatened her, he would never tell, never, he would grow up and take care of her and do everything she wanted and even Clara herself would never know that he knew. He had years to do it in. . . . There was an excitement in him that was like breathing in the glare of the sun itself, something too big and too strong for him but filling all the same.[17]

Privy to the thoughts and assumptions of the characters in these novels, the reader still has the process of coming to these realizations handed to him by Oates; knowledge in Oates' early novels is presented didactically. By the time of *them*, 1969, she has modified her third-person exposition enough to rely a bit more on the image and scene conveying meaning. Here, Jules and Nadine have just finished making love:

> Jules saw the pillows for the first time: white with dark green stitching on the edges. Everything was strange. He felt the slim curve of her body with his hands, fascinated with her skin. He could not remember any other woman, was not certain that he had ever done this before. Everything was washed out of his mind; there was nothing authentic in his experience; what was his personal history might have been stolen from movies and books, the imaginations of other people.[18]

What is most impressive about this scene is that one feels some authenticity to Jules' reactions; Oates seems to be relying on his fantasies rather than on her own need to convey information. The prose rhythms are much like those from the passage quoted about Swan, but the direction of the content makes it a different kind of passage. For all its third-person perspective, it resembles the kind of stream-of-consciousness she used in *Expensive People* and would use to a greater extent in *The Assassins: A Book of Hours* and *Childwold*.

> God speaks. In these voices. Haunting, tender, maddening. . . . But there is no
> God, there are no voices. There are phantasms in my brain, mere projections, shards
> of old desires, split-off fragments of my soul that yearn to coalesce, to be born. There
> is no God. I am not filled with God. I am pure consciousness trapped in time, in a
> body, I am unenlightened, I am dragged in a circle, I am helpless to fight free, I am
> licking the feet, the dirty feet, of the devils who dance about me, mocking me. . . .[19]

The possessed Kasch of *Childwold* could only be believable through an interior
monologue. Of the three novels, Oates' first-person technique works best in
Childwold, at least partly because Kasch as character is reasonably sympathetic. The same cannot be said of Richard Everett, the adolescent in *Expensive
People* who assumes he has murdered his mother, Nada; and the protagonists of
The Assassins, with the possible exception of Yvonne. Oates' change to first
person enables her to follow the non-rational impulses of her characters, to give
her readers some insight into that mysterious world of emotion that prompts
most action. For her at least, the third-person appeared to be less flexible; and
those characters developed in fiction told objectively too often remained enig-
mas to her readers. The mixture of first and third in *Son of the Morning* works
very well; this novel also has a concentration of focus on a single character that is
new to Oates' fiction.

Regardless of the difference in effect between Oates' third-person and
first-person narrative, her fiction continues to show patterns and oddities of
contemporary life. As she had announced in 1970, accepting the National Book
Award for Fiction, for *them*:

> In the novels I have written, I have tried to give a shape to certain obsessions of mid-
> century Americans—a confusion of love and money, of the categories of public and
> private experience, of a demonic urge I sense all around me, an urge to violence as
> the answer to all problems, an urge to self-annihilation, suicide, the ultimate experi-
> ence and the ultimate surrender. The use of language is all we have to pit against
> death and silence.[20]

Oates' concluding scene of the Yvonne section of *The Assassins* is a correlative
image for that demonic urge—and the lack of language to combat it. As Yvonne
lies nearly (or, perhaps, already) dead, her unnamed assassin hacks into her
wrist with an ax, and we as readers watch the inept dismemberment. The crime
is reasonless, the killers are strangers, Yvonne has no answer but silence:

> The man with the ax stood squarely, his feet apart. He raised the ax, he grimaced,
> brought it down hard on her wrist—in one stroke it cut through the bone and severed
> the hand. She could not scream. Everything slipped from her, was mute. . . .[21]

Horrifying as this senseless killing is, there is a near-parody of the traditional
American ethic of a job well done (with all the ingredients for a "Big Two-
Hearted River" scene—the powerful man, set for the task ahead, absorbed
completely in it). In fact, the scene closes not with a focus on Yvonne or on the
man's partners who are sickened by the crime, but with attention to this execu-
tioner's complete dedication: "His teeth flashed with the effort, he wiped his
forehead with the back of his hand, he balanced himself squarely on the balls of
his feet and continued his work."

What appear to be simple factual details in this scene illustrate that strain of pervasive irony Oates uses so well, even to the final emphasis on the Puritanical phrase "his work." For a writer so dedicated to shaping our vision of American culture, and so interested in revealing the mysterious forces of human response, Oates' later novels hardly diminish the bleakness of her first fiction; but their method is somewhat changed. That her canvas remains the same is more a charge to our responsibility than to hers. The guilt of *The Assassins* is, of course, everyone's guilt; and the escape for which Kasch yearns, completely understandable.

II. THE CRITICISM

Critical reaction to Oates' writing has varied unpredictably in the past seventeen years. That reaction could serve as a barometer for changes in literary taste during the 1960s and 1970s, as the once respectable mode of realism fell further and further from fashion. Even when Oates chose methods other than those ascribed to realism, critics persisted in emphasizing her early efforts, in seeing all her writing as an outgrowth of the original fiction. It seems ironic that throughout these years Oates has remained not only an important realist but a perceptive social observer; but that such designations, which were clearly positive during the mid-sixties, have become tarnished with repetition. The range of Oates' critical reception has been from enthusiastic praise to the present "faint praise" which undermines even if it does not directly attack.

Criticism of Oates' work also points out the mixed blessing of acquiring a public personality early in one's career. Less flamboyant, certainly, than Norman Mailer or Gertrude Stein, Oates has often attracted notice because of her very lack of drama. Her photograph appears frequently in news magazines, partly because of her youth but more often because the wistful innocence of her expression surprises the reader who expects some brusque physiognomy. Critics often comment on the supposed disparity between Oates' fiction and her appearance—the classic account being Alfred Kazin's "Oates" in *Harper's* (August, 1971)—as if certain literary techniques demanded stereotypical physical and psychological qualities.

By the North Gate, Oates' first collection of stories, received consistent praise for its unflinching realism. Critics responded favorably to her choice of mundane subjects and characters, to her skill in creating "poor or at any rate not very prosperous people." As Granville Hicks continued, "They are likely to be suffering, either through physical affliction or because of some kind of frustration. Their moments of joy, if there are any, are so brief as to have a pathos of their own."[22] Edith Copeland in reviewing the collection laments the absence of joy, but praises the effect of "weariness, sadness, confusion" that Oates achieves.[23] Haskel Frankel, writing in *Saturday Review*, hits squarely the issue of Oates' use of violence:

> Though many of these stories contain violence, violence is never the author's sole concern. In story after story she fuses realism with poetry to reveal life as something always a little larger than those who live it.[24]

The recurring controversy over Oates' use of violent scenes makes Frankel's early observation impressive.

Besides being favorable, early reviews were also anticipatory; several critics said, in effect, wait till Oates' first novel. Perhaps that anticipation was one reason the 1964 *With Shuddering Fall* was tepidly received. The convention of praising Oates-the-short-story-writer while criticizing Oates-the-novelist was born here (and continues: in 1971 Roger Sale declared *Wonderland* "a great anguished slab of a book" but concluded that Oates "is as yet only a writer of short stories"[25]). Why the hierarchy of criticism relegates short fiction to inferior rank has never been explained but it was also the tactic taken by Stanley Kaufmann when he criticized Oates' "inflated" novel style.[26]

Part of the negative response to *With Shuddering Fall* may have stemmed from the difference between reading Oates in the short story form (she had been published since 1959, so readers had had access to her short fiction) and in the novel shape. While *With Shuddering Fall* is probably the least effective of her longer works, it undoubtedly did not deserve the relatively negative reaction it received. In contrast, the reception for Oates' second story collection, *Upon the Sweeping Flood and Other Stories*, 1966, was positive. Joan Joffe Hall commended Oates' "unquestionable power" and her intense and distinctive personal vision. An Oates' story is identifiable, claims Hall, although she questions whether or not improvements could be made: just because characters fail to understand reasons for their behavior, perhaps Oates could allow readers to glimpse some of those reasons.[27] David Madden has no such problem with Oates' characters. He complains about her studied lack of technical proficiency but concludes that "She is one of the few writers today who has the vision to disturb my sleep."[28]

In 1967 Oates began publication of the three novels which she considered a trilogy. *A Garden of Earthly Delights*, the study of migrant laborers and their children, was followed by the 1968 *Expensive People*, in which the adolescent protagonist seemingly murders his mother. That expose of suburban life was then followed in 1969 with Oates' story of inner-city Detroit and its 1967 riots, *them*. The latter won the National Book Award for Fiction and brought Oates' work to the attention of many more readers than had known her short stories.

Critical reception of *A Garden of Earthly Delights* was extremely enthusiastic. The novel impressed readers with its sustained tone of bleak deprivation, whether focusing on Carleton Walpole or his daughter Clara. Their struggle to survive during the Depression excused these characters from the moral responsibility readers tended to expect. The relationship between Oates' story of these migrants—and their accumulation by whatever means of the wealth America could provide—and the painting of Hieronymus Bosch also provided helpful insights. The lives of the characters in this novel were meant to be unrewarding, uninspiring: their mistaken search for vanities could bring them only to disaster.

Oates' shift in theme, subject, and technique made the second novel of the trilogy, *Expensive People*, one of her most controversial. Whereas *A Garden* was easily labeled realistic, even naturalistic, *Expensive People* was a montage of stream of consciousness, parody, fantasy, and juxtaposed sections of literary comment and reviews. Of her style, Bernard Bergonzi wrote, with evident relief,

> Her previous books were written in a turgid, sub-Faulknerian manner; by contrast, *Expensive People* is stylistically more relaxed and sharper. Here the mentors seem to be Salinger and Updike and Nabokov.[29]

A departure from the usual comparisons to Theodore Dreiser, Bergonzi's remarks were echoed in many reviews—but often with less than approval. Readers were accustomed to Oates as realist; they could see no defensible, or even explicable, reason for such radical change. In *Expensive People*, too, Oates abandoned her usual omniscient point of view to write in the first person of the murderer-son, Richard Everett, a character most readers found reprehensible. Even though she was using a technique that usually allowed readers to identify with character, the very nature of that character here prevented easy identification.

Reviews of *Expensive People* showed that, by 1968, Oates' reputation had grown increasingly vulnerable. If she adhered to the style that had become recognizably hers, readers could charge her with lack of innovation; and during the 1960s, innovation was primary. If she tried different approaches, as she had in her recent novel, readers were bewildered and took refuge in unanswerable questions—what was the purpose of this novel of violence and tragedy? Of any such novel? Indeed, what was the purpose of fiction? As Bergonzi had evasively asked, "Miss Oates' talents are evident enough, but the real question is what she intends doing with them, and whether she can see herself going beyond the imitation of established masters and the reenactment of familiar cultural myths." Most writers would be glad to be credited with "the imitation of established masters and the reenactment of familiar cultural myths."[30] It was clear that Oates was being asked to live up to excessive expectations.

With *them*, the 1969 completion of the trilogy, Oates moved to a generally realistic approach. Regardless of style, however, *them* caught the interest of the American public at least partly because the Detroit riots were still so vivid. This was fiction with social comment, social and political identity; Oates was apparently trying to record the contemporary scene as well as explain the characters involved in creating that scene. Both in event and psychology, *them* was timely. It was, however, also subject to a surprising range of critical reaction. G. W., writing in *Newsweek*, exclaimed,

> This novel is a charnel house of Gothic paraphernalia: blood, fire, insanity, anarchy, lust, corruption, death by bullets, death by cancer, death by plane crash, death by stabbing, beatings, crime, riot, and even unhappiness.[31]

Simultaneously, Dorothy Curley was writing in *Library Journal* that *them* was "a rather sadly old-fashioned novel about a poor family." The novel "tries to be contemporary and ends up expository and romantic and earnestly out of it. . . .

somehow her vision of what people feel now in the inner city in riot areas is as naive as a proto-Martian's might be."[32]

For most critics and readers, *them* is a well-executed novel with several interesting plot lines and strong, comparatively sympathetic characters. Maureen Wendell, the former student whose letters supposedly give Oates the idea for the story, is "the crown of this book and its reason for being; she is one of the enduring women of contemporary American fiction." L. E. Sissman sees Maureen as being an image for "the whole truth of the book," both in her character and "her despairing, hopeful attempts to escape the cage of her life— and the cage of her person—as she grows older." In his respect for the novel, Sissman stresses that "it succeeds in reproducing the psychological tenor of poverty—a series of stultifying routines interrupted irregularly and arbitrarily by radical change and blinding violence—and its stunting effect on the emotional scope of the poor."[33]

Despite the fact that *them* won the National Book Award for Fiction, the divided critical response to Oates' writing continued. Of the 1971 novel, *Wonderland*, the reviewer for *Times Literary Supplement* ranted, "Virtually any page taken at random . . . would almost certainly put the majority of readers . . . off exploring further." Aimed for "the sensation-mongering American market," the novel is "an impressionistic exposure of what is wrong with American society today." The apparently British reviewer warned in conclusion that any reader would have to "wade through the gore and guts and passion."[34] For S. K. Oberbeck, *Wonderland* is "a sepia-toned, small-town American *Buddenbrooks*," replete with black humor and grotesque social commentary, with Oates' target this time being the medical profession.[35] In her alternation between novels about poverty and novels about affluent Americans, Oates may have been suggesting that corruption and despair exist everywhere. That her technique varies with the subject of her work may have suggested as well that one method is hardly adequate for treatment of every theme, portrayal of every kind of character. Whatever the cause of her alternating subject matter, readers appeared to be more receptive to her stories about poverty. *A Garden of Earthly Delights* and *them* were consistently better received than *Expensive People* and *Wonderland*, just as *Do With Me What You Will*, another novel given a quasi-realistic treatment, was better received than the more experimental *The Assassins: A Book of Hours* and *Childwold*.

Another reason for the approachability of *Garden*, *them*, and *Do With Me What You Will* (1973) might be their focus on female characters. While Oates has never been considered a feminist writer (indeed, she has sometimes been criticized because her women characters are seldom self-realizing, and often victimized), she does frequently write about women. Many reviewers have commented that this female character or that in Oates' fiction is particularly sympathetic; considering that Oates is not usually praised for creating characters with whom one can feel sympathy, such a pattern of commentary is significant.

There is little question that Oates has long been interested in the roles of women in modern society. If her early work had portrayed women as victims, often unknowing victims, perhaps that picture was credible. As Mary Allen concludes in her recent study, *The Necessary Blankness: Women in Major American Fiction of the Sixties,*

> . . . no one is better at showing the female consciousness aware of the possibilities of rape than Joyce Carol Oates. She is a master at depicting women's anxieties of many sorts, and she makes a striking contribution to our understanding of contemporary America as seen by women. Here is an author to read if one dares to know the particular fear there is in being a woman. . . .[36]

Allen stresses, too, Oates' insistence that most people's characters and lives are determined by their economic position. She finds that Oates consistently admires poor women who manage to bring themselves out of poverty, even if misguidedly. Oates' sympathy often colors the creation of these characters so that in her fiction, Allen finds, "The women of the middle and upper classes seldom come to life as her lower-class women do."[37]

Reviews of Oates' *Do With Me What You Will* and *The Goddess and Other Women*, her 1974 story collection, pivot on these issues of her choice and treatment of women characters. Elena Howe, protagonist of the novel about the Detroit legal profession, is only faintly self-actualizing but the fact that she does act—in leaving her possessive husband and coercing her lover to come with her—is both positive and, given some of Oates' earlier women characters, unexpected. As Mary Ellmann observed in *The New York Review of Books*, "Elena Howe moves only a little in the novel," but to move at all is crucial: the title comes from her husband Martin Howe's phrase *nolo contendere* (the client's putting himself or herself at the mercy of the court); and what Oates continuously emphasizes is that Elena "rejects that solution" and manages to contend with the two seemingly stronger men who would manipulate her life. For Ellmann's tastes, the novel is an all-too-accurate picture of women's dependent position in modern America, though she finds the ending unjustified: "For all her modesty, Joyce Carol Oates is a hortatory feminist. She enforces her convictions upon a heroine unsuited to them."[38]

Charles Shapiro and other readers disagree that Elena's metamorphosis is surprising. Shapiro describes Elena as

> a woman who seems always to be used, almost a parody of the women who exist only as defined by others. But she is much more. She has, in literal fact, lived through the nightmares that lie just beneath the surfaces of too many lives.[39]

Elena has the courage to change her life because of her knowledge of these past realities. Oates' presentation of Elena is, then, another image of the appearance-reality theme that suffuses so much of her fiction, a theme which is particularly relevant to her women characters since the modern culture—for all its rhetoric about liberation—relies heavily on appearance.

Several critics admired *Do With Me What You Will* for its structural finesse, a change in opinion about most of Oates' novels. Walter Clemons termed it "a striking gain in intellectual poise and control."[40] J. A. Avant praised its structure as paralleling the court presentation and the attorneys' summing up.[41]*New Yorker*, however, considered such a parallel "gimmicky," called the novel "mawkish" and described it as "a numbingly long nineteen-seventies version of 'The Sleeping Beauty.' "[42]

The same kind of widely-divided opinion greeted *The Goddess and Other Women* the following year. *The New Republic* called it "her worst"[43]while Canadian novelist Marian Engel, writing in *The New York Times Book Review*, termed it a "magnificent achievement."[44] Bruce Allen considered it "a terrible and exciting book"[45]while Edward Bartley found it repetitive.[46] As Robert Phillips pointed out in his *Commonweal* review, Oates' story collections are "carefully constructed totalities, works in their own right."[47] In *The Goddess* "we are given a succession of vital occasions in the lives of women of all classes and mentalities, often pitting the dichotomies of passivity versus destructiveness. . . . These stories counterpoint beautifully, though the long book at times seems unrelieved by humor or optimism. As a total, *The Goddess and Other Women* is a thought-provoking document on love, hate, and pain in women's lives."[48]

As with Elena Howe in *Do With Me What You Will*, the protagonists in the stories of *The Goddess* demanded some identification from readers. Readers disinterested in women's lives would more than likely be more hostile to the collection than those who found the subject matter vital. This element of reader identification surely underlay the wide divergence in critical opinion about the collection, and probably colored reaction to Oates' 1975 novel, *The Assassins: A Book of Hours* as well.

The pattern which seemed to mark the review of Oates' fiction during the 1970s was repeated in the reception of *The Assassins*. Many critics voiced disappointment. Brian Weiss, writing in *Best Sellers*, said simply that the novel fails. Suzanne Juhasz was disturbed by the length of the book, the garrulousness of the prose. A. P. Klausler counts the novel a failure because we do not care about any of the major characters, although he also finds it "a parable for our times."[49] This was the positive tactic taken by such reviews as that in *Time*, that Oates is to be commended for undertaking these portrayals of "the violence that lodges in the American heart"[50]; similar comments greeted the 1978 *Son of the Morning*.

The pervasive tone of reviews was, however, much less charitable and tended to echo an earlier comment of Michael Wood, writing in *The New York Times Book Review*, when he terms Oates' fiction "self-indulgent, a refusal by the writer to know what she knows."[51] Even *Time* was not above referring to Oates as "the somewhat too prodigious Joyce Carol Oates" and suggesting that she needed to "steady her grip" on her writing.[52]

There were good reviews yet to come, as when Bruce Allen wrote of *Childwold* in 1976 that it was "a remarkable feat of construction" written in "a striking departure from Oates' usual methods: it is a compressed, impressionistic portrayal of a lonely madman's encounter with a beautiful teenage girl . . . highly organized and stylized."[53] For the most part, however, at this point in the late 1970s, criticism of Oates' fiction seems to be divided into three camps. There are those critics who staunchly commend whatever Oates writes: "a master,"[54] declares William Abrahams; a "great writer,"[55] J. A. Avant; "one of America's best writers of short stories,"[56] says Robert Phillips. There are others, often academic critics, who find satisfaction in disliking whatever Oates writes—as when Josephine Hendin comments about Oates' "raw spleen"[57] or Helen Vendler takes her roundly to task for the quality of her poetry.[58] The third set of critics seems willing to judge each book on its own merits, although the tendency has been, with the most recent books, to announce both disappointment with the writing at hand, and fear that Oates' subsequent fiction will be even less satisfactory.

Clearly, Oates' critical reputation will profit from the book-length scholarly studies now either in preparation or recently published. The first of these, Sister Mary Kathryn Grant's *The Tragic Vision of Joyce Carol Oates*, appeared in 1978 from Duke University Press. By placing Oates' fiction within the genre of tragedy, Sister Mary Kathryn stresses that although Oates uses violence and spiritual poverty in her fiction, her purpose in that use is to move the reader toward a new consciousness.[59] This reading would seem to be in line with Oates' own comment, "With *Wonderland* I came to the end of a phase of my life, though I didn't know it. I want to move toward a more articulate moral position, not just dramatizing nightmarish problems but trying to show possible ways of transcending them."[60] Other books establishing Oates' aesthetic and philosophy will be those by Joanne Creighton, whose study in the Twayne United States Authors series will appear soon, Ellen Friedman, and G. F. Waller. Chapters from each of those manuscripts are included in this collection, so that readers can preview the approach and method of these competent and perceptive critics.

In addition, this collection of criticism includes a sampling of reviews contemporary with each of Oates' novels and some of her story collections; as well as major critical statements about her work from such esteemed critics as Alfred Kazin, Walter Sullivan, Granville Hicks, Benjamin DeMott, Irving Malin and others. Peter Stevens' essay discusses all of Oates' poetry; G. F. Waller's places her later writing in a context useful to any reader of contemporary fiction. It is a useful book, and I am thankful that so many excellent critics allowed their work to be included in it. But it is a collection that comes near the beginning for Oates' career: it attempts to chart those beginnings, and to give some indication of possible directions; but the wise reader needs to keep in mind Oates' own explanatory warning, that much art is incapable of being explicated fully:

> Every person dreams, and every dreamer is a kind of artist. The formal artist is one who arranges his dreams into a shape that can be experienced by other people. There is no guarantee that art will be understood, not even by the artist; it is not meant to be understood but to be experienced.[61]

My thanks to all the critics included in this collection, to James Nagel for suggesting what has been a most useful project, and to Ms. Oates herself for her suggestions, and most of all for her work.

LINDA W. WAGNER

East Lansing, Michigan

Notes

1. Quoted by Walter Clemons in "Joyce Carol Oates: Love and Violence," *Newsweek*, December 11, 1972, p. 72.

2. Quoted in "Author Joyce Carol Oates on 'Adolescent America,' " *U.S. News and World Report*, May 15, 1978, p. 60.

3. Oates, *U.S. News and World Report*, p. 60.

4. Joyce Carol Oates, *The Edge of Impossibility: Tragic Forms in Literature* (New York: Vanguard Press, 1972), p. 225.

5. *Edge*, p. 118.

6. Quoted by Joe David Bellamy in *The New Fiction, Interviews with Innovative American Writers* (Urbana: Univ. of Illinois Press, 1974), p. 31.

7. *Edge*, pp. 4, 6.

8. *Edge*, pp. 141, 137.

9. *Edge*, p. 161.

10. *Edge*, p. 157.

11. Joyce Carol Oates, "Fiction, Dreams, Revelations," preface to *Scenes from American Life: Contemporary Short Fiction* (New York: Random House, 1973), p. viii.

12. Oates, "Fiction, Dreams, Revelations," p. viii.

13. Joyce Carol Oates, *A Garden of Earthly Delights* (New York: Vanguard Press, 1967), p. 213.

14. Joyce Carol Oates, *Marriages and Infidelities* (Greenwich, Conn.: Fawcett Press, 1972), pp. 352, 329.

15. *Marriages*, p. 350.

16. Joyce Carol Oates, *Where Are You Going, Where Have You Been? Stories of Young America* (Greenwich, Conn.: Fawcett Press, 1974), p. 11.

17. *A Garden*, p. 303.

18. Joyce Carol Oates, *them* (Greenwich, Conn.: Fawcett Press, 1969), p. 358.

19. Joyce Carol Oates, *Childwold* (New York: Vanguard Press, 1976), p. 103.

20. Quoted as an appendix in Sister Mary Kathryn Grant's *The Tragic Vision of Joyce Carol Oates* (Durham, N.C.: Duke Univ. Press, 1978), p. 164.

21. Joyce Carol Oates, *The Assassins: A Book of Hours* (New York: Vanguard Press, 1975), p. 413.

22. Granville Hicks, "Fiction That Grows from the Ground," *Saturday Review*, Aug. 5, 1967, p. 23.

23. Edith Copeland, review of *By the North Gate*, *Books Abroad*, 38 (Summer 1964), p. 313.

24. Haskel Frankel, review of *By the North Gate*, *Saturday Review*, Oct. 26, 1963, p. 45.

25. Roger Sale, "What Went Wrong?" *New York Review of Books*, Oct. 21, 1971, pp. 6, 5.

26. Stanley Kaufmann, review of *With Shuddering Fall*, *New York Review of Books*, Dec. 17, 1964, p. 22.

27. Joan Joffe Hall, "The Chaos of Men's Souls," *Saturday Review*, Aug. 6, 1966, pp. 32–33.

28. David Madden, review of *Upon the Sweeping Flood, Studies in Short Fiction*, (1967), p. 370.

29. Bernard Bergonzi, review of *Expensive People, New York Review of Books*, Jan. 2, 1969, p. 40.

30. Bergonzi, review of *Expensive People*, p. 40.

31. G. W., "Gothic City," *Newsweek*, Sept. 29, 1969, pp. 120–21.

32. Dorothy Curley, review of *them, Library Journal*, 94 (Oct. 1969) 3469.

33. L. E. Sissman, "The Whole Truth," *New Yorker*, Dec. 6, 1969, pp. 241–42.

34. Review of *Wonderland, Times Literary Supplement*, July 7, 1972, p. 765.

35. S. K. Oberbeck, "The Life Force Gone Wild," *Book World*, (Oct. 10, 1971), 4.

36. Mary Allen, *The Necessary Blankness, Women in Major American Fiction of the Sixties* (Urbana, Ill.: Univ. of Illinois Press, 1976), p. 159.

37. Allen, *The Necessary Blankness*, p. 133.

38. Mary Ellmann, "Nolo Contendere," *New York Review of Books*, Jan. 24, 1974, pp. 36–37.

39. Charles Shapiro, "Law and Love," *New Republic*, Oct. 27, 1973, p. 26.

40. Walter Clemons, review of *Do With Me What You Will, Newsweek*, Oct. 15, 1973, p. 107.

41. J. A. Avant, review of *Do With Me What You Will, Library Journal*, 98 (August 1973), 2336.

42. Review of *Do With Me What You Will, New Yorker*, Oct. 15, 1973, p. 185.

43. Review of *The Goddess and Other Women, New Republic*, March 29, 1975, p. 30.

44. Marian Engel, review of *The Goddess, New York Times Book Review*, Nov. 24, 1974, p. 7.

45. Bruce Allen, review of *The Goddess, Library Journal*, 100 (Feb. 1, 1975), 311.

46. Edward Bartley, review of *The Goddess, Best Sellers*, Feb. 1, 1975, p. 483.

47. Robert Phillips, review of *Night-side, Commonweal*, Sept. 15, 1978, pp. 601-02.

48. Robert Phillips, review of *The Goddess, Commonweal*, April 11, 1975, p. 55.

49. Brian Weiss, *Best Sellers*, 35 (Feb. 1976), 334: Suzanne Juhasz, *Library Journal*, 100 (Nov. 1975), 2174; A. P. Klausler, *Christian Century*, Dec. 17, 1975, pp. 1164–65; all three reviewing *The Assassins: A Book of Hours*.

50. Review of *The Assassins, Time*, Feb. 23, 1976, p. 65.

51. Michael Wood, review of *Marriages and Infidelities, New York Times Book Review*, Oct. 1, 1972, p. 6.

52. *Time*, Feb. 23, 1976, p. 65.

53. Bruce Allen, review of *Childwold, Sewanee Review*, 85 (Fall 1977), pp. 93–94.

54. William Abrahams, review of *Marriages and Infidelities, Saturday Review*, Sept. 23, 1972, p. 76.

55. J. .A. Avant, review of *The Wheel of Love and Other Stories, Library Journal*, Sept. 1, 1970, p. 2829.

56. Robert Phillips, *Commonweal*, April 11, 1975, p. 55.

57. Josephine Hendin, review of *The Hungry Ghosts, New York Times Book Review*, Sept. 1, 1974, p. 5.

58. Helen Vendler, review of *Angel Fire, New York Times Book Review*, April 1, 1973, p. 7.

59. Sister Mary Kathryn Grant, *The Tragic Vision of Joyce Carol Oates* (Durham, N.C.: Duke Univ. Press, 1978).

60. Quoted by Walter Clemons, *Newsweek*, Dec. 11, 1972, p. 77.

61. Oates, *Scenes from American Life*, pp. vii–viii.

REVIEWS

By the North Gate

James McConkey[*]

Traditionally the novel has been built around a cause-and-effect narrative, one involved enough to allow for a variety of characters and episodes but not yet so involved as to prevent the writer, with the help of a coincidence here and there, from bringing his people and strands of action together in some ultimate resolution. Traditionally the short story has tried to bring off, usually at a specified moment in time, the single effect. Hence the traditional novel and the traditional collection of stories have had structurally little in common.

At the present moment, though, the differences are much less pronounced than formerly. For one thing, the "single effect" of short fiction is beginning to sound dated. With the major exception of that grand story "The Dead," Joyce's stories, with their epiphanies at the end, are coming to seem, as a friend suggested to me recently, overly calculated. Joyce has selected with such extreme care the details which are to lead to the final awareness that the stories too often seem the victims of artifice. For another thing, the novel clearly is losing, or perhaps already has lost, its lengthy backbone of causal action.

The modern story and novel alike often are composed of a variety of blocks, many of which look backward rather than forward. If a character—and, by implication, his creator—is unable, through an act of will, to determine his future he can still relate the present moment to the experiences of the past. Memory can make the disorderly, often violent present moment more explicable than would otherwise be possible. Not explicable enough, perhaps, so that the conflicting strands can be brought neatly together, but explicable enough for the showing forth of some tension between oppositions, for some "opening out" larger than that provided by the epiphany or the tidy resolution.

Joyce Carol Oates' stories, are, in general, connected through their impulse to make order through the use of memory, and they can be read like a novel, as a single unit. Her characters are caught by the past, they are bewildered by the intrusions of the past upon the present, and yet it is in that flow of past experiences that they are given meaning and identity. Furthermore, the stories are bound together by what is, in essence, the same kind of emotional problem or obsession. Often there is an act of violence, usually committed with a knife. Often, in the foreground or background, is a brother who, whatever his dis-

[*]Reprinted with permission from *Epoch*, 13 (Winter 1964), 171-72.

honor or brutality or breach of trust, is a crucial part of the memories and values of the central character.

Miss Oates' talent is a considerable one, a fact which enables me to make some reservations about it. That is, there is something of such underlying value in these stories that one can discuss the extent to which the fiction fails to attain the intensity of the vision out of which it was written—a kind of criticism impossible to use with a writer of lesser promise.

The relationship of past to present, the sense of disorder and violence in both past and present and the urgent need to construct something rational out of one's movement in time—these are crucial themes, and the intelligent and perceptive young writer is likely, at least at first, to be influenced by the work of other twentieth-century writers who have been haunted by them; as I commenced to read this collection I heard echoes of certain southern writers—Faulkner and Flannery O'Connor in particular. The locale in most of Miss Oates' fiction is the same, it is a region of farming country and small towns, and I found myself wondering now and then if the countryside and its inhabitants weren't a bit too much of a literary construct, one based not on western New York—where the author grew up—, but on writers she had read. As I continued to read, my reservations of this sort began to vanish; the landscape ultimately became more what it should have been from the beginning, the landscape of Miss Oates' own mind. I liked in particular "The Fine White Mist of Winter," "In the Old World," the title story, and—in spite of the above remarks—the first story, "Swamps."

Fatal Fascinations

The lovers in Joyce Carol Oates's first novel are every bit as combative as Miss Perutz's and a good deal more mystifyingly compelled: where Luke and Judith talk their way to predictable deadlock, Shar and Karen go in for blind, impulsive woundings. Their relationship involves not so much a manufactured clash of attributes as a total antagonism between two different techniques of despair. Shar is presented as dark, metallic, brutal, a racing driver of immense daring and indifference; the girl whose private, pointless world he violates is fair, ethereal, neurotically withdrawn. There is a near-parody upsurge of Southern violence in which Shar seduces her, crashes his car, cruelly wounds her father and then burns down the hovel containing his own dead father's corpse. In some extremely unobvious way he spends the rest of the novel failing to escape the consequences of this feat and failing also to make clear what made him do it in the first place. Karen, in oblique revenge as well as new-awakened passion, commits herself to him, and he discovers that he too is bound to her. A dazed, gloomily malevolent affair ensures which we are meant to see as a necessary imprisonment from which neither will escape until despair is clarified into disaster.

Being unshakably doomed and inscrutably motivated, the flickerings and simmerings of their involvement are a good deal less absorbing than they are clearly meant to be; we mark time until the final conflagration and note that when people are made the toys of some vague, impending awfulness it is better that they move about in crowds. Miss Oates's panoramic shots of race meetings and (the other sort of) race riots are superbly done, though by extending Shar and Karen's special claustrophobia into a general plight she runs the risk of seeming to embrace an over-facile explanation of it. But any explanation is better than none, and those passages in which there are no individual agonies, no private struggles to escape, in which apocalypse takes over, do almost seem to justify the drawn-out tremblings of anticipation.

[*]Review of *With Shuddering Fall*, reprinted with permission from *New Statesman*, 71 (Jan. 14, 1966), 55.

Upon the Sweeping Flood

David Madden°

The legend is that Joyce Carol Oates's extraordinary stories are produced upon the sweeping flood of an apparently inexhaustible creative energy. Frequently come the nights when she locks herself in an upstairs room, to emerge not long afterwards with a finished story. One sees copious evidence everywhere to support this legend. To read an Oates story, it is not necessary to buy this latest volume. Go to any newsstand and pick up copies of *The Atlantic*, *Harper's*, or *Cosmopolitan*; then go to a bookstore that stocks the *Kenyon*, *Southwest*, and *Southern* Reviews, and one will have one's own collection before Vanguard can assemble the third. As I write, she has won the O. Henry Award for this year; for the past three years, both the O. Henry and the Foley collections have included her stories. Several years ago, one of her plays was produced off-Broadway. In the library, one may encounter her essays on Melville, Fielding, Becket, and English and Scottish ballads (with which her own stories compete in star-crossed loves and bloodshed) in such scholarly journals as *Renascence, Texas Studies in Literature and Language*, and *The Bucknell Review*; her special critical intelligence is revealed also in a brilliant essay on James M. Cain, soon to appear. She teaches, in no danger of perishing, at the University of Detroit. Miss Oates's talent will probably mature slowly—a prospect of limitless expectation when one learns that she is only twenty-eight.

My own review, in the second issue of this journal, of Miss Oates's first volume of stories, *By the North Gate* (1963), was one of many that welcomed this new talent to a form that she has certainly enlivened, if not transformed. Somewhat appalled by serious styllistic and technical faults in a creator of such convincing characters and situations, I nonetheless predicted that she would soon produce a major novel. I was wrong. *With Shuddering Fall* (1964) is an attenuated short story that soars on wax wings. Reviewing the novel elsewhere, I observed that "it is much too early to expect genius from one who has so recently shown signs of it. . . . One can only hope that she will find the time to devote greater attention to style, technique, and structure without diluting the intensity of her vision or scaling down the magnificent terror of her themes." Steadfastly refusing to listen to critics, she goes right on producing stories of an excellence approached by no one else. She "turns out" (to use a phrase normally reserved for commercial hacks) stories that project the raw vitality of sup-

°Reprinted with permission from *Studies in Short Fiction* 4 (1967), 369–73.

pressed desire, impulses, urges, and instincts that suddenly explode in acts of violence. This fiction appears upon a literary scene ready to receive and praise yet another one-dimensional "pop art" novel, social problem novel, anti-hero novel, anti-novel novel, with all the fervor of a fashion-mongering galaxy of coteries. But there is nothing new, nothing avant-garde, camp, pop, absurdist about Miss Oates's stories; reading them is like reading deeply between the hieroglyphic lines of fossils found on lonely landscapes. These stories offer no isolatable, exploitable elements on which fashion might thrive; nor is the author's personality an exploitable by-product of her work. She is one of the few writers today who has the vision to disturb my sleep, to frighten me when, in banal moments, I involuntarily recall a mood from one of her stories. After reading Miss Oates, one's casual moments are not one's own.

It is difficult, if not foolhardy, to discuss these stories as literary fabrications. If they have form, it is so submerged in "experience" as to defy analysis. Out of such visible lack of formal assertion comes most of the bad writing of nontalented people, and, once in a generation, a writer of Miss Oates's stunning potential. In a time when writers master form before they imagine anything that can *live* in it, Miss Oates's shotgun approach to her targets is magnificent, if not aesthetically sublime. Because of their lack of shape and focus, some of the stories linger on as though they were real events one wants to forget.

In many of her stories, Miss Oates sets up a situation, a character relationship, a state of mind that is conventional, circumscribed, made predictable by a rigid ceremonial frame—then chance violently intrudes. Some aspect of the family context usually serves as a frame. In "Stigmata" and "In the Seminary," the family exists within a larger, religious context (Catholic). In "Stigmata," a family gathers at Easter around a patriarchal father whose palms bled for a few hours the previous Easter, and who has become famous, who is on the threshold of sainthood. His son, Walt, is the unpredictable intrusion. It is to Walt, alienated from society and family, that the old man confesses: "I hurt." The look in his father's eyes moves Walt to cry out that God is punishing his father for taking the love of his children without reciprocating. In "At the Seminary," the focus is on brother and sister. Sally, with her parents, visits her brother Peter at the seminary where he is studying; he is undergoing what is glibly referred to as a "spiritual crisis." Wearing sunglasses and a sneer, carrying her martini, Sally follows the priest and her family on a tour of the seminary. The priest proudly shows the cold, antiseptic new buildings, ending in the chapel, where a white, immaculate Christ hangs. The element of chance that intrudes upon this dehumanizing atmosphere and that replaces Sally's superficial contempt of it with purposeful awe is her own menstrual blood, which suddenly begins to flow. To shock them, Sally stomps about behind the priest and her family until the blood seeps into her shoes and marks the clean marble floor, and provokes her brother out of his pale, bloodless, smothering rituals of withdrawal, he had fled his domineering mother, his timid father, his masculine sister. But the shock of blood forces him to share this secular equivalent of a vision; so boldly smitten by womanishness, he takes it by the throat. Sally's blood is nature's cry of outrage against the artifices of man that substitute for vital human and spiritual events. Sally's response to chance provides herself and the others with an opportunity for seeing their lives in relief, within the family and religious context. Miss Oates suggests that they all but miss this moment, as man has all but missed the greater exemplary moment on Calvary.

In "The Death of Mrs. Sheer," Miss Oates parodies her own preoccupation (shared with many twentieth-century writers) with the search for a father and with the significant consequences of chance. This is a grotesque, rural, Faulknerian black comedy, a story of absurd surfaces, shuffled about with gusto, like a mover in a dream throwing tacky furniture about in a loft.

Focussing on father-son, sister-brother, brother-brother, mother-son, mother-daughter relationships, Miss Oates constructs the entire web of blood-ties, and examines the hatred, spite, strife, conflicts, traps, anguish, and guilt in family love. In "The Survival of Childhood," Carl has escaped the ugly back-woods life, "the curse of his family." His younger brother Gene "had always evoked in his parents and brothers and sisters fierce conflicts of love and hate." Suddenly, enigmatically, Gene appears in Carl's life, strangely in need of some kind of help. Carl returns to his family to "endure them," to free himself of them. All Miss Oates's stories do violence to the reader somehow, and the final ten pages of this one are virtual agony. Carl sees that Gene's wild life was a reaction against his avoidance of death the day Carl almost shot him, accidentally. In "Norman and the Killer," Miss Oates examines a similar brother-brother relationship. In their childhood, Norman and his brother were suddenly attacked by a gang of boys, and the brother was killed. Years later, Norman, by chance, recognizes his brother's killer. He feels compelled to exact justice even though he did not particularly like his brother: "they were doomed to be brothers forever and could do nothing about it." He resents the responsibility, and feels guilty because his own life has not justified his survival. For violence and suffering, within the family and outward into the family of man, each man blames another. Though one person appears to be responsible, his act is simply the hub, and Miss Oates traces all the spokes that make the wheel turn toward the precipice; and thus all men are seen to be, to some degree, both guilty and innocent.

What is it in human nature that produces, needs, thrives on violence, personal and vicarious? What control has morality and convention over it? How, indeed, does morality contribute to it? How is it aggravated by the violent impingements of chance? In exploring these questions, Miss Oates runs the risk of melodrama. But in a decade that has witnessed the behavior of Whitman, Oswald, Starkweather, and the killer of the Chicago nurses, that is a relevant risk to run. In her depiction of motiveless violence, an extreme form of behavior, she suggests that much human behavior is apparently motiveless at bottom. "The Man That Turned Into a Statue" concerns a thirteen-year-old runaway girl and a forty-year-old drifter, whose life is full of bad luck. When his plea for help is rejected, he plunges a knife into a man's throat. The incredible irony of this situation is that while the killer has a very deep sense of compassion for the girl, he can easily butcher a father, his wife, and child, then sit down with the girl to gobble up the meal his knife interrupted. "You know how it is," he tells the girl. After reading Miss Oates, *the reader* certainly does.

A typical Oates beginning is "Just around the turn, the road was alive." "First Views of the Enemy" is the story of a superficially secure, undemonstrative young woman's realization of the savage in her domesticated little boy, provoked by a chance encounter with some boisterous Mexicans who block the progress of her Cadillac. Another highway encounter with the vicious poor occurs in "Upon the Sweeping Flood." One of Miss Oates's favorite situations is that in which a man who thinks of himself as routinized and gentle encounters violent, unfeeling, crude people and ends up taking on their characteristics; this process is provoked in this story by a rainstorm and flood, which also aggravate the worst in the girl and her simple-minded brother (who, along with similar characters in other stories, is a human representation of the mindless, valueless forces in nature that work on men who try to live within some rigid context). The good Samaritan is so transformed by psychological and natural disruptions that he is moved to try to kill the boy and the girl he has risked his life (and neglected his own family) to save; thus a man's impulsive altruism is converted by natural and human violence into hatred and homicide. He cries to the rescue boat, "Save me!" (from himself and the forces he has experienced).

Miss Oates examines the operation of love and chance in the lover relationship also. In "Archways," she depicts ways in which seemingly unrelated events somehow juxtapose in the mind so that they trigger changes and action, and shows how one moves through the archways of other lives onto one's own steady course. "What possibility of happiness without some random, incidental death?" In "Dying," one of several stories in which people are physically, emotionally, or spiritually ill and wasting away, Miss Oates depicts a relationship in which a girl maintains her own health by prolonging a degrading friendship with a man who once loved her, and who is now dying, very slowly. In all relationships, one lives, to some extent, upon the dying of another. "What Love With Death Should Have to Do" begins: "At last, she said. 'I'm bleeding.' " The image of a young couple in a motorcycle race, the girl bleeding, the boy not hearing his wife's cries, is excruciatingly appropriate for Miss Oates' world. "But what has this to do with Love, Mae thought dizzily, what has blood to do with love and why did they go together?" In these stories, blood marks the spot where love and violence contend.

These stories show that Miss Oates has yet to achieve a style as commanding as her raw material, themes, and creative voice. That a style so often clumsy distracts no more than it does is amazing. She seems to have no ear for the cadences of good prose. (*Too* fine a style, granted, would distract also.) The following examples come from one of her finest stories, "Stigmata": "Walt was met inside by a young nun"; "Walt's blood throbbed foolishly"; "there were a large number of cars parked there"; "welcomes were general"; "the well-fed voice"; "a dull red flush overtook her cheeks." Too frequently "this" is used vaguely, without an object: "everyone murmured over this, perhaps agreeing, perhaps disagreeing." One senses an innate control, but conscious control is also needed to augment the sheer, overwhelming power of her talent. A frenzied, reluctant, upstate-New York Cassandra, Miss Oates seems compelled to get it said, to hack a path through dense thicket to some place of desecration.

Miss Oates's is a stark authorial authority. She never uses the first person, and in six of the present eleven stories the main character is a man. One feels along one's spine and scalp the heat of creative energy as she violently renders the involvement of her characters in their miserable predicaments, yet her cold objectivity expends no warmth upon the characters. Though she apparently writes in a burst, gives birth to her stories (to resurrect the original vitality of the cliché), she is a genuine prophetess, for her utterances belong to the mysterious force that produces them, and there is no subjective indulgence in the act—the creature born, the cord cut, it lives its own life.

Versions of Rural America

Richard Clark Sterne*

These two authors respond very differently to the sinister dreariness of a Muzak-and-murder society, in which we all tend to the condition of displaced persons. While Miss Oates's characters, whether migrant farm workers or men of property, move and have their restless being in a kind of torture garden that we see as through shattered glass, Mr. Berry's rural figures live an essentially ordered life, in whose course not only birth and familial love but the pain of grief over death by flood and in war imply the author's rejection of "absurdity" as the inevitable human condition. A *Garden of Earthly Delights* is a mechanized domain of witches who sometimes transform the despised poor into the despising rich; A *Place on Earth* is a Virgilian landscape, painted to suggest what a sane life might be.

Miss Oates's novel, its title borrowed from Hieronymus Bosch, focuses disturbingly on three generations of an American family—from unlettered, indebted and openly violent migrant laborer to literate, power-fearing, power-loving landowner. Carleton Walpole, the first member of the family we meet, carries with him as he travels with his wife and children from Arkansas to South Carolina to New Jersey to Florida in the late 1920s and early 1930s, a yearning memory of his Kentucky home and land. Dying of cancer while futilely searching for a daughter who has run off with a man, he feels he must go on living because his death would be the death of his memories:

> It terrified him that people and places and dates should fly off into nothing ... belonging to no one and making no sense—who else could know what that photograph meant ... and who else could remember his father's face, who else could remember the mistake he'd made with Rafe that time, ending up with Rafe dead and for what reason? ...

His runaway daughter, Clara, knows only that she wants "somethin'." Her home has been one migrant labor camp after another; she has been called "white trash" by a schoolteacher, and Carleton has taken a mistress—after his wife's death—who is almost as young as she. The young vagabond to whom Clara succumbs, after being struck by his resemblance to her father, acts almost paternally toward her. He makes her wash herself, and teaches her to read—at the level of romance magazines. But he is restlessly violent and suddenly takes off for Mexico, leaving her pregnant, in a Southwestern town called Tintern. With no Wordsworthian remembrances to help her see "into the life of things,"

*Review of A *Garden of Earthly Delights*, reprinted with permission from *The Nation*, April 1, 1968, pp. 448-49.

Clara becomes the mistress of a wealthy, sanctimonious married man—Revere. This somber personage sets her up with a car and a house, believes the child she gives birth to is his own, and marries her seven years later, after his own wife's death.

Clara calls her child "Swan," although his legal name is Steven, because swans "look real cold, they're not afraid of anything." Significantly, she has thought of "Clara" (the name of one of her father's sisters) as having "nothing to do with her at all." And "Swan" proves to be shrinkingly apprehensive rather than intrepid. Thus, in the course of three generations, from Carleton Walpole who vividly recalls his father, to Clara who has mixed feelings toward hers, to the illegitimate "Swan" who comes only to suspect who his real father is, names become increasingly dissociated from the persons who bear them.

Coincident with this incremental dissociation is a growing preoccupation with power and status. Carleton took pride in his own physical strength and his superiority to "Niggers" and "Mexes"; Clara becomes intensely possessive of her house and garden (as a little girl she had stolen an American flag from the porch of a middle-class house), admires strength wherever she finds it, and is contemptuous of her son's timidity. "Swan" early in life sees power as the deepest reality in human relationships, and because of his inability to reconcile his fear of having it with his drive to possess it, he goes mad. In his childhood he has been, and felt, responsible in an ambiguous way for the accidental death by shooting of one of his three foster brothers. In his early 20s, torn between his "strange mystical love" for the Revere land of which he has become a kind of steward, and his desire to "destroy everything," he kills the foster father who incarnates power, then kills himself.

At the end of Miss Oates's impressive *lumpen-Buddenbrooks*, the middle-aged Clara has moved to a nursing home, where she is visited frequently and "for the rest of Clara's life" by her oldest foster son, whom she had once encouraged to try to make love to her, and then rejected. She does virtually nothing except watch television:

> She seemed to like best programs that showed men fighting, swinging from ropes, shooting guns and driving fast cars, killing the enemy again and again until the dying gasps of evil men were only a certain familiar rhythm away from the opening blasts of the commercials, which changed only gradually over the years.

There are flaws in the novel. The last third of it, dealing chiefly with "Swan" and Revere, seems diffuse, less carefully worked out than the superbly controlled first part about Carleton, or the complex, vivid second part which focuses on Clara. The symbolism is sometimes too blatant, as when the saturnine Revere makes love to Clara—who is thinking of her lost young lover—in a parlor, their bodies surrounded by "drifting bunches of dust and the corpses of insects and odd pieces of furniture hunched beneath soiled sheets." But this book, which is reminiscent of at least one of Miss Oates's short stories, "First Views of the Enemy," is not only distinctly better than her first novel, *With Shuddering Fall*, but constitutes as penetrating an examination of our American sickness as the best work of Dreiser, Fitzgerald or Faulkner.

What Is Reality?

Granville Hicks[*]

Several reviewers of Joyce Carol Oates's *A Garden of Earthly Delights* described the novel as naturalistic, and some compared it to the work of Theodore Dreiser. "Naturalism," as used in literary criticism, has always seemed to me a slippery word. Beckson and Ganz's *A Reader's Guide to Literary Terms* defines it as "a literary term related to and sometimes described as an extreme form of realism but which may be more appropriately considered as a parallel to philosophic realism. This doctrine holds that all existent phenomena are within nature and thus within the sphere of scientific knowledge; it maintains that no supernatural realities exist." The entry goes on to speak of Zola as the principal theorist of naturalism. Dreiser sometimes writes as a naturalist, in the latter sense of the term, and sometimes doesn't. (The same may be said of Zola.)

Miss Oates is not that kind of naturalist, and to say that she is the other kind doesn't mean much. What is "an extreme form of realism"? In practice, I suppose, it is a realism that deals with matters the reader would rather not hear about.

Until now Miss Oates has been a realist in the sense that she has taken the evidence of the senses pretty much at face value for the purposes of her fiction. But I am sure she has always known that in the twentieth century it is not easy to say what reality is. Physics and psychology agree that things are seldom what they seem, and novelists have been experimenting with surrealism and with such devices as myth, allegory, and fantasy in the attempt to suggest the protean nature of reality.

I do not depreciate the kind of realism Miss Oates exhibits in *A Garden of Earthly Delights*. In my review of that book (*SR*, Aug. 5, 1967) I said that the novel "grows out of the ground," and I spoke particularly of the credibility of her people. I am pleased with her new book, *Expensive People* (Vanguard, $5.95), not because I think the method she there employs is inherently superior to her former method but because I rejoice in her versatility. She has proved that she can do something different and do it wonderfully well.

The story is told in the first person, and the narrator warns us at the outset that he is a strange fellow and perhaps not to be trusted: "Look at my hands tremble! I am not well. I weigh two hundred and fifty pounds and I am not well, and if I told you how old I am you would turn away with a look of revulsion.

[*]Reprinted with permission from *Saturday Review*, October 26, 1968, pp. 33-34.

13

How old am I? Did I stop growing on that day when 'it' happened, note the shrewd passivity of that phrase, as if I hadn't made 'it' happen myself, or did I maybe freeze into what I was, and outside of that shell layers and layers of fat began to form?" He confides in us: "And it's possible that I'm lying without knowing it. Or telling the truth in some weird, symbolic way without knowing it."

The theme of the novel, from one point of view, is the emptiness of suburban life—a familiar subject and in many hands a dull one. Miss Oates, however, does not pile up a mass of closely observed details in the O'Hara manner. She occasionally introduces a few such details with great effectiveness, but what we chiefly have is the impact of suburban life on the sensibility of the narrator, Richard Everett, and the impact on us, as passed through him, is terrifying.

To all intents and purposes there are only three characters: Richard and his father and mother. Richard is eighteen at the time he is writing the story; he was eleven when "it" happened. The father is a prosperous businessman engaged in some mysterious operation that perhaps contributes to the war machine. He rises from position to position, and moves from one expensive house to another that is more expensive. He is a stereotype and is meant to be, for all Richard is aware of is the noisy braggart who drinks too much and quarrels with his wife. The mother, as the narrator finally learns, was christened Nancy but calls herself Natashya; she asked Richard as a child to call her Nadia but what he came up with was Nada. She has literary as well as social pretensions, and she seeks relief from boredom, as Richard is aware from an early age, in infidelity. If Richard paints a distorted picture of his father because he hates him, his account of his mother is blurred by love and jealousy.

Richard, who, as he points out, is extremely precocious, plays games with his hypothetical readers. He talks, for instance, about how to write a memoir, commenting sardonically on books and articles that offer advice to the would-be writer. "I do indeed promise violence," he assures us, "yes. VIOLENCE . . . VIOLENCE (this is for people standing at *Browse & Leaf* shelves in clean suburban libraries). I offer to them also ECSTASY . . . MORAL ROT . . . ANGST . . . KIERKEGAARD . . . and other frauds." He quotes from his mother's notebooks, and even includes one of her published stories, which he interprets as referring to him. He presents reviews of his memoir such as might appear in the *New York Times*, the *New Republic*, *Time*, and a highbrow quarterly. (*Time* says: "Everett sets out to prove that he can outsmarte Sartre but doesn't quite make it.") In an amusing extravaganza, after the family has bought and moved into a new house, Nada calls employment service, a plumber, garden service, an insurance company, the gas company, the garbage service, the sanitation department, the Good Will Mission, the high school, the bank, a dentist, an oculist, a skin doctor, the electric, water, and telephone companies, a window washer, a drugstore, a television and phonograph shop, a beauty parlor, a key maker, and various others. (We know this is fantasy because she gets every number she calls.)

As we come closer to the climax, the question is whether Richard did commit the crime to which he confessed or was as deluded as the examining psychiatrists believed him to be. In a sense it does not matter what the "reality" is, for the murder is real to him, and therefore his guilt and remorse are real.

Miss Oates has written: "*Expensive People* is the second of three novels that deal with social and economic facts of life in America, combined with unusually sensitive—but hopefully representative—young men and women, who confront the puzzle of American life in different ways and come to different ends. A *Garden of Earthly Delights* was the first novel." The impressive thing about *Expensive People* is that "certain social and economic facts of life in America" do become clear in spite of Miss Oates's oblique method. It is also true that the characters do come to life, even though they are seen only through Richard's distorting lenses. (After what we have seen of Nadia, a few pages at the end about her early years serve to make her whole life history an open book.) The success of Miss Oates's technical experiment is a joy, and those who have admired her talents from the beginning, as I have, are going to have great hopes for her future.

Mirage-Seekers

John L'Heureux*

Them, the final volume of Joyce Carol Oates's trilogy about life at various cultural and social levels in the United States, is intricate, alarming, a total success.

A Garden of Earthly Delights, the first volume, chronicled the migrant worker and one woman's overpowering drive to rise above her doomed class. *Expensive People* investigated the superrich, the pursuit of something intangible in a world of tangible meaningless wealth. *Them* explores the classes in between, the lower middle class particularly, swallowed by a mechanized society.

It is the history of Loretta Botsford and her children, Jules and Maureen, beginning during the Depression with the murder of Loretta's lover as he lies beside her in bed and closing with the Detroit riots of 1967. At sixteen, Loretta, who lives "in an eternity of flesh," marries Howard Wendall, the policeman who had found her murdered lover. She leaves her drunken father and her brother Brock, who committed the murder for the simple reason that he was born to be a killer, and she moves into an emotionless Eden of raising her babies, gossiping, going to the movies. This will never end, should never end, she thinks. But then Howard is fired for involvement in a prostitution ring, and they move to the country with their children, their disgrace, and with Mama Wendall.

Loretta's life becomes at once tedious and terror-ridden. There is no one to share her gossip, no one to appreciate her voice of indignation or of sympathetic anger switched on to make her life interesting and endurable for herself and her city friends. And within or behind the tedium there looms the awful presence of Mama Wendall. When Howard is drafted and sent to Europe, Loretta flees this shrewd and domineering woman and takes her children to Detroit, where on her second day in the city she is arrested for propositioning a plainclothesman. This is her return to civilization.

But in Detroit Loretta finds life repeating itself. Howard returns from Europe—he is the kind of man nobody ever kills—and sometimes works but always drinks. Her life, exactly like the lives of her neighbors and friends, has been burdened by too many children, too much work, too little enjoyment, and at its end she is just what she has been throughout it: loud, hopeful, eager for

*Reprinted with permission from *The Atlantic Monthly*, Oct. 1969, pp. 128-29.

something to laugh at, undefeated only because she has never known the terms of the battle.

Maureen and Jules, so different from their mother, are in fact mirror images of her. Aspiring to rise above the pettiness and stinginess of their lives, they remain victims of their society. Both see money as the key to power and power as the key to escape; both are betrayed by their vision.

Them clearly and completely reveals the minds of people whose reactions and aspirations are dictated by a machine-oriented culture of radio, film, television. Thus robbed of imagination and genuine emotion they are condemned to the death of faith and the death of love. Religion becomes merely another description of one's background: where he is from, who his uncle was. Love cannot even be learned: "There is no time for love to rise in her; she does not know how to work it up, cultivate it, she's heard too much about it from her mother and other girls and from the movies." Their culture has produced people who are not unfeeling, not unconcerned; but their feelings are made in Hollywood and their major concern is for something stable.

Very near the end of the novel Jules crosses the street near a broken-down building which houses the "Students' Revolt Against the War in Vietnam," and the narrator tells us that "in their front room a few days ago one of their people had been killed, an organizer shot to death. An angry cab driver had run in and shot him in the chest. Dead. The cab driver told newspaper reporters that he had a son in Vietnam and was proud."

In a novel of over five hundred pages, this is the only mention of the house, the organizer, the cab driver. But it is typical of Joyce Carol Oates's vision. She sees contemporary America as a country in which the improbable, the chaotically and violently improbable, constantly reroutes purposeful lives and sometimes destroys them. John Kennedy, Robert Kennedy, Martin Luther King: their murders are only paradigms for a language of random destruction.

Them is written in the fluid, refined style that characterizes everything by Joyce Carol Oates. But this novel has a more elaborate and more symmetrical structure than any of her previous works. It is a study in surfaces because the characters know only the surfaces of their lives; the painful core of their experience never reaches them as being what their lives are about. They see only the flesh, the face in the mirror, the shifting image on the television screen, and these become the radical metaphors of the novel. But they are more than metaphors; they localize and define the characters themselves. The sixteen-year-old Loretta combing her hair before the mirror becomes the twenty-six-year-old Maureen; the mother's attempt at prostitution becomes the daughter's success. The Loretta-Brock relationship becomes the Jules-Maureen relationship, and Brock the murderer becomes Jules. The characters, so very unalike, beneath their surfaces are the same. The mother *is* the daughter, and all their lives are only random segments of a blind social continuum. They are them— those nameless others. And, by implication, so are we.

Taken together, the three books in Miss Oates's trilogy are insightful, tragic, and finally illuminating. If there is a certain slackness in the third volume, it is because the author has put everything in: the sloppy apartments with their endless catalogue of rags and mops and coffee tins and tissues and bread crusts, the banal conversations of women whose dreams are purchased at the hairdresser's, the smells and tastes of violence. And if now and again dialogue slips from conversation to exhortation, it is because in so large a book directions are easily lost.

Them is a history, I have said. History, not story, because we come to see not only who these pitiable people are and how they became that way, but also the social and psychological pressures which afforded them little opportunity to be anything else. And we see beyond them the unpredictable violence that threatens at every moment to enter and engulf their lives. Set in the foreground of wars, assassinations, violent and inevitable death, *Them* coldly calibrates the moral irresponsibility of two generations. It is an extraordinary and frightening work.

The Necessity in Art of a Reflective Intelligence

Benjamin DeMott[*]

Miss Oates's prefatory "Author's Note" to *them* points at some difficulties of her situation that have general cultural significance. The Note addresses the question how a professor of literature could come by the knowledge that lies at the heart of this tale. (Joyce Carol Oates teaches at the University of Windsor in Ontario; *them* deals chiefly with the experience of truck drivers, counter girls, parking-lot attendants, prostitutes, hapless aged in homes and welfare clinics, slum-dwellers, murderers, looters, rapists, and thieves.) The author has raised similar questions before, in relation to her earlier books, usually answering by speaking about slogging up source material in libraries. (The racing-car background in her first novel, *With Shuddering Fall*, for example, is said to have been pulled from trade journals.) But *them* is a different story. In writing it, says Miss Oates, she had the help of a former student—a young girl with a "disadvantaged" past who provided a generously detailed autobiographical confession, and at length became the central character of the book:

> ... the "Maureen Wendall" of this narrative [was] a student of mine in a night course, and a few years later she wrote to me and we became acquainted. Her various problems and complexities overwhelmed me, and I became aware of her life story.... My initial feeling about her life was, "This must be fiction, this can't all be real!" My more permanent feeling was, "This is the only kind of fiction that is real." And so the novel *them*, which is truly about a specific "them" and not just a literary technique of pointing to us all, is based mainly upon Maureen's numerous recollections. Her remarks, where possible, have been incorporated into the narrative verbatim, and it is to her terrible obsession with her personal history that I owe the voluminous details of this novel.

Miss Oates acknowledges that the personal history wasn't in every instance allowed to stand, on the ms. page, in the form in which it first became available to her. "... the various sordid and shocking events of slum life, detailed in other naturalistic works, have been understated here, mainly because of my fear that too much reality would become unbearable." She adds, somewhat obscurely, that "certain episodes [were] revised after careful research indicated that their context was confused." But she repeatedly stresses that, in substance as in detail, *them* is no imaginary voyage. The basis of the whole was solid fact—so furious

[*]Review of *them*, reprinted with permission from *Saturday Review*, Nov. 22, 1969, pp. 71-73.

an outpouring of fact, indeed, that, as the author tells it, her own life and sense of self almost vanished in the welter:

> For Maureen, this "confession" had the effect of a kind of psychological therapy, of probably temporary benefit; for me, as a witness, so much material had the effect of temporarily blocking out my own reality, my personal life, and substituting for it the various nightmare adventures of the Wendalls. Their lives pressed upon mine eerily, so that I began to dream about them instead of about myself, dreaming and redreaming their lives. Because their world was so remote from me it entered me with tremendous power, and in a sense the novel wrote itself.

Read in their entirety, the remarks just quoted seem a shade disingenuous. Occasional shakiness of tone, for instance, hints that Miss Oates might have hoped, by writing the Note, to disarm speculation that "Maureen Wendall" was in any sense herself, and that her conversancy with conditions of mean life was bought at a personal cost. (The jacket copy for *them* speaks only of Miss Oates's university degrees and literary honors; promotion for her earlier books, though, made much of her humble beginnings—early life on a farm outside a factory town, education in a one-room schoolhouse, escape via state scholarship to an undistinguished nearby university, etc.)

And the insistence on the "verbatim" character of the transcript also stirs mild skepticism. Whoever "Maureen Wendall" was, it's clear that Miss Oates's skill in shaping and pacing a narrative exceeds that of any conceivable non-literary mind. A family chronicle covering three decades (1937-1967), *them* shuttles between the life stories of a working-class mother, Loretta Botsford, and two of her children, Jules and Maureen. (The major settings are a small industrial canal city—it resembles Lockport, New York, where Miss Oates grew up—and Detroit before and during the '67 riots.) All three stories are clotted with violence. The book begins and ends with killings; parental beatings send children to the hospital for months; there are police clubbings, car and airplane crashes, barn burnings, bombings, stabbings . . . All three characters live for long moments on the chased side of the law, as thieves or prostitutes or rioting revolutionaries. And, to repeat, the crises of these lives—a series of desperate flights from one or another murderous pursuer—are recounted with speed, breathlessness and a communicated sense of anxiety that non-professional confessions (lax, rambling affairs that rarely attach themselves vividly to any particular instant of feeling) never attain. In short, facts of art as well as of life diminish the credibility of the author's account of her sources.

Yet her comments, as indicated, do possess interest. These fumblings with the "problem of esthetic distance," this uncertainty about how that problem can be met—both are signs which, when considered together with the public reception of Miss Oates's work, constitute a portent. Miss Oates's way of meeting the problem of "distance," her way of asserting her separateness as an artist, is to announce that she's writing a true story—about another girl, not herself. And implicit in that explanation is obliviousness to a series of truths about writing which, once familiar and well respected, have lately lost visibility and authority. Chief among them is the truth that it's unimportant whether "the experience" is or isn't the writer's own. What tells is whether the writer has achieved comprehensive power in, through and over the experience, whether he has terms for considering the experience, understanding it, registering its meaning and value, comparing it with other possible kinds of experience.

"Achieving a distance" means, in other words, holding in mind other possible responses besides those of a particular character, even in the act of representing the particular character's responses exactly; it means, more generally, maintaining a constant alertness to life-possibility, the possibility of stronger, worthier, more life-enhancing patterns or forces than those which may momentarily, by necessity, be represented. The prime requirement for achievement of distance in this sense is the possession, as a result of toil, meditation and risk, of a wider knowledge and deeper sympathy than are found in most men. And the purpose of laboring to attain it is to carry forward the endless work of enlarging human understanding.

To say that these commonplaces have lost authority for Miss Oates isn't to say that *them*—or any of her previous books—lacks narrative vigor. It is to say that she continues to appear as an *un*developing talent, a writer making no apparent advance toward reflective intelligence. *them*, like Miss Oates's earlier books, registers no distinctions among qualities of experience. The crudities and flatnesses of its characters' responses never are set in any perspective broader or subtler than their own. More important, at those moments when one or another of her people moves tentatively toward a dilation of mind or feeling—becomes for a moment, say, an enthralled reader of a classic novel in a quiet library—Miss Oates ruthlessly suppresses the sense of possibility, cutting and fitting the occasion to a systematic, schematic, reductive version of things.

The single principle or assumption carried in the texture of her narrative is that in every instance, every circumstance, the poor are vicious, their inwardness is blank; and the mind of the narrator, the teller of the story, is seldom tempted to move a step beyond this hopelessly abstract and restrictive vision. The book's epigraph does, to be sure, question the moral necessity of such a continuum of brutality and blankness. ". . . because we are poor, shall we be vicious?" (John Webster, *The White Devil*.) But in the body of the work there's no suggestion that alternatives to viciousness—or, at the least, interruptions of it—could exist in the presented world. And, saying it again, the novelist is utterly unwilling to allow herself to "stand in" through nuance or gesture for the intelligence or humane response "necessarily" erased from her story because of the nature of her characters. Not once, not even in the tone-shattering, clumsy moment midway in the book when Miss Oates enters in her own person and speaks of "Miss Oates" and of "her" student Maureen, does she enable her reader to believe that a mind subtler than that of the characters has been silently viewing the action with an appropriately compassionate and critical decency.

Why does this matter? says a voice. Miss Oates is thirty-one, enormously energetic and ambitious: is it not oversolemn to be foreclosing on her, denying the likelihood of a development? On its face, yes. At closer glance, though, the problem does look serious for although Miss Oates is young, facts both of the contemporary literary culture and of her own special situation as a writer appear to be working against her chances. Her six books, most of them published while she was in her twenties, have been enthusiastically received. Reviewers have assigned one of her novels a place on a level with Dreiser's *An American Tragedy*. Two of her books have been nominated for a National Book Award, and it's probable that *them* will win the prize in 1970. Her fiction is sought after by the imposing literary reviews of the day, journals whose editors take firm, well-publicized positions on television against the corruption of literature by Miss Jacqueline Susann. Few of the living writers whose work could provide invaluable models for Miss Oates have sufficient fame to compel her eye. (For keys to the humane penetration of lives lacking in privilege, Miss Oates could study the stories of Tillie Olsen; for knowledge of how to sustain an evaluative perspective on public events of a magnitude comparable to that of the Detroit riots she could study Anthony Powell's *The Military Philosophers*; for a model of natural, reflective sensibility, she could study John Barth's *The Floating Opera*.) Those who praise Miss Oates, moreover, do so in a vein that encourages her to regard an inability to perceive or create meaning as a virtue—a "courageous" eschewal of judgment, a new foray into the meaning of meaninglessness. And this "critical line" is but part of a wider body of conviction throughout the culture at large—conviction hostile to the sequential and the reflective, impatient with effort at discriminating the quality of this or that response to life on the ground that such effort is un-involved, secondary, less like an action than an imitation of an action, hence unproductive of excitement or profit or pleasure.

And then beyond all this—a further obstacle to Miss Oates's development—there's the matter of her sense of herself as a teacher of literature in a university. Speaking of this subject without wallowing in self-elevating self-hatred is, for the present writer (himself a professor), no easy trick—but still it's wrong to evade it. The case is that people paid to ruminate about books in front of young people are powerfully tempted to believe they have entered the penetralia of art, have learned "the secrets," know the thing from inside. And this knowingness inevitably complicates a writer's proper understanding of himself as an apprentice. And knowingness does cast a shadow everywhere in Miss Oates's work. It shows itself sometimes in needlessly pretentious titles and epigraphs. Sometimes it takes the form of displays of self-reference—allusions in her own stories to the progress of her literary reputation, quotations from her earlier work, etc. (see Miss Oates's *Expensive People*). On still other occasions it surfaces as a pretense of bored superiority to mere reviewers—as when Miss Oates included in a novel parodies of the reviews she expected in various magazines. (The parodies weren't neatly executed—Miss Oates's writing lacks wit and grace—but their effect on her book wouldn't have been less disastrous if they'd been clever.) In sum, the severest handicap facing this writer may well be her obligation, as a member of the professoriat, to patronize her own insecurities, to adopt a posture of scoffing self-certainty and assurance before her own writing desk.

Pause, reflect, and you see at once the relevant contradictions and intricacies. Miss Oates "must" strive for a range of penetration and compassion beyond that of other human beings. Miss Oates "must" also labor to overcome a professional tendency to regard the teacher as superior to that which is taught. Hard counsel. And no way to ease the contradictions except with the worn reminder that being a writer, a useful contributor to human understanding (as opposed to Making It), is difficult work. At this hour in her career Miss Oates resembles, speaking harshly but I believe truly, a female James Jones donning and doffing, by turns, an unseductive doctoral hood. There is nothing mysterious about her emergence as writer or teacher, nor are the anti-élitist elements of contemporary culture responsible for that emergence without exception negative, regrettable influences. But seeing Miss Oates merely as part of a whole cultural configuration is, in the end, unjustifiable; hers is an individual human situation and, as such, deserves respect and understanding. The primary fact about that situation is, perhaps, that only an exceptional creature—someone combining in himself extraordinary will, intelligence and humility—could, given its nature, win through to a significant literary achievement. There would be richer rewards than have ever been forthcoming from prodigies, publishing phenomena and the like if Miss Oates could find such resources within herself. Best therefore not to quote odds; best simply to wish her well in what cannot fail to be a long and arduous search.

Vivid and Dazzling

Calvin Bedient*

In 1966, a former student of Joyce Carol Oates wrote to tell her how much she hated her, envied her too, for her control in the classroom, for being "filled in" where the human ache should be, and for "knowing so much that never happened," for believing—so academically, so ignorantly—in literature and its "perfect form," when in reality the world is crazy and out of control. "I lived my life but there is no form to it," she challenged. "You write books. What do you know?"

Them is the story of this girl, here named Maureen Wendall, and of her brother Jules and her mother Loretta. Set in Detroit—that "hole with a horizon"—in the last three decades, it is, in part, a story of the crush of family life among the urban poor and, more deeply, of the radical anguish of all human relationships. *Them* is also a story of the folly and cruelty and, for the poor, the desperate necessity of the American dream of betterment. The book drills through almost immediately to that nerve of anxiety that forms part of all human beings simply by virtue of their being alive, subject to change, unsafe. And to Americans, especially, the Wendalls—so vulnerable in their self-conceited dreams of the future, so prone to defeat—will seem frighteningly familiar, nightmare versions of their own worst fears.

As the book opens, Loretta—16, pretty, naive, a child of the movies—exults that "anything might happen." Alas, only too true; impulsively, she invites a boy into her bedroom, and near dawn, while both are sleeping, her older brother shoots him in the temple, then runs off. Loretta wakens, screaming, to an explosion near her ear—and this book of disasters has begun. Fleeing out into the streets, she happens, at length, upon Howard Wendall, a young policeman whom she has known for years, and returns with him to the apartment. Howard, "agitated, red-faced, very strange," saves her. The price is marriage.

Sixteen years and three children later, when Howard is still climbing on top of her—"that fat bastard"—Loretta will lie about during the day puffy-faced in her soiled bathrobe, resting her can of beer on her belly; but like a hardy weed she'll still be hoping, in her own eyes pretty and 16 forever: "I want to get dressed and walk down the street and know something important will

*Reviews of *them* and *Anonymous Sins and Other Poems*, reprinted with permission from *The Nation*, Dec. 1, 1969, pp. 609-10.

happen." she will say to her children, "like this man who was killed because of me . . . I wasn't meant to be like this—I mean, stuck here."

Her daughter Maureen, cold and intent, knows that at least *she* is meant for better things: in the 9th grade, feeling "nothing at all" like her mother at 16, she sells herself and hides her earnings in a book of poetry, living for the day that she can make her escape. Before this can happen, however, her mother's second husband spots her in a stranger's car, finds her money, awaits her return, bloodies her with his fists. Regardless, at least a part of Maureen *will* be free, will not be stopped—the part that soon thereafter steps down to the curb and "becomes vivid and dazzling, standing on the sidewalk with her head turned back at a painful angle, looking at Maureen on the bus, her face guilty and wild."

Even from this point, Maureen has far to go; and meanwhile her brother Jules—though more lively, charming, quick—fares no better. Every prize he reaches for comes down on his hand, a clamp; and of these the most binding is the rich girl he loves, who teaches him—what Maureen has also learned—how good it is to close one's spirit and go to sleep. Jules will wake again, and so will Maureen: testifying, possibly, to the stupidity, but also to the resilience, the heartbreaking heroism, of the human spirit.

Them has the historical validity and something of the factual discipline and verbatim reportage of a documentary—but how much more rare and deep it is than this black-and-white, shopworn term can suggest. For what *Them* really amounts to is an almost uncanny act of dramatic self-transmutation: it is not so much a literary performance as the compulsive product of a possession. Except for a few paragraphs of direct address—in which Joyce Carol Oates, that irrelevant personage, sounds quite outside her subject and unequal to it— the novelist, as such, does not exist in her novel. Neither stylist, architect, judge nor philosopher, she is simply, and astonishingly, *them*.

Had "Maureen" actually read her teacher's "books," she would have known that precisely such indifference to "perfect form," to wrought sentences, verbal tapestries, consoling symmetries of design, has been the risk and virtue of all Miss Oates's published work. The striking quality of this writer's imagination has always been its kinetic aspect of grip and gland, its way of entering her characters and grappling out their lives with them, its instant access to the psyche's confused and impossible needs, to the pain both of being connected and of standing apart. Above all, the pain of connection: for Miss Oates's characters almost always move in a thick, down-dragging element of human relationships, exposed, gasping, embattled, yet now and then surprised by their own cunning or violence, as if by some monstrous stranger in themselves who is yet more themselves than any conscious self they have known.

The history of the Wendalls thus came to Miss Oates as virtually an extension of her own imagination, like a novel that, terribly and unwittingly, she had somehow thought into actual life. So immediate, so relentless an imagination, is obviously limiting; it has no distance, no "order," no leisure for disporting with ideas or for making words couple with the alarming jolt of joining railway cars—no mind for tricks or patterns or any of the cross-word paraphernalia of sophisticated modern fiction. On the other hand, a novel like *Them* makes one realize how predictable and tiresome the artful novel has become, how it caters to both the novelist and the reader's pride in his own ingenuity, how merely life-dabbling it tends to be. *Them* reduces "literature" to virtually the dramatic level alone, but at that level it is so emotionally demanding and successful, so "hot" with life, so imposing that, brought within its range, philosophical or aesthetic schemes, no matter how profound or elaborate, would shrivel at once, unable to bear the temperature.

This is not to say, however, that *Them* is a book without form. For Miss Oates's student was wrong; though her life was "endless," as she insisted, it did indeed have at least a narrative form, and Miss Oates not only adeptly makes her chapters rise to a climax, to still another fumble or recovery in the Wendall lives, but with great naturalness and surprise suddenly brings her novel round to what feels like a "close"—to a fragile, tender, shared moment of reprieve in the lives of Jules and Maureen.

When Miss Oates's potent, life-gripping imagination and her skill at narrative are conjoined, as they are preeminently in *Them*, she is a prodigious writer, one of the best we now have. But she is not often at her best, and has perhaps published too much, too quickly, been too little self-critical. She seems not to know when one or the other of her powers has gone dead. What must be said of *Anonymous Sins*, her first collection of poems, which has just come out in a handsome volume, is that the most important of her gifts, her dramatic imagination, seems shut off. Though about emotional experience, the poems do not connect with it but lie on top of it, curious inorganic aggregates of words:

> *We in love are a series of sleep*
> *like ridges of rock moulded to the*
> *soft convulsions of the brain.*

Unfortunately, there is neither music nor sense here, and poetry must have one or the other.

The truth would seem to be that, a born novelist, Miss Oates needs the distance of objective characters—that distance which she so astonishingly overcomes—in order to get her powerful imagination off the ground. And then how greatly her words take hold and matter, colorless though they may be in themselves. So it is with the words in some of the short stories, in parts of one of the earlier novels, *A Garden of Earthly Delights*, and above all and very wonderfully in *Them*.

The Terror of Love

Charles Lam Markmann[*]

In a very short time Joyce Carol Oates has produced an astonishing number of books and received an amazing amount and variety of acclaim. There is an age-old belief that anyone who does so many things so quickly must of necessity do them badly or superficially or otherwise reprehensibly; and it is regrettable to observe how much loyalty this folk notion commands even among the otherwise intelligent and discriminating. There is a parallel belief—strongest, it must be confessed, among just those intelligent, discriminating persons—to the effect that anyone who attracts more than minimal and esoteric praise must be second-rate. True believers would therefore be morally obliged to reject *The Wheel of Love* and its author out of hand.

Nothing could be more mistaken. Every one of these twenty stories is at the very least a respectable creation, and a surprising number deserve to be called accomplished in every sense of that word. There are a density and force in each of these compact works that come from a touch with words as sure as Richter's at the piano. No word is ever superfluous, as no image is either forced or flat. Form and content alike are constant in their intensity.

This is indeed as it should be, since the subject of all the stories is love—whether the love of men and women, the love of parents and children, the love of friends, or the love of love. All Miss Oates's characters may fairly be said to be, as she herself describes one of them, "trapped in love, in the terror of love." In every ecstasy there is a terror, and it is the terrors, not the ecstasies that contain them, with which these stories are concerned.

In almost every case it is the terrors in the minds of women that are foremost—their own and their perceptions of those of men. These are rarely, in either gender, spectacular, of the kind that can afterward be recollected and savored in tranquillity; they are chiefly the chronic, unvarying terrors to which in real life there is never an end, only an occasional intermission. None of these is exploited, in the vulgar sense: very often their full import is not stated and indeed is not grasped until after the story has been read, and its people have thrust themselves into our world.

Miss Oates's characters—the unfaithful wives, the "delinquent" girl, the victims of parents, the frightened solitaries, the self-indicting mothers—have no connection with the movement for women's liberation, yet it is difficult to

[*]Review of *The Wheel of Love*, reprinted with permission from *The Nation*, Dec. 14, 1970, pp. 636-37.

conceive of more convincing arguments for a new sexual polity than these stories, so compassionately yet relentlessly uncovering the erosions wrought on women and men alike by our best-of-all possible arrangements. Like so many women in life, Miss Oates's fictional personages recognize how much weaker men are than they. Some, like Nina in "The Heavy Sorrows of the Body," are driven to win and can say of a union, as Nina says of hers with Conrad, "It was a duet, a duel." Others, like the anonymous narrator of "I Was in Love," must lose by punishment of self or others because they cannot punish husbands or lovers, and in the end the weak must have the victory or (what they so frequently confuse with it) survival.

The inner struggles of the parent with his contesting drives toward child and lover are nothing new, and indeed get little attention from Miss Oates— who, on the other hand, magnificently if mercilessly presents the matter from a small boy's viewpoint in "Wild Saturday." She is equally effective in creating women whose love for men is to be realized only at the expense of guilt toward mothers or fathers who, for more reasons than the banally Freudian, will not let go. Two stories in particular, "Demons" and "Matter and Energy," are almost archetypes of such situations.

Though one of the least successful stories is told from a man's rather than from the prevailing woman's viewpoint, this is not to be taken to mean that Miss Oates is precluded by gender from successfully creating male characters. Often, it is true, the men in her stories are secondary, sometimes even shadowy. In "Convalescing," on the other hand, she has fashioned a thoroughly credible figure—David, the victim of an automobile accident that has reduced him almost to nonbeing. This story is one of her best. In a few hundred spare words she creates—she imposes—an automobile crash a thousand times more overwhelming than the painstaking accumulation of those in Godard's *Weekend*. The story develops and modulates like the movements of a symphony, with a flow and a logic that are incontestable.

Often Miss Oates's perceptions are clinical in their thoroughness and accuracy, yet they are never without tenderness, no matter how unfashionable that quality may have become. Never does she permit herself, however, the vulgarity of sentimentality; all the more reason why one will not forget the jealous daughters, the tortured wives, the frightened widow who knows, opening the door to a virtual stranger, that "she will see his eyes and the eyes that are inside them." The title of that story is "What Is the Connection Between Men and Women?" The reader of all these stories learns a good deal about what is the connection between person and person. The wheel of love does not stop turning; and everything before it, whether yielding or defiant, it runs over.

Everyday Monsters

[Peter S. Prescott]*

Some of us, in these degenerate times, find that our fantasy lives have been overtaken by headlines. I drive home alone from the station, improving the idle minutes by wondering whether, this evening, my driveway will be full of police cars, rotating lights, short men with bulky cameras. Joyce Oates whispers in my car: "Yes, yes; that's the way it is!" Neighbors, standing on my lawn by the overturned tricycle, nudge each other and stare at me. The state trooper advances cautiously: "Mr. Prescott?"

"Gothicism," Joyce Oates wrote two years ago, "is not a literary tradition so much as a fairly realistic assessment of modern life." Gothic fiction, then, becomes realistic fiction, with grotesque people—monsters, really—devouring each other in a welter of everyday detail. We are used to it in newspaper reports and in our more fanciful nonfiction, but with novels one usually makes a choice: Gothic fiction (imperiled maidens in windy castles) over *here*; realistic fiction (junkies in slums) over *there*. Miss Oates's combination of the extravagant and the familiar comprises a perspective on fiction that is both personal and exciting.

A chart of one of her novels would look like an electrocardiogram gone berserk: a plateau or two and a few longueurs scattered among a dozen or more horrendous, superbly dramatic set pieces, self-contained episodes so securely crafted that they often appear elsewhere as short stories—which is perhaps not entirely salutary. "Wonderland" is as impressive, as admirable, as her other fiction, but perhaps those who will admire it most will be those who don't know her other work. For those of us who do, a certain sameness, certain patterns, are beginning to come clear. The connecting themes and images in "Wonderland"—of personality and the possession of one's self, of the devouring father and the parricide—recur throughout the novel without development. A suspicion grows: perhaps the truth of Joyce Oates's novels is no more than the truth of journalism; perhaps the anguish behind the melodrama, for all the talk of fate and destiny, has not yet found a full articulation. Partly for this reason, "Wonderland's" parts seem greater than the whole.

DESPAIR:

The story begins in 1939, in upstate New York, with Jesse, a 14-year-old boy, about to flee his father, who has just slaughtered his family, and who will

*Reprinted with permission from *Newsweek*, Oct. 11, 1971, pp. 96, 100, 101A, 102.

try to get Jesse, too, before turning his gun upon himself. Jesse flees: he is a survivor, an Oates hero, typically desperate, blood throbbing in his ears, fear banging in his brain, a scream rising in his lungs. Inside, Jesse is empty, his despair a hollowness like hunger. As an adult, Jesse would remember that he "did not have a personality. He did not want a personality. His heartbeat told him always: *here you are, here is Jesse, a survivor.*"

Other men, father figures to Jesse, try to fill his emptiness by making him grow into their own images. "He will become the complete form of the self I have imagined for him," says his adopted father. Jesse flees him, too. Another, a surgeon who takes Jesse on as a protégé, denounces personality as something monstrous: "We each have a hidden obsession, I suppose, a kind of monster that has made our facial structures what they are . . . and we try to keep this monster secret . . . This is the personality people defend." Not profound, perhaps—it is a bit like the lines they feed to Vincent Price in movies—but it is melodramatically effective, nonetheless. Again, Jesse presses for survival at the expense of personality. In time, his daughter will accuse him of seeking to devour her, will make her own break for survival, and the Kronos myth, always a highlight of Miss Oates's fiction, will be even further extended.

TENSION:

Miss Oates writes impeccably, as always, linking with metaphor her human and geographical landscapes: "this backyard of junk, the odor of smouldering rubber from a fire that is perpetually burning invisibly . . . " As always, she compresses much emotion in small space. In a brief paragraph, for example, she shows us fright, hurt, anger, love, impotence and hostile weather, a tension between people that kills communication. She writes about the ordeal of interns and the hippie scene in Toronto: the kind of fictional journalism that she does so well, so much better than she does her characters with theories to expound (in this she shares a kinship with de Sade). She has a genius for the horrific detail: the medical student broiling and eating a woman's uterus, the girl at the vivisection lab brushing a piece of intestini from her hair.

Long sections are absolutely marvelous—stories, as I have said, that stand by themselves—but somehow, from a writer of Miss Oates's talent, it is not enough. We have had this, theme and variations before. No one can ask a writer to write books other than those he knows how to write, but by establishing a pattern, a writer invites a closer scrutiny. Although I enjoyed "Wonderland" thoroughly, I am beginning to have doubts about the links Miss Oates establishes between melodrama and significance: they are not quite convincing.

Only Prairie Dog Mounds

Ronald De Feo[*]

Most of the people in Joyce Carol Oates' latest short-story collection, *Marriages and Infidelities*, a huge, disappointing volume, seem to be dangling from very thin, worn threads that are about to snap. They are either married and miserable, engaged in extramarital affairs and miserable, or divorced and miserable, and they are all courting crisis and breakdown. Though Miss Oates tries hard, playing up melodrama, occasionally tossing in a shock effect (a man fascinated by the newspaper photo of a mutilated girl, a couple getting revenge on a hated woman by making love in her death-bed), she generally fails to interest us in her dreary lot.

At this point in her writing career Miss Oates seems more concerned with describing extreme emotional states than with conveying character. All well and good, one may say. But how can a description of a crisis period impress and move us if we care little about the individual living through that period? In "The Metamorphosis," for example, Miss Oates produces a car salesman suffering a breakdown. She describes the process well enough, but who cares about the salesman? It is not simply that her people are humorless (Dostoyevsky's characters, after all, aren't exactly jovial types), determined to wallow in misery or else so limited that they must accept misery as a norm, but also that they are terribly one-dimensional and unbelievable. Though we realize they are suffering, experiencing frustration, guilt and depression, we never quite understand why. Too often these people are reminiscent of actors who find themselves in an unmotivated drama and overact to compensate for the shallow, improperly defined material.

Miss Oates is basically a traditional writer, so when she tries to broaden her technique, toy with experimental forms, as she does, for example, in "The Turn of the Screw" and "Inventions," the results are usually awkward. The best story in the collection, "The Children," is a very fine traditional piece—carefully paced, suspenseful and concluding on just the right note.

What is particularly distressing about this collection and Miss Oates' other recent work is that it seems quite inferior to her early work (*By the North Gate, Upon a Sweeping Flood*). The writing in the early work was much more artistic and memorable; the work had much more resonance. In the recent volumes we find merely efficient, colorless, flat prose; unsubtle, forgettable characterizations. We feel that the writer is hurrying along at careless breakneck speed. Miss Oates is one of our most prolific writers. I admire prolificacy. But, then again, I admire quality and care even more.

[*]Reprinted with permission from *National Review*, Nov. 24, 1972, p. 1307.

Two Major Novelists
All by Herself

Sara Sanborn°

A nervous doctor asks a little free legal advice. What should you do if the Attorney General is bringing suit against you? Marvin Howe, invincible trial lawyer, answers out of the abyss of his experience with criminality. You have the same choice you would have in a suit brought by God himself: "Plead *nolo contendere* and hope for a very sharp ax." *Nolo contendere*—"Do with me what you will."

God, the Law, the death sentence imposed on all men and stayed or executed by other men, guilt and innocence, power and subjection, the saving or murderous pull between men and women are the concerns of this huge novel. It is a novel of force, of natural forces. It moves toward its conclusion like a glacier; sometimes slowly, always inevitably, and the spectacle is awe-inspiring.

The story is that of Elena Howe, "Elena the Queen of Sleep," and her awakening into "criminality." Three times in her life, Elena dares to venture outside of innocence. The first time she is 7 years old and crawls under a schoolyard fence dragged from its posts and held off the ground by her crazy father, who kidnaps her for a stumbling, cross-country odyssey that leaves her nearly dead of neglect in a dingy rooming house in San Francisco. She is worth dying for, her father swears, but it is Elena who almost dies. Ardis, the hungry and driving mother who retrieves her from the welfare hospital, promises, "Nothing will ever happen to you again." During the dreamlike years that follow, while she is set before mirrors and cameras for the reflection of her incredible blonde beauty, Elena assuages her panic with the magic phrase: "Nothing will happen." Mirrors, cameras, tape recorders—devices for mediating experience—are the controlling images of the novel, and Elena is the Lady of Shallott who sees only in a glass, never face to face.

She loved the drunken, driven man who cut across her childhood like a disease and left her half alive; a few years after the kidnapping, she is unable to distinguish between the words "afraid" and "ashamed." At 17, she awakens momentarily from her beautiful, marble sleep in the presence of Marvin Howe, savior of homicidal husbands and wives. In answer to a question from the others

°Review of *Do With Me What You Will*, reprinted with permission from *The Nation*, Jan. 5, 1974, pp. 20-21.

at the night-club table as to whether his acquitted client was guilty, Howe explains patiently:

> There are no guilty people. The law establishes their guilt, it establishes whether they have violated a law, the decision becomes a matter of public record and you can look it up.

Elena asks falteringly, "Everyone is the same? Everyone is innocent? . . . Not just the bad people, but the people they do it to . . . ? I mean the victims. . . . They're innocent too . . . ?"

Ardis has planned to marry Elena to a third-rate racketeer, but Howe determines to have her. First he taps the mother's telephone and has them both followed for several months. Ardis refuses to allow him "access" to her daughter until she is satisfied with his offer. Men seek "access" to Elena as if obtaining right of way to a body of water, and that is how she thinks of herself. Howe draws up an elaborate and unbreakable marriage contract (there are to be no children) and establishes Elena in his baronial mansion, imported and rebuilt stone by stone in Detroit. There he calls her three times each day; she dresses her waist-length hair and reads the letters addressed to her by his vindictive mistresses around the country; and she counts ten sailboats on the lake each morning as a promise that there will be no danger that day.

Elena is compassed about with protectors, those who want to feed on her unearthly beauty and her utter lack of involvement with the world of exigency and contingency, mortality and decay. One day, back in California, she walks away from a secluded estate and a bodyguard, wearing another woman's clothes, to telephone a young lawyer whose name she does not know and summon him to San Francisco. Her crime is adultery and she knows she should die—if only someone will kill her like all of the beautiful strangled women in the newspapers.

Jack Morrissey, her lover, calls himself a "nigger lawyer"—and not even a high-class one because he is white. He loves to fight and win for self-confessed rapists and thieves caught with the goods; he loves to defend the guilty, because the best he can get for the innocent is what they deserve. He can't defend, can't even tolerate the innocent.

> Uh. . . . You going to make a deal with them, then?
> I don't have to make a deal. . . . She has to testify against you, and she has to convince a jury that she didn't deserve to be followed by you, that she didn't entice you, she didn't smile at you. She has to convince a jury that she didn't deserve whatever happened to her. . . .

Morrissey learned his art from Marvin Howe, seduced on the witness stand as a boy by Howe's power to create the exonerating myth, the way that everything must have happened, his miraculous power to take away guilt. The trancelike purity of Elena maddens Morrissey. She is the Unmoved Mover, like her namesake in *Faust* a beautiful vision forever untouchable. She is "a dead thing," he finally shouts at her. Morrissey understands guilt and loves it. Howe rejects the entire category of guilt, and nearly strangles Elena to save himself from sinking in corruption. Finally, at last, knowingly, Elena walks away again from her deadly safety, determined to embrace desire and crime, to be "selfish . . . evil [and] adult." She will reach for what she wants and fight for it. This she decides, is what men do.

Oates herself has described this novel as treading the path between two traditional American "ways," the way of Law and the way of Romance. It is a good description, as far as it goes. Morrissey's wife Rachel, a fiercely deliberate and knowledgeable romantic, carries one strand of the theme. Rachel seems incapable of loving, only of smearing herself like a slogan over the public domain, "Make love not war." She and her political friends ignore Jack when he begs them to take a little care of the law. Mered Dawe, radical lover of the world, entrapped into touching a marijuana cigarette by a police agent, is an incorrigible innocent who defeats Morrissey's efforts to hammer out victory in the courts. Romance versus the austerity of the legal system provides the basic conflict. But the legal system itself is vulnerable to romance in the shape of the public happy endings dictated by American myths.

We must cherish the law and protect it, Marvin Howe insists—it is what we have now instead of God, the only source of divinity. Both lawyers in this book are lords of creation; they shape characters out of common clay for a brief hour on the stage. They know their clients better than the wretches know themselves. They demand total subjection and truth, and in return they create their clients' histories, memories, experiences, personalities. The purpose is the new redemption, wresting from the arbiters in the jury box a verdict of Not Guilty, "the greatest gift you can hand another human being." But the greatest gift, paradoxically, that Elena's father and Morrissey, her lover, hand her is that of being guilty.

Oates has explored themes of guilt, innocence and victimization before; no one knows as much as she does about the relentless energy with which adults use children to save themselves. Here the theme is carried further. Far into her adult life, everyone wants to use Elena as profane object or sacred symbol; she sees in the eyes of men in the streets their imagination of the things they could do to her. In her fascination with the things that are done to women and children, Oates brings the fearful closeness and power of the Victorian novel into contemporary fiction. Indeed *Do With Me What You Will* extends a line that begins earlier still, with *Clarissa Harlowe*, and runs from *Daniel Deronda* through *Portrait of a Lady* (with a beautiful sport in *Lolita*), the story of women captured by powerful men backed by the forces of society. Unlike such nice American girls as Carol Kennicott of *Main Street* and the many mad housewives of today, these women are not trapped by the obviously inferior spirit of the times and the neighbors but by their own impulses and the devouring determination of the people closest to them.

For her emphasis on self-seeking ferocity we call Oates "Gothic," but she is perhaps better understood as a contemporary heir of the Great Tradition. Like Austen, Eliot, or James in their various ways, but with a gift for violence, she aligns the moral and the social. There is in her books a heaviness, density and pressure that we are not much accustomed to. Her characters are not people we easily identify or identify ourselves with, but something near to archetypes—people placed at the breaking points of society and carrying the grains in themselves. She has a tendency to announce her themes on brazen trumpets; whenever the word "innocence" appears in this novel, it seems to be in metaphysical bold face. Flannery O'Connor thought it necessary to exaggerate in order to draw anyone's attention to ontological issues, and perhaps Oates faces the same necessity. Her themes are always in the major key, imposing, and they are always thickly imagined in the minds and senses of the characters.

At times it seems that there is too much in this book, too many words and ideas; Oates leaves nothing unattended to. The novel is like Marvin Howe's warehouse, crammed with the possessions of his murderous clients, from priceless antiques to personal photographs—"We won. But they had to sign everything over to me." At times it seems that too many implications are started with hunting horns but not pursued to the end. But as the book moves on its way, gathering in, churning under, and offering up again everything in its path, it achieves necessity. Finally, everything in this book belongs, everything matters.

The novel has its flaws, like most big efforts, but they are scarcely worth discussing next to its achievement. Commentators on the sad state of our culture frequently refer to the fact that we have so few major novelists. Let Joyce Carol Oates count for two.

The Hungry Ghosts
by Joyce Carol Oates

John Alfred Avant[*]

Joyce Carol Oates has written strong novels, but she is best in the short story. Her most characteristic stories read like dreams or nightmares, urgently written in order to release the dreamer. She writes, as she has said, compulsively; and the failure of the poor or partially achieved stories seems the result of haste. But when her stories work, when all the elements come together, the same compulsiveness is present. The perfection seems accidental, even when the stories are structured in labyrinths.

The stories in *The Hungry Ghosts*, attractively brought out by a small California press (but with too many typos), lack the immediacy of Oates' major work. They don't grip us as visions, but some of them are extremely funny, which is surprising, since the awesomely serious Oates hasn't been deliberately funny since *Expensive People* in 1968. These "seven allusive comedies," with titles like "Democracy in America" and "The Birth of Tragedy," are set on and around university campuses. Oates intends them to be satiric, and most of them succeed as satire.

Oates, who in one area of her life is a full-time professor, has written academic stories before; and she can distance them as she can't others. They've always been a world apart from her stories about tabloid sensationalism and sexual obsession. In the typical Oates story wealthy girls go klepto and nympho for their drug addict lovers, or housewives bring their guilty adulteries to peaks of apocalyptic violence. This is the stuff of pulp, but the best Oates is pulp transformed into a unique American vision. Oates' endless expensive cars, lipstick tubes and nervously clutched purses become Kafkaesque emblems of horror. She can be shattering like no other writer—an American primitive.

Oates doesn't charge her academic stories as she does her pulpy visions; but *The Hungry Ghosts* crackles with tension and wit, and its subjects—the foibles of academia and the literati—are tantalizing. "Rewards of Fame" has potentially the richest subject: the poets who try to keep out of debt by signing up for package deals to read their poetry at colleges. In Oates' conception the college poetry reading circuit isn't very different from the old vaudeville circuits that used to squeeze name poets in between dancers and comics. The poets tear each other down and hate themselves because they aren't as popular with students as

[*]Reprinted with permission from *New Republic*, Aug. 31, 1974, pp. 30–31.

the McLuhan figures who share the billing. They also hate themselves for succumbing to poetry groupies, who love to get famous poets drunk so they can sleep with them. This is a wonderful satiric idea, one that might move from satire into tragedy. Most of "Rewards of Fame" is very good. But Oates, who brings her poets to the point where some revelation, some event, is needed to illuminate their dilemma, fails to supply the illumination. The story just goes limp, as though Oates lacked the patience to finish it.

Most of the other stories seem finished and amazingly well crafted for Oates, who is rarely a conscious craftsman. Several stories cover the same specific terrain: the English department of the fictional Hilberry University in Southern Ontario (Detroit and America lurk across the lake). "Pilgrims' Progress," which, under another title, appeared in *Playboy* and won an O. Henry Award, is a swift, hard story that focuses on academics who are so unstable outside their scholarship that they are vulnerable to any strong wind that makes them feel committed. Their lives and careers fall apart when they are sucked into radical politics by a charismatic figure.

The two best stories are the funniest. "Up from Slavery" is an audacious treatment of a young black professor who "hastened to put all white people at their ease . . . by emphasizing the scorn he felt for anything 'black' . . . he preferred the more sanitary and middle-class 'Negro.' " Franklin Ambrose has a white wife whom he despises, and he is driven to sleep with his attractive white female students. Had Oates written about Ambrose straight, not satirically, she might have emphasized his sexual desperation and taken it to melodramatic heights, or she might have tied in his black skin's erotic appeal with the hidden death wishes of his young girl students. Instead she turns the tensions into comedy, which she hilariously resolves with a sexual put-down by another faculty member. The laughter is healthy.

"A Descriptive Catalogue," an even funnier story, has a marvelous big scene in which a faculty committee investigates a plagiarism suit brought by a jealous professor against the department's prolific poet-in-residence, who has managed to publish 358 poems by transposing the good poems of dead poets into McKuen-like banalities. The main satiric object is the publish-or-perish threat that looms over professors' heads; but the comedy is rooted equally in Oates' portraits of the investigating committee members, who are precisely caricatured. The caricatures are venomous but not offensive. Caricature seems natural in a campus setting, because academics often see each other as caricatures and can spend hours creating verbal cartoons out of their colleagues' idosyncrasies. The secret of this story's success is that Oates knows how hilarious professional bitchiness can be.

It's good to know that Oates, who comes off so solemnly in interviews, can be funny; and the assuredness with which she controls the stories is gratifying. *The Hungry Ghosts* must have been restful to write and much easier to take than the fictive outbursts of the more familiar Oates, that tawdry Cassandra.

The Assassins

Anonymous*

The somewhat too prodigious Joyce Carol Oates, 37, whose fiction has exploded with gunshots, stabbings and bombings, also sets off booby traps in the mind. Her seventh novel is a meditation on assassination and the violence that lodges in the American heart. This is her roughest, most repetitious read, yet it is difficult to suggest a briefer way to tell such a complex tale.

When Andrew Petrie, a former right-wing U.S. Senator, is assassinated in his sprawling New York farmhouse, the list of possible left-wing assassins is all but endless. A reactionary advocate of population control, Petrie was also the nettlesome gadfly editor of a scholarly monthly journal. At the time of his murder, he was composing a treatise on the failure of the American experiment. The reader is compelled to ask if the megalomaniacal Petrie was 1) a mere crackpot, 2) a latter-day Henry Adams or 3) a pernicious William F. Buckley minus the charm. The novel is slowly unraveled by three highly inflamed, profoundly disturbed minds. Each version of the events needs the other two to make literary and psychological sense.

Author Oates is best understood alongside the 19th century's great moral improvers. She is sister-in-arms to Melville, Hawthorne, Twain and Mrs. Stowe. All wanted their writing to better the public they were writing for—even when they despaired of civic improvement. Oates has yet to write a book that liberates as fully as it lacerates. But she cares about the national identity as no other living American novelist does. If she can steady her grip on her terrifying, transmogrifying wit, there may yet be a great novel in the already vast Oates canon.

*Reprinted with permission from *Time*, Feb. 23, 1976, p. 65.

Possessive Material

Irving Malin[*]

The Poisoned Kiss is a remarkably unified collection of stories. In the epigraph Joyce Carol Oates alerts us to the obsessive, dominating, possessed qualities we should expect. St. John of the Cross writes—the translation is by Roy Campbell—that "darkness" is dearer than the "morning's pride." He prays to the night: "Oh night that joined the lover/ To the beloved bride/ Transfiguring them each into the other!" These lines are an invocation; they suggest that "opposites"—"lover" and "bride," night and day, deity and worshipper—melt into each other; the world is a confusing tangle. The epigraph forces us to look closely at the title, "poisoned kiss," in which the same marriages are apparent.

The matter is even more complicated and playful. Oates gives us a "note" before the stories; she tells us that they are "translations" from an imaginary work, *Azulejos*, by an imaginary author, Fernandes de Briao. "Without his very real guidance I would not have had access to the mystical 'Portugal' of the stories—nor would I have been compelled to recognize the authority of a world-view quite antithetical to my own." The note is written as a clear explanatory introduction, but we see that it deliberately undercuts our usual separations of worlds; it is, if you will, an echo of the title and the epigraph—it insists upon joining opposites. "Translations" force us to remember "transfigurations"; there is an effect of "crossing the border" (another Oates title) and a suggestion that such crossing is *necessary, unplanned, compelled.*

The stories vary in length, but they are all told from an off-center position. In one of the best, "Our Lady of the Easy Death of Alferce," the statue observes her worshippers and, in an odd way, begins to become more human. *Stone turns to flesh.* She narrates the story, almost confessing her weaknesses; she recognizes that she must move and touch and comfort the worshippers. Oates makes us even more uncomfortable—and attentive—by using such words as "film" and "swaying of flames." The atmosphere is "transfigured" because of the changing, drifting union of worlds—a "union" which can never really take place? By opening and closing the story without fixed points—we are thrust into the middle of sentences—Oates intensifies the effect.

I am reminded of Poe and Borges by this story (and indeed, by the whole

[*]This essay was written specifically for this volume and is published here for the first time with permission of the author.

collection). The real and unreal continually assault us—there are various *violations* in every story—and we cannot be sure about the sources of such "enchantment." Thus it is not surprising after the first few stories that "secret mirrors" (another possible clue) abound. In one story a man stands before an "actual" mirror and dresses as a woman—he loves the otherness of the garments, the shadow-self. (There is a striking parallel to the Lady's lament I have already mentioned.) But at the same time he knows that he cannot *become* the woman despite all his efforts. He is trapped, especially when "the reflection in the mirror begins to weep." Oates doesn't stop here. We are left wondering about the "you." Isn't the reflection more real (when the weeping occurs) than the observer? And does it matter that we make a distinction between the woman in the mirror and the man dressed as the woman? Isn't the same person involved in the ceremony?

I have suggested that these two stories are ritualistic; they concentrate on "still points" which are achieved—only briefly!—by elaborate, compulsive, "excessive" pursuit of details. The "perverse" quality is heightened by the matter-of-fact, dry style; Oates' sentences apparently explain why the man dresses as a woman or the Lady mourns the human condition. But the deception is purposeful. She implies that her style is another reflection of her characters and themes—all, indeed, come together so that we are baffled. We want to know more; we want to move beyond rigid lines of explanation and "let go" of our public, daylight selves to understand the "mysteries" of "translation."

Although the two stories can be read as "religious" or "psychological" meditations on the nature of the self/the real world, they gain their effect by resisting easy division. The Lady is like the man—both are eager to get through the mirror—and it is dangerous to use words from theology/psychology to explain their secret longings.

Oates offers several stories about art—the collection itself is an act of homage to "Fernandes"—and in one of them, "Plagiarized Material," she mystifies us brilliantly. As we read about Cabral and his work, we begin to wonder about him. Is his work the product of genius, insanity, self-love, pure adoration of the other? The story includes details from his work—work that questions the usefulness of explication—and we are led to believe that Cabral is a reflection of other writers and, I may add, other worshippers in the collection. Before he dies, he writes his obituary—it "seemed to him unassailable, perfect. Perfectly opened and perfectly closed." He dies with an "Amen." There is a marriage of life and art, openness and closure, and this compels us to return to the title and the opening of the story. "Plagiarized material" refers not only to the obvious use of others' work but to the world itself. The world (material) is a reflection *and* possession of some other world; we may write about "Portugal" but our "Portugal" is not the real country—we use it (or are used by it) for our ceremonies.

When Oates writes her "afterword" she maintains that she, like the Lady and Cabral and the man dressed as a woman, was possessed by another consciousness—that of Fernandes. He came out of nowhere; the stories did too. She tells us that she was violated; she had no intention of creating another personality, another author, another country. All of the stories belong to Fernandes/ Oates; consequently, they reflect the ceremonies of creation—sexual, artistic, theological. Oates cannot accept rational explanations. (Perhaps my abrupt explanations are simple.) But she also cannot accept glib pronouncement about other worlds. She, the "creator," finds that she was *created*.

In the last sentences of the afterword, Oates tells us that five years later she is tempted to see the collection—and the experiences which created it—as a literary device, a "metaphor." Nevertheless, she knows that such critical explanation is false—as is all criticism?—because "in truth none of it was metaphorical, any more than you and I are metaphorical."

Oates' afterword and note at the beginning reflect the stories I have summarized. They subvert conventional truth—and book design—by leading us into alternative worlds. *They are marvelous, disturbing ceremonies*. We can analyze the Lady or Cabral or Oates herself but our very acts of explication are colored. We are so moved by the powerful marriages recorded here that we begin to lose our identities. We merge with the stories; we are "poisoned" as we admire their craft and mystery and wisdom.

Night-Side

Robert Phillips°

Ever since her miscellaneous collection, *The Wheel of Love,* Joyce Carol Oate's story collections have been more than "mere" collections: they have been carefully constructed totalities, works in their own right. *Marriages and Infidelities* was an appropriate title for the plots of the stories it contained; *The Goddess* stories all concerned women or girls; *The Hungry Ghosts* of the collection of that title were all critics, academics or writers; and *Crossing the Border* is a meditation on just that.

Oates's newest collection is also more than a grab-bag. This time the interrelation of the stories is not occupational, geographical, or sexual. It is psychological. All eighteen tales are concerned with borderline reality, what the author has called "that mysterious realm of the paranormal." *Night-Side* differs considerably from her early novels in that almost all the violence is mental rather than actual. With the exception of "The Blessing" (the volume's weakest story), these are interior tales—stories of individuals haunted by their own uneasiness and anxieties. What is striking is the way Oates manages to reconstruct the dreams and nightmares which afflict us all, reminding one of Henry James's statement, "The extraordinary is most extraordinary in that it happens to you and me." *Night-Side* is not, however, a book of the occult. Joyce Carol Oates's ghostly tales are related to the tradition of realism of Daniel DeFoe's "True Relation of the Apparition of One Mrs. Veal" rather than to the chains and clanks of Walpole or Mrs. Radcliffe.

It is impossible to "review" eighteen stories in this space. I will say that *Night-Side* contains some of the best work of one of America's best story tellers. Anyone interested in her must read the title story, which is as gripping as a thriller. Others which intrigue are "The Translation" (in which a man's conception of his beloved, a foreigner, is shown to be only a manifestation of his translator's skill); "The Sacrifice" and "Exile" (in which alter-egos or exterior projections of interior conditions lead the protagonists to their fate); "Further Confessions" (in which one man outwits Fate); and "Daisy"—a study of the untenable position in which the "sane" are placed when their next-of-kin are judged "insane." They are asked to play God.

"Daisy" explores this relationship in the lives of Bonham, an artist, and Daisy, his talented but disturbed daughter. In a state of weakness Bonham signs

°Reprinted with permission from *The Commonweal.*

a paper to commit her to a mental institution. Afterward he perceives the terrible things they have done to her:

> How she had suffered, and for what cause? Seeing her, he had burst into tears and demanded that she be released in his custody at once. No more of this!—no more. "From this day forward," he had shouted at them, "let everyone be free of pain! Let there be no more agony inflicted on human beings by human beings—do you hear? Do you hear? I'll make you hear!"

Bonham in his rage, and Daisy in her infirmity, recall James Joyce and his daughter, Lucia Anna, who (in the words of Joyce's biographer, Richard Ellmann), "was to affect Joyce's life much more deeply than he would have believed possible." The disarray of Lucia Anna Joyce's mind and its possible sources in Joyce's own strange and nomadic life is at the heart of this accomplished tale, one of the best in an important collection.

Hungry For God

"Son of the Morning" spans, in true Joyce Carol Oates style, more than 30 years of American experience, ending in the 1970's. And the novel takes as its subject the hero or victim of another particularly American phenomenon, the world of Pentecostal religious fanaticism—small-town revival meetings, healers, inspired local preachers. The boy Nathan, brought up by his grandmother in the foothills of the Chautauqua mountains, is the fruit of the savage rape of a teen-age girl: he becomes a provincial messiah. Between the ages of 5 and 34 he experiences seven revelations when "God seized him in the flesh." He becomes more than a charismatic preacher; he is possessed by God to the exclusion, in the end, of all else: "Salvation had nothing to do with human relationships, the believer's allegiance was to God. . . ." Becoming superhuman, he sees nothing of the human pain and corruption in the vast organization—the Seekers for Christ—that his charisma has spawned. Finally, like Icarus flying too near the sun, he is destroyed.

It is a hugely ambitious novel. Clearly well-researched, it could serve as a basis for the sociological study of the theory and practice of Pentecostal religion. It explores the phenomena of "revelation" and mystical experience with an extraordinary imaginative thrust. It poses, without answering, questions about the nature of Christ, the church as an institution, and whether there is God or only the desire for God, leading to madness; and whether he is a God of Salvation or a vast metaphysical appetite for souls, a destroyer. The story is told in the third person but, one gradually gathers, the narrator is Nathan himself, apostrophizing God as "You" as he goes along. Nevertheless the narrator knows, or intuits, a great many things that Nathan could not have known. "Is this a revelation, I ask myself. Or an aspect of my punishment."

This is a bare and inadequate plot summary, for the author enters into the heightened feelings and experiences of nearly every character in the large cast—except God's. But the girl's memories of the rape, Nathan's relationship with God, his grandmother's supernatural adoration of him as a child, his grandfather's desperate stoicism, the hysterical fervor of the prayer meetings, and the physical hardware of everyone's ordinary life, are all felt and described with a sustained virtuosity. The language, fittingly enough, is biblical, apoc-

°Reprinted with permission from *New York Times Book Review*, Nov. 26, 1978.

alyptic, intense. For me the book is a little too long: compression is not high on the author's list of priorities.

The sharp edge of irony, however, tempers the intensity when the venality of hypocrisy of the "normally" religious is revealed, without comment. The successful preacher Beloff, for example, Nathan's patron, who travels round in a Rolls, makes salvation a commercial deal with the Almighty: one "cannot *miss* being taken up by the Lord into His Kingdom under these conditions!" More subtle is the way in which Nathan's grandmother, after teaching him that we can talk to Jesus and that Jesus is always with us, is embarrassed and discomfited when the child finds this to be literally true. Her discomfiture, though it does not loom large in the story, is fascinating; most believers *do* prefer God to be strictly notional, and judging from the experience of Nathan, who fell into the hands of the living God, their instinct is a sound one.

Echoing Nathan's hunger for God, and God's for him, there is throughout the novel a harping on the huge, crude hungriness of nature, the vicious circle of hunter and hunted. The novel opens with the exterminating of a dangerous pack of starving wild dogs, abandoned by their masters, each "nothing but a certain length of guts about which the animal skeleton and flesh moved, frantic with desire." It ends with Nathan's collapse at a mass meeting, when he sees the congregation as "a great hole," a greedy mouth to devour him, and the mouth is the mouth of his ravenous God. After this vision he too is abandoned, lost. His doctor grandfather, much earlier, sees his demanding patients as "the ava-lanche of sheer rapacious nature," and studies Marcus Aurelius to preserve himself, in vain.

There is a hungriness in the writing of Joyce Carol Oates, too, an appetite for huge themes and violent emotions, in seeming tension with her analytical, academic side. It makes for great vitality; it also breeds a slight resistance in the reader, as does her extraordinary fluency and productivity. Can so regular a flow of novels, stories, poetry and criticism all be in the first class? Of course they can. Costiveness is not necessarily a literary virtue. The problem for the contemporary reader, however, is that it is hard to see the trees for the forest. We cannot know whether it is her whole oeuvre that will seem the sum of her achievement in the eyes of our grandchildren, or whether one novel, a Great American Novel, say, will survive as a classic, and the rest be unread except by thesis writers. It doesn't matter; "Son of the Morning" is a rich stew that will be devoured by the hungry faithful.

ESSAYS

Only Control: The Novels of Joyce Carol Oates

Robert H. Fossum*

To say that Joyce Carol Oates is the best woman novelist in America today is like saying that Jane Austen was the best woman novelist in England in 1815. For Oates may be the finest American novelist, man or woman, since Faulkner and surely the best to appear in the past decade. She is at least the most prolific, having brought out six novels,[1] four collections of stories, three volumes of poetry, and a book of critical essays since 1964. Oates differs from many of her less productive contemporaries in a more important sense, however. Unlike Philip Roth, say, she has not turned to parody or black comedy. Unlike a Thomas Pynchon or Donald Barthelme, she has not violated the conventional structures of language. Nor has she so lost faith in the power of realistic narrative that she feels compelled to undergird it with the mythical dimensions by which some of our postmodern novelists (Styron, Updike, the early Malamud) give significance to the commonplace. Although her fiction sometimes fails to capture the peculiar social texture of a given time and place, it brilliantly illumines the emotional lives of her characters, be they migrant workers or wealthy farmers, suburban executives or lower class urbanites, and evokes an overwhelming sense of those psychological pressures in American life which produce our obsessions and frustrations, our dreams of love and power, our struggles to understand the world and ourselves.

Oates has said that art "must deal consciously with emotions that are . . . 'unimagined,' not yet rendered into coherent images by most people," and hence "dangerous."[2] If "all human beings are artists, whether consciously or unconsciously," Oates's characters are notably unsuccessful artists. Their imaginations stunted or impoverished by circumstances, they experience few epiphanies and few visions beyond those induced by American advertising. Ignorant of the causes of their feelings and actions, they exist in a state of bewilderment, a waking dream punctuated by moments of restlessness, impotent rage, or violence. Unable to " 'write one book, get everything into it' " (*GED*, p. 291),[3] they feel like actors in a script written and directed by someone else. And their emotions become, as a result, dangerous indeed.

These emotions and the conflicts between them are fundamentally the same from novel to novel. Repeatedly, Oates's people crave an order associated

*Reprinted with permission from *Studies in the Novel*, 7 (1975), 285–97.

with "home" and the loving protection of the father. Repeatedly, this conflicts with a yearning for the "road" and freedom from the father. And both are expressions of a struggle to control their own lives against the forces of "accident," circumstances, other people. Oates's fascination with the depression clearly stems from the collective impotence and bewilderment characteristic of that period. Her preoccupation with control accounts for the importance she places on childhood, not only because the parent-child relationship typifies the conflict but because she believes that early experiences become internalized fatalities. It also accounts for the much-remarked violence in her fiction. Rarely premeditated or fully comprehended by its perpetrator, violence is a response to thwarted attempts at self-determination, a response which becomes, ironically, one of those accidents defeating the attempt at control. Still, violence is not her characters' only response. Retreats into somnolence, into gluttony, into self-fabricated worlds designed as fortresses against fatality are almost equally common.

With Shuddering Fall introduces the basic design which Oates's subsequent novels embroider more elaborately. Shar Rule's flight from home to become a racing car driver was not originally a rebellion against a "life dominated by fathers" (*WSF*, p. 173) but a repudiation of the senior Rule's attempt to impose order on the "insane pile of debris" (*WSF*, p. 8) inside his tarpaper shanty. It is only when his desire for Karen Herz is frustrated that Shar erupts, setting fire to the shanty and beating up Karen's father. Karen, however, is from the beginning torn between father and Shar, home and road, a desire for order and the desire to outrun time. She chooses Shar, but rather than resolving the conflict, her choice simply changes its form. For Shar, who is "happy only when in control" (*WSF*, p. 188) and whose command of the racing car gives him the illusion of immortality, is invincible only so long as he remains independent of other people. Karen, who feels she is "nothing in herself" (*WSF*, p. 82), is beguiled by Shar's ability to dominate and by his emotional aloofness. Yet just as Shar is both attracted and challenged by Karen's passivity, so the qualities which draw her to him also threaten her. She hates his "strange world that she cannot control" (*WSF*, p. 109) and knows that only by imitating his "icy reserve that controlled the game" (*WSF*, p. 117) can she acquire sovereignty over him. She succeeds all too well. Because each wants total domination of the other, true communion is impossible, victory for either a defeat for both. Thus the "communion of pain" (*WSF*, p. 174) effected by Karen's miscarriage gives Shar to her but does not give Karen to him. Emotionally involved, he has lost that which made him indispensable to Karen. " 'What do you want me to do?' " he asks. She answers, " 'You make me sick' " (*WSF*, p. 181).

Shar for the first time now feels drawn to other people by a sense of their common doom. To give oneself to another is to be mortal; for "death to auto racers came not through surrender to the center"—that is, themselves—"but through surrender to . . . centrifugal force, a sudden careening off the track" (*WSF*, p. 80). There is only one possible act of self-determination left to Shar. Driving his car into the retaining wall, he kills himself. His life, the meeting with Karen—they may have been accidents; but " 'he made his death for himself' " (*WSF*, p. 191). Shar's death also returns Karen to father and home, where in the timelessness of the Church she finds relief from her awareness of mortality, in subjection to God and her father the "greater presence of someone to acknowledge her" (*WSF*, p. 111). For Karen, communion and identity have been achieved, but at the cost of control and self-affirmation.

Of Oates's first five novels, only *With Shuddering Fall* begins and ends with home. Although the Boschean title of her second novel refers most specifically to the various plots of domestic order which Clara Revere cultivates, *A Garden of Earthly Delights* begins on the road winding through a larger and not very orderly garden: the America of the 1930s. It is the road traveled by migrant workers, Clara's father Carleton, and his family among them. A victim of natural and economic forces beyond his comprehension or control, haunted by thoughts of the home he has lost, Carleton responds with sporadic violence aroused by thoughts of the "bastards who ran things" (*GED*, p. 113); by trying to arrange his memories "into something that made sense"; and by clinging to the little he owns, for to lose anything would make it "harder to get home again" *GED*, pp. 22–23). After Clara runs away with Lowry, Carleton searches for her as if she were his lost youth, only to recognize finally that he will never untangle his life, that his quest for home has ended where it began: on an empty highway.

As ambivalent as Karen, Clara considers Lowry both an escape from and a substitute for her father. Unfortunately, for all his apparent independence, Lowry is also homeless, dispossessed, and cannot finally control even Clara, since when he takes to the road, she casts aside his belief that one's fate is determined by accident. Going to bed with the unhappily married Curt Revere, she finds a father for Lowry's unborn child and a means of bringing "all those accidents into control" (*GED*, p. 189). For Revere not only brings to life the picture of a father in her grade-school reader; as an agent of the economic power ruling the Carletons and Lowrys of this world, he establishes her in a house which fulfills the American Dream symbolized by the flag she once stole as a child. Here, in contrast to her life on the road, are permanence and possession. Here, she can tend a small garden symbolic of the order and control she wants. Here, she can even refuse Lowry when, psychologically wounded and craving Clara's earthy simplicity, he returns from the war to reclaim her.

Her eventual marriage to Revere brings Clara and her son out of their insulated Eden and into the expansive domain of Revere's family house. From its windows, they "cannot see the horizon" (*GED*, p. 263) beyond which lies a past they cannot change. a future they cannot foresee, a world without limits. It is an ominous sign. Clara can control the phlegmatic Revere better than the restless passion whose claims she denied in renouncing Lowry. Unable to handle words, which "betrayed her" (*GED*, p. 132), Clara cannot create a metaphor by which she might understand and give coherence to her emotions. She can only arrange objects, enlarge the "garden room," plan additions to the house—all based on magazine advertisements and calendar art. More dangerously, she releases her "unimagined" emotions in affairs bitterly witnessed by the son she both loves and resents. Naming him after the indomitable white birds, Clara wants Swan to be a "person to whom everything would make sense, who . . . would not just control his own life but other lives as well" (GED, p. 201). Ironically, the zeal for control which led her to Revere has taken Swan's destiny partially out of her hands, while her uncontrolled promiscuity contributes to her son's equally uncontrollable emotional turmoil.

Contrary to a jacket blurb assertion that he exemplifies the "terrible innocence of natural evil," Swan is no Claggart. True, he sometimes feels impelled to fulfill Lowry's prophecy that he will be a killer and unconsciously feels responsible for his stepbrother's accidental death. But more often he is nauseated by violent death of all kinds. That the impulsion eventually triumphs is primarily the result of his thwarted desire for total control. The desire has not been satisfied by reading, which he gives up when he realizes that he can never command all "that vast systematic garden of men's minds" (GED, p. 361), nor by usurping Revere's economic control of Eden County, that "garden so complex" (GED, p. 347). Indeed, nothing short of total control would seem to suffice. The impulsion, on the other hand, is compounded by his intuitive sense that the prophet hovering over him like a hawkish Fury is his true father, Clara's true love and master. It is compounded further by his belief that Revere will disown a son who is not a hunter. Thus both fathers deny him a home, both (along with Clara's lovers) deny him control of his mother's affections, and both urge him toward violence.

Swan can morally justify his intention to kill Clara on the grounds of her "bitchery," his suicide on the grounds that he willed his stepbrother's death. But just as Shar, the father-killer, kills himself rather than Karen, so Swan cannot shoot Clara. Instead he shoots Revere—usurping father, mother's lover, arch-controller—before killing himself. Clara, in turn, ends like her mother, underscoring Oates's recurring insistence that the past is fatality: in a mindless state dominated by television dramas in which violence invariably destroys evil and rewards good.

Expensive People begins with a confession of violence. Its narrator, eighteen-year-old Richard Everett, announces that he is a child murderer. Not, he points out, someone who has murdered a child (his parents have in effect accomplished that) but a child who has committed murder. In this and other ways, Expensive People thematically resembles A Garden of Earthly Delights. Technically, however, it is more broadly satirical, more blatantly symbolic, and more contrived than either of the earlier novels. It is also more ambiguous, since the psychopathic Richard is hardly a reliable narrator; we are not even sure that he has in fact killed his mother.

We are more certain that Richard's discussions of the art employed in writing his "memoir" are not merely occasions for Oates to expound on her own craft. In practicing his writer-mother's profession, Richard is trying to re-create the person he thinks he has destroyed as well as seeking to order and control his life, past and present. His mother had also tried to do the latter. Nada Everett's stories about childhood are analogues of her attempt to create a coherent, self-determined personal history through possessions and social status. Like Richard's memoir, they may or may not be "true." Indeed, the relationship between the freedom-loving Nada who sometimes abandoned home and Richard for the road and lovers, and the devoted mother who, he says, was an "embryonic creature of my own" (*EP*, p. 100), parallels the relationship between reality and art, fact and imagination, the uncontrollable and the controlled. Granted, Richard sometimes suspects that art too is an "accident," as devoid of order as life itself, or, if either has an order, that it is effected by some unfathomable and omnipotent Artist. Nonetheless, the memoir is undeniably his attempt to impose form, to become the governor rather than the governed.

However manipulated by Richard's imagination and Oates's satirical purpose, Richard's world is that of upper middle-class suburbia, a "domestic American darkness" (*EP*, p. 145) in which parents are their children's "molesters" and expend souls in expending money. Richard says at one point that "Fernwood is Paradise" (*EP*, p. 123), adding that "it means nothing" (*EP*, p. 120). A garden of earthly delights, it is a spiritual hell, tolerable only if one maintains the illusion that possessions are all. To give up the illusion would mean "the end of western Civilization!" (*EP*, p. 142); it would also mean the end of a world dominated by women. At the library, one of Nada's friends peruses a book called *The Care and Feeding of the Middle-Aged American Male*. At a beauty parlor, Richard sees in *Vogue* pictures of women who have assumed male roles. At his office, Richard's father has power; at home he is nothing. And except for an occasional rebellion against the " 'lousy American father bit' " (*EP*, p. 235), Everett accepts his emasculation. Victimized by his "extravagent . . . love for Nada" (*EP*, p. 22) and the void her name suggests, he and his male counterparts assert their will to power in their interchangeable executive jobs, in ownership of their interchangeable houses, in driving their interchangeable cars, but never as husbands and fathers. So Richard, like Swan, sometimes doubts that Everett is his parent and longs to hear the "strong, hard, even brutal voice of my true father" (*EP*, p. 26). So too Nada cherishes her material Eden yet periodically seeks the excitements of the road.

Nada is, in fact, simply a more elegant, imaginative Clara. The child of immigrant parents, she has vowed to create herself anew as part of a "world that owns and controls everything" (*EP*, p. 56), thereby escaping from history into a realm of expensive things which "seemed emanations of a higher existence" (*EP*, p. 116). But the realm proves to be a trap, she herself both a personification of its emptiness and a sometime rebel against it, a woman alternating between greedy acquisition and flights to strange lovers in strange and distant cities. Her husband (like Revere to Clara) is at once her liberator and her jailer, her son (like Swan to Clara) at once a creature to be shaped in her image of perfection and an obstacle to her freedom.

Whether Richard actually kills his mother or not, his motives are clear. Bright as he is, he can never be as bright as she wants him to be; loving as he is, he cannot stop her from leaving him. Only when the real Nada is dead can he imaginatively engender a mother tamed by his "power and love" (*EP*, p. 21). Still, if Richard's violence, real or imagined, sometimes seems to him proof of free will, at other times it seems proof of foreordination. He remarks early on that a madman cannot " 'commit' murder," that "it gets done somehow, with or without his volition" (*EP*, p. 31), and later inverts Dostoevsky by observing that "no one was ever responsible for anything" (*EP*, p. 141); he implies elsewhere that he has made it happen. Even at the end of the novel he is unsure: "This is the only consolation I have, my readers: the thought of my free will. But I must confess that there are moments when I doubt even this consolation" (*EP*, p. 256). No matter. The important thing is what he wants: not "accidents" but a "murder committed by a child in full possession of his wits" (*EP*, p. 10), a murder which is also an attempt at creation.

The contrivances of *Expensive People* are absent from *them*, Oates's best novel so far. Good as it is, however, the work is not entirely satisfying. Set in Detroit, it proceeds from the mid-1930s to the mid-1960s yet evokes no strong sense of temporal flow. Its characters are products of the depression, yet the economic forces affecting them seem shadowy and unsubstantial. They live through World War II, yet it means no more to them than some Latin American revolution. If *them* is a historical novel as George Lukács has defined the mode, it is history in "personal perspective," that of Oates's characters, most of whom regard urban reality as a beast emitting the "foul stench of failure" (*T*, p. 267), or as "them," the people who threaten to control their lives.[4] To Grandma Wendall, "them" means Loretta, the mayor, the governor. To Loretta, it means Grandma, blacks, "foreigners." To the children, it means their parents. Finally, near the end of the novel, the attitudes of the Wendalls find their middle-class variants in the hostility of young revolutionaries toward all authority.

However threatened, Loretta and her children maintain a typical American reluctance to admit their helplessness. Loretta doggedly waits for an apotheosis promised by the movies which shape her values and dreams; failing at everything, she is "always ready to begin over again" (*T*, p. 142). As a young girl, she has seen her mother go insane, her father become a hopeless incompetent, her brother murder her lover. Later, she watches her husband drift into a vegetable passivity and die from an industrial accident. None of these destroys her belief that the world is divided between "hopeless bastards" and people who are "going to get somewhere" (*T*, p. 18) because they will not let themselves be "pushed around." Her unflagging quest for a permanent home and a strong husband reflects her faith in the possibility of self-determination and ultimate order. And though sometimes, like Clara and Nada, she longs for the excitement of the road, neither her longing nor her will to satisfy it is as strong as theirs.

Her son Jules is not so limited, but he shares Loretta's belief that desire is fate. For him, the symbols of mastership are money and a car on the road. The "imperial crest of the Cadillac" his only "coat of arms" (*T*, p. 258), the "golden ceiling of the bank" (*T*, p. 255) his only church, Jules believes that with money and wheels he would be "fated to nothing." He is a "true American" (*T*, p. 357), reaching for a future whose spatial analogue is the West and confusing it with an equally dreamlike past, that of his boyhood rural home. In such a past recaptured in the future, this latter-day Gatsby thinks, he "could change himself to fit into anything" (*T*, p. 109). The more worldly Faye warns him that there is nothing out west. But whereas the magic in American eyes generally "wears out quickly" (*T*, p. 410), in Jules's eyes it endures.

A typical Oatesean youth, Jules considers home and family to be heavy fleshly garments restricting his soul's freedom; at the same time, he wants the order and communion they represent. His conflicting desires for road and home are associated with an accident witnessed as a boy: a man's head is split in two; Jules suffers nightmares about it; and he comes to associate it with another childhood experience in which a policeman clubs him on the head. Later on, his brief affair with Faye temporarily heals the split. Offering him communion, she also epitomizes the freedom he seeks, having severed her own family ties. Furthermore, she introduces him to the wealthy Bernard Geffen.

Even Geffen's violent death and Faye's disappearance do not destroy the dream which her name connotes. Like Scott Fitzgerald's sad young men, Jules continues to search for a woman "with the gray-green metallic odor of money" (*T*, p. 247) and thinks he has found her in Nadine, the girl from Grosse Pointe. Personification of a "made-up imagined" fate comprised of money, power, and beauty, Nadine too wants freedom from parental control. The haven she imagines, however, is " 'somewhere empty' " (*T*, p. 291) as herself. The Jules who wants communion is eager to penetrate "her deepest silence," to "lose himself" (*T*, p. 381) in the emptiness of the American Dream which her name suggests. That side of Jules which wants freedom recognizes, on the other hand, that his soul is endangered by this woman "prodding him with the toe of her expensive shoe," this "opening . . . into nothing" (*T*, p. 355). Indeed, when she cannot draw his power into herself, she shoots him, and the "spirit of the Lord departed from Jules" (*T*, p. 403).

It returns during the riot. One of those apocalyptic, collective eruptions which frequently constitute the penultimate episodes of Oates's novels, the riot is fomented by university students venting personal frustrations under the guise of ideological revolution. Jules shares their frustrations but not their self-deception. His vision of "some clearing in the midst of the cities" (*T*, p. 503) temporarily replaced by the actuality of excavation sites and dead-end streets, the riot reawakens the "violence that had become his . . . emergency instinct" (*T*, p. 469). Earlier he has picked up a runaway girl, an upper-class version of his sister Maureen and a more helpless counterpart of Nadine; by subduing her, he has broken the grip in which each, in her own way, had held him. Now, during the riot, he kills a policeman and avenges the head-splitting blow dealt him as a child. Both acts are affirmations, he believes, of the essential, autonomous Jules.

Nonetheless, Oates's suggestion that Jules will someday write his own version of *them* is unconvincing. Rather than resulting in self-understanding and a coherent metaphor of his emotions, his violence appears merely to revive his dreams of making money, marrying Nadine, and finding the Great Good

Place in California. Maureen's choice of home rather than road seems even less likely to provide the means of self-determination. Possessing the passive power of Oates's women rather than the power of her men, Maureen also believes in an open future, money as freedom, the opposite sex as salvation. Her two selves, as she thinks of them, are in fact reflected in Jules and Loretta. Jules is her "darker self" (*T*, p. 266), a "free body, running away" (*T*, p. 318). Loretta is the self wanting to "arrange her life the way she arranged her kitchen" (*T*, p. 136). Because she cannot control this duality, she prays for some external unifying law to declare itself or, failing that, for self-obliteration in an abyss of love.

Maureen's rage for order, which eventually defeats her desire for liberty, prompts her to enroll in writing courses, first with Oates, then with Jim Randolph. But her compositions are as inchoate as her existence. At times, she even defends their jumble. If literature gives form to life, she asks, why is that better "than the way life happens, by itself?" (*T*, p. 338). The similarity between Maureen and Oates, which they both sense, lies in their comparable perception of chaos. Even assuming that life has some form, Oates's easy assertion that literature provides it is obviously wrong, as Maureen recognizes; all literature can do is discover the figure in the carpet. And if the carpet has no figure, literature can only mirror the chaos or provide a form not inherent in its raw materials. Maureen's compositions do the former. Oates's novel mirrors the chaos, discovers the emotional patterns to her character's lives, and creates a work of art having its own formal pattern.

In a sense, Maureen's marriage to Jim Randolph is her work of art, a carefully fashioned stay against the confusion of the formless. The difference between her work and Oates's is of course obvious: people and circumstances in a novel are controllable, those in real life frequently not. Jules recognizes the latter, at least. For when Maureen urges him to go away because he is one of "them" she would exclude from her new order, he reminds her that she herself is one of "them." She is that, certainly, to Randolph's children and former wife, whose domestic order she has disrupted to create her own. She is, moreover, Loretta's daughter and Jules's sister, sharing traits which, though repressed, may ultimately subvert her control. So Clara and Nada discovered. So Jesse, the protagonist of *Wonderland*, will discover.

Wonderland comes close to fulfilling what Oates has called her "laughably Balzacian ambition to get the whole world into a book." Paradoxically, it may also seem her least "realistic" novel, because its perspective is largely that of characters who, in a more sophisticated way than any in the earlier works, substitute self-created hermetic worlds for formless, accident-prone reality. Doctors and scientists, they are too "civilized" to indulge in the violence of a Shar, too strong-willed to lapse into the somnolence of a Howard Wendall, too ambitious to settle for those "tidy rooms in Bedlam" furnished by a Clara or Maureen. Yet these very qualities give birth to wonderlands more remote from mundane reality than anything their predecessors could conceive, to hospitals and laboratories where human personality can be scientifically controlled.

The novel begins in familiar Oatesean fashion: during the thirties, in a town ominously named Yewville, with a violent response to biological accident. Jesse Harte's father, maddened by his wife's latest pregnancy, slaughters the entire family except Jesse, who escapes. Bereft of parents, and thereafter of a grandfather who rejects him, Jesse feels that he no longer exists, that he has been excluded from the human family and denied the past upon which identity depends. To remain sane he must repress the image of the slaughter and re-nounce everything "dragging Jesse back to Jesse's . . . childhood" (W, p. 173), including the self his father had tried to murder, his grandfather repudiated. He must find new parents, a new home, a new self. That Oates considers this to be figuratively true of all young Americans is implied by the title of the first book: "Variations on an American Hymn"; but in Jesse's case the process of "inventing himself" (W, p. 271) continues beyond boyhood.

After Dr. Pedersen adopts him, Jesse establishes a pattern he will follow from then on. Modeling himself on a surrogate father, he seeks his identity within a family. *"Let me be like them, let them love me, let everybody know that I am one of them,"* he prays, so that he can know "precisely who he was" (W, p. 86). Like them, he voraciously consumes food and information as urged by the Doctor, who thinks to control everything and everyone by engorging them. Pedersen's other children defeat him by retreating into their own won-derlands, Hilda's built with mathematical, Frederick's with musical symbols, while his wife periodically escapes into disorderly drunkenness. Hence, Ped-ersen's hopes focus on Jesse, whom he tries to mold into the " 'complete form of the self I have imagined for him' " (W, p. 127). But in spite of the boy's willingness to be formed, his compassion for Mrs. Pedersen leads him inadver-tently to oppose her husband, to be repudiated, and to be told once again that he does "not exist" (W, p. 184).

Pedersen continues to exist for Jesse, however. Although he changes his name for the second time, this time to Vogel, Jesse retains his stepfather's ideals. He too becomes a doctor. Believing that man's fate is ultimate perfection, he too wants to " 'organize the future' " (W, p. 77) not only for himself, his family, and his patients but even to the extent of saving " 'everyone from dying' " (W, p. 171). Dr. Perrault is simply a less Dickensian Pedersen, and by imitating him, Jesse turns himself into a " 'copy of a copy of a human being' " (W, p. 313). A machine operating on patients whom he views as machines, Perrault considers the distressingly unstable human personality an enemy, and while insisting that one person cannot own another, his actions reflect the contrary assumption. Science in general and Perrault's aims in particular appeal to Jesse for obvious reasons. "Isn't the great lesson of science *control*," he thinks. "*Control*. That was all he wanted" (W, p. 197).

What distinguishes Jesse from his surrogate fathers is that he seems less concerned with control of others than with control of himself, less intent on ridding others of personality than on destroying his own. He "did not want a personality" (W, p. 322), because personality is based on memory and Jesse's memory is full of monsters too horrible to contemplate. Now even as a scientist, Jesse suspects that the past is ineradicable, arguing in a medical journal that earliest memories are most staunchly retained and collecting news clippings associated with his own buried life. Still, he tries to believe that he need remember only "as far back as he wanted to remember—that is, as far back as he had been Jesse Vogel" (W, p. 236)—thereby purging himself of a personality he dreads. In performing brain surgery, he is then vicariously trying to remove the "poisonous little beads" (W, p. 435) from his own head. The result is not health but fragmentation.

Because salvation as Jesse conceives it also demands freedom from emotional involvement, he withdraws into the laboratory, the operating room, the study, where he can disregard his patients' "personal history" (W, p. 209) and love them only in the abstract. Trick Monk is quite correct in saying that Jesse " 'aspires to a condition of personal bloodlessness' " (W, p. 237). Monk's friendship must be abjured, in fact, not only because he would emotionally involve himself with Jesse but because he is a " 'kind of equivalent' " (W, p. 456) of the "other Jesses . . . sinister and unkillable" (W, p. 190) who must be kept buried. A doctor turned poet, Monk addresses his *Poems without People* to Jesse, who, in his way, also constructs "poems" devoid of disturbing human presences. The difference between them is that Monk knows his wonderland is imaginary and affirms personalities by pretending to exclude them.

Oates has said that "without personality there cannot be art," for without it we cannot imagine the existence of others or create the metaphors needed to understand ourselves.[5] Jesse's memory, one of the bases of personality, is too mutilated even to understand literary plot, the "necessary pattern . . . that demanded completion." He believes that all stories, like his own life, are "fragments from shattered wholes" and not, in any case, " 'believable' in the way his medical texts were believable" (W, pp. 228–29). Thus he would like to replace "trivial human language," another basis of personality, with the language of the surgeon's hands, the psyche, container of all time, with the "inviolable . . . timelessness" (W, p. 311) of the operating room. Neither replacement is possible. Like Maureen, the other Jesse struggles to find the "exact words that would explain his life" and waits "for someone else—a woman, perhaps—to draw these sacred words out of him, to . . . redeem him as Jesse" (W, p. 349).

His wife cannot help him. Recognizing that Jesse is a " 'jumble of men' " (W, p. 350) who, seeking integration, wants to *be* his wife and children, she also realizes that her own identity is too shaky, her own head too filled with unformed words to elicit any from him. The only woman who might have succeeded is Reva. As her name implies, she is more dream than reality, more *anima* than a simple, separate person. This is why Jesse thinks he has known her before, why her name is "made up," and why he feels that by possessing her he would "penetrate . . . all parts of himself" (W, p. 377). Reva herself believes that together they could complete a plot and bring about a new start. But Jesse cannot afford union with Reva, for that would mean acknowledging Jesse Harte and "slaughtering" his family. Instead, he mutilates himself once again. It is indeed "The Finite Passing of an Infinite Passion": the sacrifice of an integrated passional self to the gods of his domestic and scientific wonderlands.

Both fail him. He gives a scientific name to a patient's uncontrollable mental disorder but senses that it should be called *The Tragedy of Joseph Ross*. After his daughters are born, he thinks that finally "his life was in his control" (*W*, p. 314) but soon learns that he can control neither his children nor his emotions toward them. Shelley disobeys his command, an echo of Dr. Pedersen's, that she " 'speak only in complete sentences' " (*W*, p. 404) and is frightened by *Alice in Wonderland* because she sees herself diminished and dragged through the air by her father. The Kennedy assassination disturbs them both—Jesse because it was a death he could not prevent, Shelley because her father cannot alleviate her terror. Moreover, when she runs from home, she not only repeats Mrs. Pedersen's flight but seeks in drugs what the latter sought in alcohol, Jesse in his work: darkness without memory, the destruction of personality.

Jesse is condemned to relive his past in another way. He is now the pursuer rather than the pursued, acting out the role of Pedersen in trying to repossess the rebellious object of his possession and swearing that " 'Nobody is going to die tonight' " (*W*, p. 479). To Noel, her presumed saviour, Shelley even echoes Mrs. Pedersen's words to Jesse—" 'he gets into my head' " (*W*, p. 172) and is similarly reclaimed by her would-be owner. Actually, she had achieved no more freedom than the Doctor's wife. Haunted by thoughts of her father, she needs Noel as Mrs. Pedersen needed Jesse. In treating Shelley as his property, Noel is a surrogate father; in proclaiming that passion is fate, he is the other Jesse. The combination is irresistible to Shelley, representative of a "Dreaming America" desiring both autonomy and communion, self-assertion and loss of self, the restoration of the past and freedom from it.

The period when Jesse was a member of a family has been temporarily recaptured, but so has the past he hoped to escape. Shelley has in her way dissolved the family; Jesse is now tempted to repeat his father's violence by slaughtering his wife, his children, humanity itself as exemplified by a youthful Chicago mob. Hating its "formlessness," he wants to "destroy them all . . . . So much garbage in the world," he thinks, "And most of it human!" (*W*, p. 499). Although he resists that temptation, the ending to the novel is hardly happy.[6] Jesse has not only failed to "catch up with his own consciousness" (*W*, p. 396); he has failed to discover the wonderland of controlled order that he has envisioned for so long. Like Oates's other novels, *Wonderland* begins in violence and ends not with the restoration of order characteristic of tragedy but with the exhaustion born of defeat. In her world, the only order is that of art, the only one in control the artist herself.

Notes

1. The sixth, *Do with Me What You Will* (New York: Vanguard, 1973), appeared after this article was written.

2. Letter to *Times Literary Supplement*, 13 April 1973, p. 420.

3. In the parenthetical page references throughout, titles are abbreviated as follows: *WSF* = *With Shuddering Fall* (Greenwich, Conn.: Fawcett, 1964); *GED* = *A Garden of Earthly Delights*

(Greenwich, Conn.: Fawcett, 1967); *EP* = *Expensive People* (Greenwich, Conn.: Fawcett, 1968); *T* = *them* (New York: Vanguard, 1969); *W* = *Wonderland* (Greenwich, Conn.: Fawcett, 1973).

4. Ambiguous as Oates's other titles "them" also suggests the differences initially felt between ourselves and the characters which the novel as a whole tries to dispel.

5. "Art: Therapy and Magic," *The American Journal*, 1 July 1973, pp. 18–20.

6. The original Vanguard Press edition ends with Jesse and the dying Shelley adrift in a boat, the former crying that everyone has always abandoned him, even the "undefiled Jesse." In the ending to subsequent editions, Shelley is alive and Jesse in love with "this control, this certainty" (*W*, p. 478). Yet when his daughter says he is the devil, Jesse, still uncertain of his identity, can only reply " 'Am I?' " (*W*, p. 479).

The Language of Tragedy and Violence

Mary Kathryn Grant, R. S. M.*

But what must also be said, as we see this new structure, is that the most deeply known humanity is language itself.

Raymond Williams, *The English Novel*

The verbal ambiance of Joyce Carol Oates's works is violent. Her choice of images, figures of speech, and her basic rhetorical devices support and confirm her underlying concern with the violent and the tragic. Most activities in her fictive world are performed violently; conversations are angry and charged with hostility, the interaction between characters is often brutal and savage. Beneath this ambiance is the persistent and gnawing fear that one will be destroyed and the corresponding necessity of establishing or maintaining a sense of order and meaning in one's life. The resultant tension is electrifying.

A subtle type of violence Oates uses in her fiction is the deliberately annoying and disconcerting absence of a resolution in many of her pieces. The reader is teased into involvement with and concern for a fictional character or situation, only to be confused by an artistic statement which refuses to make sense. Oates acknowledges in "Fiction Dreams Revelations," the preface to *Scenes from American Life*, that art is often mimetic.[1] Because "nothing human is simple," that art which endeavors to speak to human experience will not necessarily be explicable or satisfying. Her own fiction, consequently, is often violently, annoyingly uncompleted. Her characters do not act; her plots are frequently unresolved; certain of her stories do not make sense.

By means of such devices as the imagery of shattering glass, of jigsaw puzzles, and of entrapment, through the repeated and powerful technique of describing even the most trivial objects and events in terms of violence, together with the rapid pace at which her tales are narrated, Oates creates her own unique language and aesthetic tragedy and violence. Careful always to skirt the potential dangers of mere sensationalism and horrific titillation, she generates an ambiance of violence integral to her tragic vision. She is thoroughly imbued

*Reprinted with permission from *The Tragic Vision of Joyce Carol Oates* (Durham, N.C.: Duke Univ. Press, 1978), pp. 93–116.

with the fact that the value of aesthetic violence lies in its power to bring man to an awareness of his own mortality.

As John Fraser notes in *Violence in the Arts,* "some violences make for intellectual clarity and a more civilized consciousness, while others make for confusion."[2] If Oates's fiction leads to a sense of confusion, this is so in order to reflect the confusion inherent in human life and to push on toward a new consciousness. Only when one begins to ask how life can be lived or to wonder if a careless move can unhinge the universe can he begin to see how he can take hold of his life and avoid the careless move.

One mode of rhetorical violence in Oates's work is the technique of excessive concern for detail which creates an effect like that of a camera refusing to move to another scene; the reader is forced, as it were, to keep watching despite his desire not to see any more. This attention to detail, Oates explains in her review of Carlos Castaneda's *Tales of Power,* is part of Western rationalism. She describes this condition as "the system of perceptions and verbal descriptions of the world that, in our culture, is a social convention." But art is "not mere reportorial observation," because it "resists and transcends conventional categories of labeling, like Norman Mailer's poetic journalism and Truman Capote's 'non-fiction novel' *In Cold Blood.*"[3] Although written in defense of Castaneda's works, the statements are equally applicable to her own writings.

In the world of her novels, people make love, play pianos, and eat violently. Music explodes, grins shatter, grease spatters maliciously as Oates uses every rhetorical device at her command to create an explosive atmosphere. By not relying solely on the narration of violent actions but supplementing this with rhetorical violence, she succeeds in generating a highly charged fictional environment. Her narratives mirror the turbulence and disorder of this nightmarish world. By repeatedly describing even the most ordinary of human actions in terms of hostility, brutality, and truculence, Oates creates a totally violent fictive world. There is no relief, and there are few comic interludes; once the tragic tale is initiated the tension escalates through greater and more tense scenes, most often culminating in murder, suicide, or riots. Infusing every detail of the narrative with violence, Oates leaves her reader exhausted.

She adeptly sets an ominous tone in the description of the night club where Shar, Max, and Karen celebrate Shar's recent racing victory. "Music from the jukebox exploded into the room. Mosquitoes and flies scattered to the ceilings" (WSF 143). One of their party is with a woman who appears "teased into prettiness" by "a violent, exotic outlining of her lips." Couples, dancing in one corner of the room, seem to "gallop together, violently" (WSF 144). The cumulative effect of these images carries forward the tension created in the preceding scene in which Shar has killed another driver during the race and prepares for the violence soon to come in the narrative. Oates directs the reader's attention to every charged detail as she describes even the most ordinary and commonplace things, such as lipstick and jukebox music, in terms of violence.

In one of the episodes just before Shar's death, a similar device is used.

While visiting taverns along the beach, Shar and Marian encounter a foreign couple shouting at each other in rage. The sun next affects Shar so that he begins to feel excited for a violence his body "craved and strained for"; then he is tempted to attack a young woman bather. Finally, he oversees two young boys "fighting viciously . . . with terrible hatred" (WSF 218). The mounting details help to generate a tension in the narrative paralleling the increasing rage in Shar until the "desire for violence had grown so strong in him that tears of rage and lust had forced their way into his eyes" (WSF 223). By heaping scene upon scene of violence—the angry argument in a foreign tongue, the urge to attack someone, the youths' vicious fighting—the episode creates in the reader an explosive urgency, the sense of having arrived at the brink of imminent action or disaster.

Likewise, the events which lead up to Nadine's shooting of Jules are described with rhetorical violence. Jules senses as they embrace that they are "fated for some final convulsion, locked in each other's arms, their mouths fastened greedily together in a pose that neither had really chosen—like gargoyles hacked together out of rock, freaks of mossy rock" (*them* 314). The effect of the language, "a convulsion, kissing like gargoyles," prepares not for a romantic reunion but a turbulent encounter. After several days, when they meet again in the apartment Nadine had arranged for, Jules wants to "gather her violently into his arms and penetrate her to the very kernel of her being, to her deepest silence, bringing her to a release of this joy. But she seemed to slip from him, too weak or too stunned, and he felt his love emptied violently into her again while she held him, her hands tight against his back, tight as if with alarm, her own body grown rigid at this crisis" (*them* 381). Nevertheless, Jules feels the moment is "magical." The effect of alternately describing the scene in terms of magic and violence is one of sharply heightened tension, and the rhythm of violence and magic parallels the mood of the lovers as it moves from ecstasy to terror, "making them both victims" of the "tyranny in the tension . . . between them" (*them* 397). Ironically, it is Jules who thinks he might destroy Nadine until he recognizes that her "beauty had gone all into hardness, in vacuity." When she pulls the trigger, Jules sees the "sunshine shattered in the windshields of an acre of large, gleaming, expensive cars" (*them* 403). Her hardness, prefigured in the image of gargoyles, ultimately reveals her as a killer. Rhetorical violence, carefully placed in juxtaposition with the motif of magic, serves to create a tension in the narrative that far surpasses that which the mere recounting of violent incidents could create.

Clever punning achieves a comparable effect in *Do With Me What You Will*. After kidnapping his daughter and taking her to San Francisco, Leo Ross is more sick, bewildered, and frightened than ever. When he becomes particularly apprehensive about hiding out in his small apartment, he pockets his pistol and walks to the waterfront. Self-conscious, he is certain people are staring at him so he "shot them small half-mocking, half-inquisitive smiles" (DWM 33). The image of shooting smiles at questioning passersby suggests how close he is to resorting to physical violence. He is at the limits of his endurance, so armed with his weapon, he shoots hostile looks at his inquisitors. Sometime later in a park, he wants to shoot the ducks because of their annoying quacking. Inarticulate, incapable of understanding what he has done and what is happening to him, Ross resorts to the only language he does know how to use: violence.

Even Ross's metaphor for the world is implicitly—and incongruously— violent. The world is like a sieve, " 'a lot of little holes that things fall through like water, like blood . . . like blood bleeding out of your arteries while you stand there and watch . . . The world is filled with holes that surprise you every morning' " (DWM 30–31). There is nothing in the basic image of a sieve to link it with bleeding, yet as Ross elaborates on his description of the world as a sieve, he implicitly creates the image of shooting, in which out of bullet wounds one's lifeblood might pour. The image is obviously incongruous, yet here, once again, rhetorical violence inheres in every detail, every image of the narrative.

Oates draws a second image for the violence implicit in human life and living from another incongruous source, from the fair. It requires a certain acuity to recognize that "things don't stay still but are always jolting you . . . . It's my burden. Things never stay still, it's like one of them trick rides at the fair—the floor starts tilting under you and you almost fall down" (G 96). However tricky the grounding is, for Oates what is important is the recognition of the tilting floor; the rest can be coped with, if one understands and accepts this reality.

Sometimes, however, the tilting floor upends a character. The process of being reborn, of coming to terms with life tragically necessitates a breaking down, a dying. As Lea Gregg and her young friends, in the story "Free," note when discussing their own breakdowns, they need a new term like "vision" or "penetration." "Because, of course, what had seemed to be a breakdown was in reality a building up, but before any building could take place the clutter of twenty years of buried life had to be violently swept away" (G 131). The past has to be destroyed—and violently—if the phoenix of a new life can rise from the ashes. For most of Oates's fictive creations the past cannot be built on, but must be destroyed. The possibility of redemption is turned toward the future and does not affect the past.

When Oates describes the difficult and often violent quest for identity and a personality, distinct and unique, she chooses to use the word *protoplasm* to identify the existence before the creation of personality. One of the earliest uses of the word occurs in Trick Monk's poetry where it is quite in keeping with the character's nonidentity. However, to be reborn in Oates's recent fiction means to achieve one's sense of meaning, one's personality for the anonymous "protoplasm" of the present. Neil Myer, a young orderly in "Narcotic," grapples with this process when he visits a former patient, a girl who had tried to commit suicide. Besieged by doubts of his own identity, he longs to tell her of the "taunting voice in his head that told him he was *Neil Myer* and could not escape. A teaspoon of protoplasm?" (G 316). Groping for his identity, he can only find his name. And he knows "his name is not important, but sometimes he discovered himself repeating it, over and over, mechanically fascinated by its sound. *Neil Myer*. A combination of shrill shrieking sounds that were muffled by the 'N' and the 'M' but were not really silenced" (G 305).

When he leaves the hospital on his way to visit Paula, the young girl, he feels the people he passes on the street are accusing him: *"You are still Neil Myer."* When he fantasizes making love to her, he imagines "a time when he would not be *Neil Myer* but an anonymous young man, twenty-six years old, in anonymous good health, making love to an anonymous young woman" (G 313). Neil is caught trying to wrest his personality, his identity, from the teaspoon of protoplasm which is his existence and, at the same time, trying to escape that identity through anonymity.

In addition to the direct, overt use Joyce Carol Oates makes of violence are the subtle, pervasive suggestions of violence. The very pace of her narratives leaves the reader breathless; she creates a "pitch close to madness.' "[4] In just more than ten pages of the first chapter of *A Garden of Earthly Delights*, there is a collision between a truck of migrants and an auto, an angry fight between the two drivers, and the birth of a child. The rapid-fire telling of the events sets a pace which mirrors the frenzied activity of the lives of the characters. In *With Shuddering Fall*, the opening pages describe the cruel domestic setting from which Karen Herz inevitably must escape. *them* narrates in the first fifty pages the senseless murder of a young boy, the depressing domestic conditions of the Botsford family, and Loretta's rape by a policeman. Likewise, *Wonderland* recounts a mass murder and suicide all in its first two chapters. Not only are the events in themselves violent, but the very manner and speed with which they are narrated increase and tighten the tension. Critics have remarked that any synopsis of an Oates novel is practically impossible because there is a density of episodes that makes it difficult to recall and separate one event from another. These rhetorical techniques—the rapid pacing of the narration and the infusion of violence into detail—create an atmosphere of unrelieved tension: the incremental effect creates a totally violent fictive ambiance.

By her constant use of inversions and juxtapositions, Oates is implicitly violent. By equating totally dissimilar objects, she forces her reader to reexamine not only the objects themselves but the very language which can create such incongruity. " 'Bombs are poetry when they go off. Machine-gun fire is poetry. Agony is poetry' "—so Lea is told by one of her friends. "Life," on the other hand, "is ugly" (G 141). By distorting the commonplace in the heinous and the ugly into the artful, Oates constantly affects the reader's sensibilities. The marked difficulty of accepting these inversions helps to unsettle the reader's convictions about the ugly, about poetry, about life—the very effect Oates set about to generate. Finally, she calls into question language itself which can distort and misrepresent. As one of her characters bewilderedly explains, "telling [the truth] was an act of violence" (G 125). Telling the truth is the ultimate aim of Oates's fiction—however violent, however unpleasant and distasteful, however cruel and brutal that truth is.

Perhaps the most successful images suggesting the fragility of human life assailed on every side by violence are those of fine glassware and china. Reminiscent of a similar use of the images by Tennessee Williams in *The Glass Menagerie,* Oates's characters are often described in terms of fracturing or shattering glassware. The sense of holding onto one's life delicately but firmly, of trying to prevent the breakage, is poignantly captured in Jules Wendall's remarks to Nadine. Reunited after a nine-year separation, he confides to her that one thing he had come to realize during his convalescence is that " 'we all carried ourselves like glass, we are very breakable' " (*them* 363). In his short lifetime he had come to understand how very fragile a hold a human being can have on his own life and destiny, how much he is the victim of the violence and cruelty of others. He is not the complete master of his life; he never has the total control over his life which he constantly seeks. When he was only eighteen and had come to visit Maureen after her beating by Furlong, he had already experienced the unspoken feeling of his own fragility; "he carried himself up into this apartment like a man carrying something breakable" (*them* 223). This feeling of being breakable is his throughout his life.

As Richard Everett moves more and more into his tale, the awareness of his frailty grows on him. But the image of destructibility is more devastating in this narrative than in the others because the relief of "falling apart" is denied. Richard writes, "I am glass, transparent and breakable as glass, but—and this is the tragedy—we who are made of glass may crack into millions of jigsaw pieces but we do not fall apart. We never fall apart. Instead we keep lumbering around and talking. We want nothing more than to fall apart, to disintegrate, to be released into a shower of slivers and have done with it all, but the moment is hard to come by, as you can see" (EP 101). The escape, the "having done with it all," the merciful respite of forgetfulness and disintegration are withheld; the anguish and the pain of enduring as a million jagged jigsaw pieces remain.

The image of breaking or shattering into pieces is most frequently used in relation to facial expressions and suggests a fragile mask. As Carleton stands by, waiting as his wife delivers their child, he steels himself not to betray any emotion. He cannot show too much concern for his wife; men are not supposed to do that. But when she screams with the pains of labor, he must redouble his efforts "to keep his face from breaking into pieces" (GED 13). The image of fracturing, of being tested to the point of breaking, to a point beyond one's endurance, captures the tension of the moment. Carleton fears the breaking of his mask, the exposing of his feelings.

Clara, his daughter, experiences a similar tension of preserving her mask when she and Rosalie are on their little excursion to the town on Rosalie's birthday. Faced with the wonder of things she had never seen before, Clara starts to cry and feels her face breaking up into pieces. She needs to destroy the order and peace, the prosperity she finds in the town. Resisting the temptation to break the stained glass windows of a storybook house, she contents herself with stealing an American flag from the porch. Ironic as that gesture is—two poor migrant children stealing a flag from the home of more prosperous citizenry—it gives the girls great delight, and Clara runs off triumphantly with her prize.

The ability to keep her face from breaking into pieces requires great inner control. It also requires that Clara know what face to wear; it requires that she be able to judge which mask is appropriate to the occasion. Most of her life, Clara is plagued with the problem of deciding on the right face. Often, particularly during the early days of her relationship with Lowry, she confesses how hard it is "to know what kind of a face to have" (GED 150). Clara's challenge is to determine on and then to wear the right face for Lowry: the face that will keep him. So she must search for the right mask. The only time her expression is described as soft is in a photo taken on their trip to the shore. Clara's picture is vague "with a kind of beauty never hers . . . her face misty and softened by some mistake in the photographing process" (GED 195). A soft countenance could only be a mistake; Clara knows too well not to wear such a face.

Clara's fictional ancestor, Karen Herz, is actually called a "little mask" When Max knowingly tells her that he recognizes the fact she had been pampered during her life and could consequently manipulate people. She had not fooled him, however; he knows her tricks. Despite her being "very discreet and learned" (WSF 88), she is a little "persona" which Max thoroughly enjoys.

The masks, the "faces of all the world," appear to Maureen Wendall to be "frozen hard into expressions of cunning and anger." Sensitive, gentle Maureen, "having no hardness in her," is forced to creep into silence where she can wait for the day "when everything would be orderly and neat, when she could arrange her life the way she arranged the kitchen after supper, and she too might be frozen hard, fixed, permanent, beyond their ability to hurt" (*them* 136). Maureen is too simple and guileless to protect herself. Because she does not or cannot become "frozen hard," she constantly teeters on the brink of "breaking into pieces" (*them* 202). When she finally does break, she retreats behind an impenetrable wall of silence. Openness and tenderness leave her too vulnerable; as Maureen tragically learns, one can too easily be broken when one does not wear the right mask.

Forced into fashion modeling to help support her mother, young Elena Ross is taught early in life that she must *take care of that face, carry it like a crystal"* (DWM 79). She must keep her mask in place, her smile ready. Not only does the image of carrying a crystal fittingly depict the care and attention necessary to have an acceptable "face," but it also suggests Elena's various refractions of personality. Deprived of a childhood by her mother's ambitions, she is quickly married off to Marvin Howe, whom she not only does not love, but whom she does not even know. The model her mother, Ardis, offers of a confident and self-assured adult is anything but imitable: Ardis changes her name six times, undergoes plastic surgery, is continually dyeing her hair. When one's physical identity is so changeable, one's own deeper sense of identity is undoubtedly unstable. Ardis's advice to her daughter to carry herself like crystal is appropriate to the kind of life Elena is destined to lead. She must be equipped to wear many masks—until she finally does not know who she is and does not want to live. It is no wonder that with her recounting of her temptation to commit suicide at fourteen comes the recollection of her feelings of freedom.

She had pricked her wrist with a paring knife and she *"never forgot that pinprick sharp as a flash of light: freedom"* (DWM 309). When Jack Morrissey finds her in a trancelike state in front of a statue, she recalls withdrawing into peace, going into stone like the statue, but having to awake and to live. She is confused and fantasizes her own death as a way out. She has worn so many masks that her real identity has become obscured, and death looks like a long sought-after release.

Elena's fragility is almost comically noted when Jack, with a "stricken, questioning look," checks to see that she is not hurt, not damaged after they have intercourse. She is used to this kind of inspection by her husband, Marvin. Living on the brink of *"nullity"* and *"extinction,"* she needs to be constantly monitored—both her husband and her lover identify this weakness in her.

The continual suggestions of fragility and weakness, the metaphors of china and glassware, the hints of personalities shattering and breaking into pieces serve well to intensify the ambiance of violence in Joyce Carol Oates's fiction. She deftly sketches in the personalities of characters brought to the very brink of destruction and despair—all of which she skillfully works into her tales of unspeakable violence, with the effect of creating a fictive world in which violence inheres in even the most quotidian details. On occasion, she appears to mute the shocking effects of violence by draping the scenes in terms of magic. However, rather than muting the violence, the use of magic only more dramatically points to its horror.

In what is perhaps one of the most horribly explicit scenes in all of Oates's fiction—Brock's shooting to death Loretta's boyfriend beside her in bed—she has Loretta muse in stunned wonderment that "one shot had done it, like magic" (*them* 38). Incomprehensible as that event is, Loretta can only grasp its significance when she thinks of it as magic: time seems stopped; the room becomes unfamiliar. The only way she can cope with the reality is to regard it initially as magic. Gradually, however, the realization of what has happened descends on her, and she must act. Her own sense of the unreality of the situation is reenforced by the fact that the one magical shot arouses no response in anyone else. "Maybe a gunshot in the middle of the night wasn't much of a surprise after all" (*them* 37), she reflects. In stunned bewilderment, the sixteen-year-old girl must try to get her wits together and handle the situation.

Young Richard Everett speaks ironically of magic in his tale. His sense of how certain things happened "magically" belies his childlike candor and points to a fierce cynicism. When he introduces his parents into the narrative, his wry observation captures his love-hate attitude toward them: the love is magic, the hate, real. He writes, "at these special times when we were together I thought I had somehow, magically, captured a man and a woman from another land, foreign and exotic and not quite speaking my language, who were tamed by my power and love and who walked obediently after me . . . These were my true parents. The others—the dissatisfied Natashya Romanov, minor writer, and the blubbering breastbeating executive Elwood Everett—were nothing but cruel stepparents" (EP 22). Another time he describes his home as having at times a "certain soft magic, misty air" (EP 64). When things are well between his parents and between them and him, the times are like a magical dream. Yet he is fully aware that nothing is magic, so that rather than mute the horror of his story, his descriptions of magic events and situations only serve to call greater attention to the violence and chaos of his life. A departure from Oates's straightforward, stranger-than-fiction "histories," this novel parodies the creation of a novel. In so doing, those events and deeds of violence so horrifying in her other works are minimized and seemingly discredited. The underlying question of whether or not Richard actually murders his mother is never resolved and ultimately ceases to be a significant question.

With ever-greater irony, in *them*, Jules is described as a magician. As a youth, his "magic words" can make his companions perform anything he suggests. Even when it seems that nothing will ever be right in his life, he retains his belief in his magic touch. But as Maureen puzzles over his near-fatal shooting by Nadine, she comes to realize that there is no magic in America where "it wears out too quickly." She equates magic with life, being, identity, "the mysterious substance of the eye," and she is forced to conclude that it is a "terrible cruelty, because it wears out. In America it wears out quickly" (*them* 410). Magic cannot exist in her country—it is too easily killed off and destroyed.

In *Wonderland*, too, Oates ironically uses the make-believe magical world to suggest the muting of violence. The very title conveys the image of unreality and fantasy.[5] Occasional references to magic in the text inversely impute horror—not wonder—to the incidents. The ego-maniacal Dr. Pedersen declares in a guest sermon he delivers in the local church that "there is something magical about the United States. This is a time of magic . . . ." (W 113). Jesse Harte, his adopted son, is seated in the congregation and caught up with the meaning of these words. He tries to make sense of them, turning them over in his mind. For a fleeting period of his life, things do seem magical, but the spell is quickly broken when he is cast off by Pedersen and declared dead. There is no magic, no wonder in Jesse's life, only horror and pain.

Another effective device Oates uses is stark and often repulsive realism, as in the story, "Did You Ever Slip on Red Blood?" Like a refrain, the question is repeated throughout the narrative. The short fiction opens with the query, the meaning of which, again in typical Oates fashion, is only revealed at the end of the narration. Allusions to death and to a killing fill the pages of the story in a disconcerting and unsatisfying fashion and are only fully explained in retrospect. When Oberon and Marian are first described, Oberon looks at her as if [she were] centered in the telescopic sight of a rifle" (MI 339) which, one later learns, is exactly how he first saw her.

Throughout the narrative, Marian compulsively asks Oberon if he had ever slipped on red blood as she had, the red blood of the man he had shot. Marian believes that she loved Robert Severin, a man she had just met, the slain hijacker. And, as could only happen in Oates's world, Marian, the stewardess, and Oberon, the FBI agent, two lonely people, eventually get together, and believing they are in love, have an affair. Every element of the narrative creates a tension; not only the rifle, the flare which looks like a stick of dynamite, the pocket knife, but also the more subtle things like the anonymity secured through the use of sunglasses or the growing of a beard, the flight to strange cities and foreign countries, and the deep loneliness that makes strangers instant lovers. A master craftsman, Oates introduces no detail into the story that does not advance or increase the tension. Even the time sequence of the fiction is unsatisfyingly disjointed; nothing makes sense until the end, but at least in this narrative, the various elements fall into place at the conclusion. The red blood on which Marian slips is ironically—and tragically—that of a young, confused pacifist.

The fine fusion of intention and description at which Oates is so skilled is everywhere manifest in her writings. The opening story of her most recent collection of short fiction recapitulates the problem of anonymity, a theme often repeated in the volume, and does so most effectively by means of her use of rhetorical techniques and devices. The characters and setting of "The Girl" do not have names, but labels: The Director, the Cop, the Motorcyclist, the Beach, the Girl. Persons do not have identities; they merely represent functions. Nor do they relate to one another; they are only actors in a bizarre scenario. The story concerns events surrounding the making of a film during which the Girl is gang banged. When she sees the Director, some time after the filming, and tries to address him in the street, he is described as machine-like: a "kind of shutter clicked in his head" (G 13). He seems not to remember her, but she needs the assurance that the film-making had been real, that she had not imagined it, that she was the star. So out of touch with reality is she that her concern is only to establish her role in the film. Mechanical people look at each other "like on film," and people walk past them in the street as passersby "in a movie." "They are not in focus"; they are as blurred as are the events and circumstances of the story.

The story is filled with the lack of concern for and the failure to understand the effect one person has on another. The need for acceptance and sensitivity is nowhere in the story more pathetically described than when the Director blurts out, " 'I'm an orphan . . . I'm from a Methodist orphanage in Seattle' " (G 8). In response, the Cop grins and the Motorcyclist laughs. The Director's pathetic confession and the Girl's later cry for recognition are the products of the anomie of society. And Oates draws attention to this central issue through her rhetorical device of not naming her characters and of vaguely blurring the action.

Set against the fierce images of violence, the most frequent image of order and tranquility is the library. Neat, orderly and ordered rows of books stand in sharp contrast with the chaos and disorder of the world outside the library. While Karen recovers from her strange illness, Max brings her magazines and books from the local library. In her mind the library is a component of the systematic structure of city government: the order of the library is a microcosm of the system of the city. When she sees the books that Max had "checked out of the library in the city, she was struck by a sense of disorder, of wonder as if it were somehow absurd to have to see her bed and this anonymous room in relation to a larger city, a coherent world of governmental design that in turn related itself to the world of her family (WSF 163–64). The library books suggest the apparent larger order of the world outside and sharply remind Karen of the disorder of her life.

Maureen Wendall in the novel *them*, however, is more obsessively fascinated with the order of the library. Early in her life, the library had become a shelter and source of solitude. After she awakens from the catatonic stupor brought on by her near-fatal beating by Furlong, she again retreats to the quiet security of the library. She senses the world is "out of control, crazy"; only the library affords peace, tranquility, and order, a respite from the disorder of daily life. Suspicious that the other patrons of the library would like to "throw the books out the windows, break the lamps and chairs, hit one another over the head with anything they could grab," Maureen projects onto these other people her own explosiveness. She craves order amidst the upheavals and restlessness of her world and when she finds it, she feels a compulsion to destroy the very order she sought.

Maureen's brother Jules is always bothered by that "something about life [which] he could not figure out." His futile attempts to bring order into his life, like his aching to set the salt and pepper shakers side by side during a family feud, underline his own need for even just the appearances of order: "they made sense together." But Jules is doomed never to achieve this order. Eventually he comes to the insight that life is mysterious, yet he still wonders why "the mystery was cast in the forms of such diminished people." Rather than seek tranquility as Maureen does, Jules seeks escape. First he escapes from his family, an action Maureen continually dreams of imitating; then later, he uses his car as the means of escaping from everything. "So long as he owned his own car he could always be in control of his fate—he was fated to nothing . . . His car was like a shell he could maneuver around, at impressive speeds; he was second generation to no one. He was his own ancestors" (*them* 356). His car is his means of transporting himself not only from the disorder of his life but also from history, from time, from lineage. If Maureen seeks a sense of history in the library, Jules seeks to be free of history in his car. The violent chaos of their lives drives them to seek even the most superficial semblance of order; salt and pepper shakers side by side and library books all neatly arranged. Through the juxtaposition of the images of order and those of disorder, Oates increases the tension of the narrative.

When Richard Everett in *Expensive People* visits the Fernwood Public Library with his mother, he is impressed with the "homey-home" quality of the building. As they enter the cozy, inviting library, they meet Mavis Grisell, and Nada sends a "sideways glance" to her son which assures him she would never leave him again. Nada has never cared for Mavis—who ironically is the woman Elwood marries after Nada's death. The purpose of this trip to the library has been for Nada to look up an article which praises her as a promising, young author. Charged with irony, the scene picks up the various themes of the novel: the homelike quality of the otherwise impersonal library exaggerates Richard's need for a home and for a mother. The irony implicit in the meeting of Richard's mother and soon-to-be-stepmother, together with Nada's assurance that she would never leave again, mirrors the shallowness and superficiality of the relationships in the novel.

Richard explains his love for libraries, "all libraries, those sanctuaries for the maimed and undanceable, the lowly, pimply, neurotic, overweight, underweight, myopic, asthmatic . . . Few are the flirtations in a library, I insist, though Nada never had to search far for adventure. Few are the assaults, physical or verbal. Libraries exist for people like me" (EP 113). The technique of counterpointing the systematic order of the library with the chaotic disorder of the lives of the Everetts powerfully calls attention to the differences.

In addition to the images of the library and those of glassware and china is the equally powerful metaphor of consumption in *Expensive People*. Richard admits he is trying to kill himself by overeating, following the example of a relative. He has been tempted to stuff himself with money and die in that unique way, but he has not enough cash. Acquisition and consumption are all-important realities in the world of the Everetts. Devouring not only stuffed shrimp and lobster, "sinking into a slough of food," the expensive people consume one another and ultimately cost each other dearly. In their world, everything has a price tag, and the cost of living, for Richard, proves to be too high.

By means of the creation of various kinds of characters, from the gluttonous Max, who devours not only great quantities of food but also great numbers of people, through the child Richard Everett, who tries to satiate his hunger for love by eating, to the idealistic Jules who dreams of a new society, the refrain reverberates in Oates's fiction: people are fragile, easily hurt and destroyed, easily victimized. As he is wont to philosophize, Max warns Karen that " 'people are so delicate, a word misspoken might never be amended, a look of the wrong sort never negated . . .' " (WSF 184).

Using the image of a racetrack, Max also explains to Karen the order of the universe in terms of the laws of centrifugal and centripetal forces. There are " 'two pressures' " he elaborates, " 'one pushing in, the other pushing out. That's how our lives are . . . . the pressures are opposed, they fight each other. The law of the circle . . . two forces, one to live and one to die' " (WSF 140). Our lives are lived in the tension between the two forces; the universe is ordered by these opposing forces. Later, talking to her about *Paradise Lost*, " 'a long poem he had been rereading,' " Max takes pains to expound his belief that there is no paradise: " 'The only important thing is that we have no paradise: we have none' " (WSF 182). Any pulling force toward an outer world, a spiritual world is illusion. Consequently all questing for order and meaning is folly. We are trapped in a disordered world, which according to Max is the only world.

This image of entrapment is integrally linked to violence in the novel. Karen feels, when a fight erupts between her father and Shar, "once more a creature trapped within a dream, waiting for release. The unreal violence of the past few minutes rushed to a climax and exploded in her brain as she felt the impact of her father's disgust" (WSF 72). The double image of cloaking the very real violence as a dream and of awaiting release from a trap successfully

carries forward the ironically muted violence of the scene. The need for freedom suggested by the image of entrapment recurs often in the novel. Shar
clings to his freedom as Karen increasingly threatens to infringe on that freedom. She concludes that no one is really free: "If some men supposed themselves free it was only because they did not understand that they were
imprisoned—bars could be made of any shadowy substance, any dreamy loss of
light" (WSF 161). She has already surrendered her freedom by leaving her
father and following Shar; she understands something he has not yet learned:
there is no such thing as total freedom.

A suggestion of entrapment is further conveyed in the description of
Karen's feeling that "they might have been two people condemned to an eternity in each other's presence, lovers or criminals who had sinned together on
earth but who could not understand precisely what they had done, or why, or in
what way it was a sin demanding damnation" (WSF 167). Trapped, condemned to each other by their very relationship with one another, they do not
understand why they must be so punished. Fully aware of her destructive effect
on Shar, Karen understands "his hatred for her as a token of their growing
familiarity." Life has become so disordered that love destroys, reality becomes
a dream, and one is trapped in this existence.

Some of the power to give a sense of order to reality comes from that same
power of language to give some semblance of order or meaning to human
experience. The ability to name something, to articulate and record, confers on
the speaker some power or mastery over his world. Oates astutely comments on
this power of language when, discussing Harriette Arnow's book *The Dollmaker*, she notes that we are called upon to complete the characters of that
novel with words, to fill them out and to enflesh them with our own language.
The Dollmaker, she writes, "deals with human beings to whom language is not
a means of changing or even expressing reality, but a means of powerfully
recording its effect upon the nerves."[6] Language grants some measure of control over one's fate; the ability to define and to record is the first step toward
achieving that control.

Language is not only that power which elevates man above other living
things, but it is also his only weapon against annihilation and destruction. Man
re-creates the world through language, according to Oates. It is all he has "to pit
against death and silence." Silence, she maintains, is the opposite of language
and "silence for human beings is death."[7]

Implicit in Richard Everett's opening remarks in *Expensive People* is this
belief in the power of language. Discussing his rejection of various beginnings
of his novel, he writes: "If you have to begin your life with a sentence, better
make it a brave summing up and not anything coy: *I was a child murderer*" (EP
6). The pun and the posed insouciance do not mollify the impact of the statement. Richard's action of writing his memoirs, which read like a compulsive
confession, is an effort to come to terms with his own confused feelings. By
attempting to give his disordered world the order which language confers, he
tries to identify and sort out his love-hate feelings toward his parents. He speaks
of seeking a language for his memoir and of turning "desperately to the works

of 'culture' " and only finding the "same kind of seething, tortured products" as the one he is writing. Any order or beauty he finds is surface only, and he consoles himself with a quote from Tennyson— " 'We poets are vessels to produce poetry and other excrement' " (EP 103)—which undercuts his very search for a language to give order and meaning to his art by extension to his life.[8]

In *A Garden of Earthly Delights*, Lowry flees Clara because he cannot talk to her. Their relationship ends because they have run out of words to use with each other. The failure of language is responsible in large measure for the failure of their relationship; they need language to complete their love, and when they cannot find the words, when they do not have the power of language, they must separate. Lowry's son Swan realizes he has the same difficulty when he tries to talk to his girl friend, Loretta. "He did not know the style of language and behavior the other boys knew instinctively. He did not know what to say or do and the knowledge of his stupidity depressed him" (GED 399). He understands that he cannot talk to her, just as his father could not talk to Clara. The tragic inability to use language contributes to the destruction of both men.

On the other hand, Clara and Swan, in their conspiratorial relationship, achieve power over Revere by always referring to him as "he." They can maintain a distance and a noninvolvement through language. "Revere was *he* to Clara and Swan; it was an impersonal pronoun that always remained impersonal" (GED 358). Similarly, Swan assuages his conscience of any guilt in the shooting of Robert by thinking of the boy as " 'Robert,' " Although his responsibility in the death is never clearly established, he is haunted by memory of the event, until through language, he can objectify the dead boy.

Torn between his love for his mother and his revulsion at her suspected promiscuity, Swan uses language to hurt her. When Clara deposits him at the library, the paradigm of order, while she carries on an affair in town, a word forces itself out of him: " 'That bitch.' " Calling her that name empowers him to punish her because "that name was a punishment, even if she did not know what he had done." When Revere's other son, Jonathan, calls her a " 'goddam filthy bitch' " to his friends, it is not directed at the same purpose. His use is simply descriptive; Swan's is punitive.

When Swan is finally called upon to use language, he cannot. After driving all night to the home where Clara and Revere live, he cannot explain why he had come. He can only stammer, " 'I want to . . .! I want to explain something to you' " (GED 438). But words fail him again, he feels as if his lips are swollen and "too large to move," so he resorts to physical language and picks up his gun. Still unable to speak he kills Revere and himself.

Part of Howard Wendall's failure as a human being is his similar failure to use language. The Wendall menage is described as a "tomb of a house of silent men," where only the youthful exuberance of the child Jules is heard because "Howard, gone off to war, was no more silent in his absence than he had been at home" (*them* 70). A "silent and angry man," Howard is powerless to use words in any way; he merely broods and lumbers about like a dumb animal. By contrast, Jules is fascinated with the power of language. As a very small child he believes words have a magic power, and at school his classmates are captivated by his "magic words." Once when he had witnessed a hideous plane crash in which a man's head had been sheared off " 'like with an ax,' " he had hidden himself in the family barn. When Loretta finds him, he is stammering, "the beginnings of words stumbling over themselves and piling up so that nothing could get loose, as if he were choking, so small a boy suffocating with the urgency to speak" (*them* 72). He senses, as young as he is, that to be able to speak about the horror he had seen would somehow enable him to cope with it better.

In *Do With Me What You Will,* Elena Ross cannot speak of her terrifying experience of being kidnapped and neglected by her father. Suffering from both the physical and psychological effects of such an ordeal, she cannot speak. When she tries to talk the words only go around in her head and will not come out of her mouth. She mentally describes the experience as: *"There were two streams of words: one in the head, where you can feel them like stones, hard little things, getting ready to be said out loud, and one in the throat and up into the back of the mouth and the mouth itself, on the tongue, and there the words are in the shape of air. Bubbles. The two streams of words come together in the back of your mouth, where you swallow, but sometimes they don't then people stare at you. Then they laugh."* But the words in her head will neither come out nor will they dissolve. *"They hurt. Passing through the parts of the head they hurt, they swell up and get big. Words in the throat like crying, swallows of air. You swallow them by mistake"* (DWM 40). Like Jules, she instinctively realizes the power of language to help give order and meaning to even the most frightening of experiences, but she is powerless to speak. When she finally does talk, the ironic statement is made: *"And the world became perfect again."* The world never was nor will it ever be perfect for Elena, but at least the power to speak enables her to come to some terms with her world.

Words are given shape in silence; in silence, too, a deeper communication can sometimes take place. Even the erratic and irresponsible relationship between Karen and Shar has its "periods of real silence that were more intimate than anything Karen had ever experienced" (WSF 172). She does not have to tell Shar that she will not consider having an abortion, her wordless response can have no other meaning. At other times, Karen uses her silence as a weapon against Shar. She encloses herself protectively in it, beyond his reach. Clara, too, realizes that it can be a protection; locked secretively in silence she knows "that way no one could get you" (GED 136). She runs from the revelatory power of words, just as Maureen recognizes that a "private language" can separate people. Without a common language there can be no communication, no use of the power of words.

Words may also violate a kind of sacred silence between two people as in *Wonderland.* When Jesse Harte comes to live with his grandfather after the tragic death of his family, the silence between the two has a healing effect on the boy. However, once the grandfather explodes in anger to Jesse, their silence becomes "dirtied by words." Jesse cannot understand how his grandfather can speak so, "how he could be putting [those things] into words?" Their "partnership of silence" has been violated. "It was not that his grandfather had said anything wrong, but that he had said anything at all," which perplexes Jesse most. Words have become a betrayal, and Jesse knows he can no longer live in the house of his relative.

Oates consistently imputes to language antithetical powers: one to heal and one to destroy. Consonant with her use of rhetorical violence, she frequently focuses the reader's attention on the latter. When verbal language fails, her characters fall back on physical language—beating and killing—or they retreat to silence. Throughout her works, however, is the underlying belief that language has some power, some potential to help man give order and meaning to his inchoate world, if he could but find and use the right words. Her fiction itself stands as testimony to this belief.

She repeatedly affirms her belief that the "customary use of language [is] to restore, with its magical eloquence, the lost humanity of the tragic figure . . ." (EOI 12). By enriching her narratives with rhetorical violence, she reenforces her understanding that violence often becomes a substitute for verbal language. Deaths, murders, killings in her fiction are often "only paradigms for a language of random destruction."[9] By her adroit use of such rhetorical devices as employing modifiers and verbals which connote violence and hostility, describing things and people in images of shattering glassware and trapped animals, giving her narratives a breathless pace, and, while acknowledging the ordering power of language, calling attention to its equally powerful ability to destroy, Joyce Carol Oates creates a language of violence and tragedy which infuses into her narratives an horrific ambiance of violence. Not only are the central episodes violent—rape, murder, suicide, riots, beatings—but the smallest descriptive details are also. The ultimate effect of this technique is the creation of fiction permeated with violence and tragedy. Oates's works offer nothing to mollify or diminish the intensity of her tragic vision.

Notes

1. Joyce Carol Oates, ed., *Scenes from American Life* (N.Y.: Random House, 1973), p. vii.

2. John Fraser, *Violence in the Arts* (N.Y.: Cambridge University Press, 1974), p. ix.

3. Joyce Carol Oates, "Don Juan's Last Laugh," *Psychology Today*, 8 (September 1974), pp. 10, 12.

4. William Abrahams, "Stories of a Visionary," *Saturday Review: The Society*, 1 (October 1972), p. 76.

5. An unpublished paper by Ildiko Carrington, MLA Oates Seminar, December 1973, "Borges and Oates: Monsters in *Wonderland*," discusses the gothic and grotesque dimensions of Oates's novel and relates it to work by both Borges and Lewis Carroll.

6. Joyce Carol Oates, "An American Tragedy," *New York Times Book Review*, January 24, 1971, p. 2.

7. "Remarks by Joyce Carol Oates Accepting the National Book Award in Fiction for 'them' " press release from Vanguard Press, March 4, 1970, p. 2.

8. An unpublished paper by Alice Martin, "*Expensive People*," compares Oates's use of nausea with that of Jean-Paul Sartre (MLA Seminar, 1973).

9. John L'Heureux, "Mirage-Seekers," *Atlantic*, 224 (October 1969), p. 128.

The Artificial Demon:
Joyce Carol Oates and the
Dimensions of the Real

Walter Sullivan*

I

In the fiction of Joyce Carol Oates, the middle ground is a no man's land into which her characters venture only occasionally. We know that in Detroit and New York and points south and west there are millions of people living ordinary lives on ordinary incomes, committing no murders, indulging no illicit appetites, requiring no psychiatric therapy or protective incarceration. But these are not the people who challenge Miss Oates' imagination. She wants hers either rich or poor, criminal or sick or drifting in that direction, with here and there a reasonably normal human being who might in rare instances earn the reader's unqualified admiration. To take one example, in *The Wheel of Love*, a collection of twenty short stories, a cursory count reveals ten cases of insanity or neurotic disability, three suicides, two attempted suicides, two murders, one death following criminal assault, and three violent ends which do not fit any of the above categories. To what extent this list might be augmented, should one keep score through all her books, I would not try to guess, for Miss Oates is surely the most prolific writer of serious fiction working in this country today. And in my judgment she is one of the most talented.

Two immediately apparent virtues of her work are those gifts which are indispensable to all writers of good fiction: an unerring eye and an infallible ear. Start with "Where Are You Going, Where Have You Been?" which is one of her most widely reprinted stories and justly so. In its basic delineations it is an interlude of terror: it builds fearfully toward a violence so unspeakable that it must happen offstage. Two boys in a jalopy come to call on Connie who is alone at home on a summer afternoon. But one of the boys is a man, perhaps thirty, and this discrepancy in age—Connie is only fifteen—an old device used in a new way, increases the tension and deepens the meaning of the story. Youthful language and gestures employed by Arnold Friend combine with his uncanny knowledge of Connie's circumstances, the names of her acquaintances, the habits of her family, to develop a sinister adumbration. He is not what he seems,

*Reprinted with permission from *The Hollins Critic*, 9 (Dec. 1972), 1–12.

which is a familiar theme in modern fiction, and the car, the blaring radio, the clothes he has on, innocent symbols of a subculture under ordinary conditions, are made evil by Friend's illegitimate intention. This is the true terror as all good writers understand: we may be frightened by the distortions of a dream landscape; but horror resides in the transformation of what we know best, the intimate and comfortable details of our lives made suddenly threatening.

The story proceeds in conventional fashion. Miss Oates develops Connie in the opening pages and thus gives us our character over whom to grieve and with whom to suffer. We see her with her mother, with her schoolmates at the shopping center, with boys at the soda shop. The surface truth is drawn clearly and accurately and because of this some of the ambiguities of human existence—the kind of truth that the artist is trying finally to tell—begin to accrue to the story. Connie reaches out for adventure, deplores the humdrum, yearns for romance. That adventure should come in a deadly parody of romantic love is the sort of ironic trick that fate sometimes allows itself. Irony and violence are a part of life and they serve in this case to put youth in a new perspective. The young are at once more and less frivolous than we might formerly have believed, more and less innocent, but like all the rest of humanity, enormously vulnerable. Connie is helpless against the vicious Friend who enters her house and leads her away. There are to my knowledge no symbols here, but the story is rich with the imagery of life's deceptions and perils.

"Wild Saturday," which like "Where Are You Going, Where Have You Been?" appears in *The Wheel of Love*, is a story about a little boy lost in the selfishness and animosity of his parents. The mother is a cold citizen of the bourgeosie who despises her estranged intellectual husband and the feeling is mutual. Saturdays are the days that Buchanan spends with his father, and this Saturday begins as we know all the others do, with a sense of release that follows his mother's furious last kiss and the hope that this time things will be different. The usual trip to the zoo is promised, the picnic lunch, but first they must get Sonya, Dad's girlfriend, and her fatherless child, Peter. Then there is Artie, a potter, who hates children and just about everything and everybody else in the world to judge from his conversation, so as usual they do not go to the zoo, but to Sonya's apartment, where the fat girl who shares the apartment with Sonya greets them.

There is nothing to entertain Buchanan here. Sonya and Dad argue; the picnic basket yields only candy and potato chips; Sonya's flatmate claims to have flu. Visitors come and go. Wine is poured. At last Buchanan retreats to the tiny bedroom where Peter is already sleeping and sleeps himself and awakens with a cold. Peter has wet the bed; Sonya is half undressed and drunk; Dad is unconscious on the living room floor and cannot be aroused by the police who come looking for Buchanan. But to the very end Buchanan is loyal and will not admit to his outraged mother that he has not been to the zoo.

This story lives in the sharpness of its characterization. Buchanan is a perceptive, honest child, not above a thrust of impudence now and then. He is largely innocent and therefore victim: he becomes for his mother and father a weapon for each to use against the other. And what is worse, each tries to justify his own life style by imposing it on Buchanan. The story is one of selfishness compounded by dishonesty and the attitudes are so splendidly cast, the dialogue is so accurately devised that the narrative is profoundly convincing. Sonya's sympathy is engaged by strangers seen on the street, she proclaims her love for her baby when she is drunk, but she will not prepare a dish or change a bed or find a lost shoe for Peter. So it is with the others, with Dad who will not give Buchanan a moment of his undivided attention and with Buchanan's mother who wants most of all to deprive Dad of Buchanan's company forever. Except for Buchanan, who is hardly old enough to be evil, there are no good people here, and certainly there are no winners. Life that was tense and drab at the beginning of the story is worse at the end. Even the mother, who has won Buchanan from his father, has lost a little more of the slight affection her son once had for her. And of course we see ourselves here, whichever side we are on, whichever path we choose for our lives to follow.

From *The Wheel of Love,* I take a final example. "Bodies" shows Miss Oates in her bizarre dimension. Pauline, rich, young, a sculptor and instructor at an art institute, is pursued by a man of uncertain background. She does not know quite what he wants from her, other than her company which she is unwilling to give, and in a scene that is uncommon, even for Miss Oates, he accosts her. On the street, in the light of day, he cuts his own throat, sinks to his knees, clutches Pauline around the waist and lets his blood spill out upon her. The end of the story is this: Pauline, who cannot forget the blood on her stomach and thighs, believes she is pregnant and cannot be dissuaded. She is sent to an institution and is given little chance to recover.

I do not want to pursue all the ramifications of this story. The meaning of its main action is obvious at least to a point: a marriage of death and birth which issues into insanity—but an insanity modified, the irrational quality softened by its relationship to art. For the story is couched in terms of artistic representations of life, death, fate, love: and of dreams which are composed of remembered objects of art, sculpture, painting; and of visions of violence. Art, too, is perhaps a manifestation of insanity and the artist an abnormal figure in the world's eyes. Finally, we suspect that life itself, when it is seen in all its breadth and intensity is partly insane, even as it maintains our rational context. However this may be, however far we may want to proceed along this course of inquiry, of one thing we can be sure: a narrative such as "Bodies" is the place to begin. Of the three stories I have examined here, it is by far the most typical of Joyce Carol Oates' fiction.

II

It would be too much to say that the spirit of *tour de force* informs the art of the short story. Yet, we are all familiar with the difficulty the best short story writers occasionally encounter when they try to write novels. Many of the characteristics which are virtues in short fiction—the clarity of dialogue and detail, some kinds of wit—become mannerisms that sometimes test the patience of the reader when they are employed on a large scale. And technical devices that will work for ten or twenty pages, will not necessarily survive for four or five hundred. I have in mind the kinds of thing Miss Oates attempts in *Expensive People*, an early book, and in *Wonderland*, her most recent novel. *Expensive People* is a tale told by a slob, a fat and neurotic post-adolescent who cannot and is not intended to convince us that his story is true. Richard Everett begins his first person narrative with a bad pun: he calls himself a child murderer and then must explain that he means a child who kills, not one who murders children. But is he really what he claims? We never know. It is true that a sniper is loose in Cedar Grove and the fact that Richard's mother is shot to death is established. But the police do not find the rifle where Richard tells them he has hidden it, and at the end of the novel, the psychiatrist says, "Richard, let me assure you of this: hallucinations are as vivid as reality, and I respect everything you say. I know that you are suffering just as much as if you had killed your mother." So, having paid the price by reading the book in the first place, the reader can make his choice.

Miss Oates may be suggesting that objective reality does not matter, that appearance is all. But the case does not seem quite that simple. Richard calls his mother Nada—such a name can hardly be without philosophical implications—and she is a fine example of how surface impressions deceive. She presents herself as Natashya, the daughter of Russian nobility, now dead. But as we discover, she is really Nancy Romanow and her immigrant parents survive her. Perhaps then, there is no way to know reality, or perhaps reality is what we make it, what we say it is. Or maybe the book is not about the real at all, but about guilt and intention and the moral structure of the human act. Whatever the theme was meant to be, it is one that might have served very well for a short story, but it is not substantial enough to sustain a book.

Wonderland, a more difficult and more skillfully conceived book, may be even more of a failure as a novel. The volume is dedicated to "all of us who pursue the phantasmagoria of personality," and having devoted a good deal of time to Miss Oates' narrative, I am as yet uncertain as to whether I want to count myself in or out of that distinguished group. Which is to say, I do not know quite what she means. If personality is a phantasmagoria, then what is character, or more to the immediate point, characterization? If we take this as a strictly literary question, the answer will be, It depends. Short stories do not make the same demands for development and motivation that novels make. For example, Miss Oates has written a story titled "You," which exhibits her talents at their best. The main character is a television actress, aging but still beautiful, famous, but not at the center of the world's renown. She is miserable because of her selfishness and all those around her are miserable for the same reason, and nothing changes her, not even the attempted suicide of one of her daughters.

The narrative is given texture by a dual point of view. Marion tells her mother's story in the second person while she tells her own in the first and the two fictional movements form a counterpoint of carelessness and responsibility.

The two women, as well as the minor characters—the other daughter, Miranda; Peter, once the mother's lover, now Miranda's—are very clearly drawn and totally believable, as Miss Oates' people almost always are *at any given moment in their careers*. Where the mischief comes is when Miss Oates attempts to take a character such as Madeline Randall of "You" beyond the limits of a situation which is strictly circumscribed. In the novels the characters simply change. Personality does become a true phantasmagoria, not an organic development from stage to stage, but a random shifting from one manifestation of character and being to the next. As I shall try to show later, her best novels, *A Garden of Earthly Delights* and *them*, are marred by this discontinuity of attitudes and values, but what had before seemed a defect in craftmanship emerges as a philosophical principle in *Wonderland*. By a series of clever devices, disruptions based largely on chance, the main character is carried from one to another of a set of vastly disparate circumstances. With each dislocation he becomes a different person to the extent that even his name is changed. The idea is not good; it does not work; even the writing, the details of setting and action which are usually Miss Oates' strong suit, fails to convince.

III

A Garden of Earthly Delights and *them* share a common glory—Miss Oates' talent for clean fictional representation—and a common difficulty. One does not know where the focus should fall in these novels or who the main characters are. *A Garden of Earthly Delights* begins among itinerant farm workers whom we follow from Arkansas to Florida to New Jersey and back to Florida once more, and the first third of the book clearly belongs to Carleton Walpole. In the opening pages, Carleton talks of making enough money to pay off his debts and return to his small farm in Kentucky, but his ambition is soon forgotten, and the novel succeeds in showing the very directionlessness of Walpole's life. He works, breeds, drinks, fights, and his days drag on leaving him nothing to show for the effort he has put into living and no hope for a future that will bring him any sort of ease.

There is no way to exaggerate the brilliance with which the sordid quality of Carleton's existence is conveyed. The hovels in which the workers live, the food they eat, the clothes they wear—all the mundane details are drawn vividly and with economy. The dialogue rings true, the people are convincing. We see Carleton's wife grow more and more withdrawn with the birth of each of her children until she bleeds to death after her last delivery. Such a thing should not have been allowed to happen, the doctor admonishes later, but we are by this time almost inured to the unceasing agony these people undergo. Pearl is buried, Carleton finds another woman, life continues in its old pattern; the children grow up foul-mouthed and dirty and take their places in the field.

At the end of the first section of *A Garden of Earthly Delights*, Carleton dies, but by this time the emphasis of the narrative has shifted to his oldest daughter. With the help of a kind man who for a long time will not accept the physical love she offers him, Clara escapes to a small town, lives in a rented room, works at the five and ten. Once more, Miss Oates' vast talent for conveying the hard circumstances of insignificant and impoverished lives engages us absolutely. Clara strives for beauty. She skimps to buy a bedspread, sews curtains on Sunday afternoon, cherishes a cheap pair of shoes, a tawdry ribbon. It is only after she is translated from poverty to ease and security, first as the mistress, later as the wife of a rich man that the novel begins to falter.

For though life may be without purpose, as Miss Oates' fiction generally seems to assert, it nonetheless usually assumes a certain shape. Days lived under any kind of ordinary circumstances form a pattern and this pattern helps establish the texture of a novel. Motivations develop, relationships mature and shift, aims are pursued, actions are taken, consequences are suffered. But these are ends that Miss Oates will not seek in her work. In *A Gardon of Earthly Delights*, accidents happen, blood flows. One of Clara's stepsons dies in a hunting accident. Her own son kills his father, then shoots himself. There are sexual encounters, arguments, fights, accommodations, but except for the fact that we continue to read about the same group of characters, the incidents and sequences appear to be separate unto themselves. And soon, the seemingly inevitable disintegration toward mental illness sets in.

Now, I am aware of the argument, all too frequently heard these days, that in order to portray a chaotic world, we must resort to a chaotic art. There are enough writers around who have followed this notion to its conclusion to show us how fallacious it is. Art as an imitation of life does not mean art as a carbon copy of life, and one of the first tasks of the writer is to maintain some kind of control over his material. He does this by giving the material coherent shape. But of equally serious consequences to her fiction is Miss Oates' tendency to let her people go insane. Here again, I think I get the point. She is saying that we are all crazy to one degree or another, and in taking this position, she puts herself in agreement with much modern psychological and even judicial theory. There are no longer the good and the evil among us, but merely the sick and the well. This is not the place to examine such a view of human morality, but I do submit that should it gain complete hegemony it will be the death of art.

Literature requires action that is morally significant, which means that the characters must be at least theoretically free to choose for themselves. If we are persuaded that Macbeth murdered the king simply as a result of some psychosis which forced him beyond his control into regicide, then the play makes scant sense. What was true for Shakespeare is, I think, true for Joyce Carol Oates. Once a suggestion of lunacy is allowed to intrude, then doubt is cast over all the procedures of a novel. Where did the neurosis begin? What actions and choices were tainted by it? To what degree has the fiction become nothing more than a case history? Finding Clara in an institution at the end of *A Garden of Earthly Delights* gives me no sense of fulfilment. It is a sad fading away of a book that contains much that is powerful and sharp.

IV

them is more ambitious than *A Garden of Earthly Delights*—it has more characters, its scope is wider—and as a chronicle of life among the poor of a big city, it rings all too true. We are told in an author's note that the material for the book including not only the characters and plot, but much of the voluminous mass of details which give the novel its intense verisimilitude, were told to Miss Oates by one of her students at the University of Detroit. Where it was possible, Miss Oates says, the recollections of the student were "incorporated into the narrative verbatim," but this is not necessarily an easy way to write a novel. The trick is to know what can be used as is, what must be discarded, and what the author must furnish for himself. In other words, the problem of form remains, the parts must add up somehow to make a whole.

In *them*, there are a good many parts to be accounted for. The book begins with typical Oates blood and thunder. Loretta, young and poor and dissatisfied with her lot, takes her first lover and wakes the next morning to find the boy dead beside her. He has been shot by her brother. The policeman whom Loretta calls off the street first makes love to Loretta, then helps her dump the body in an alley. Later Loretta and the policeman are married and their relationship is a proper overture for the sordid scenes that are to come. In the progress of the book, Loretta is displaced as principal character by her son Jules, who in his turn gives way to Loretta's daughter Maureen. But until the last phases of the narrative are reached, Miss Oates keeps fairly good control over most of the various ramifications of her plot.

And the writing in *them* is certainly some of the best she has ever done. Maureen is a superbly drawn character. We know her first as a sad, quiet girl trapped in poverty, surrounded by loud, insensitive and vicious people. Her brother can escape by taking to the streets, but for Maureen there is only the temporary respite found in books, and her reading is continually penetrated by the complaints of her grandmother, the scolding of her mother, the verbal and physical assertions of her aggressive sister. We watch the brutalization of this perceptive and innocent and essentially decent child. When she is denied use of the library until a twenty-five cent fine is paid, she is terrified that her only solace might be taken from her forever. Having been elected secretary of her class in school, she loses the minute book and searches in vain and in agony for it. These sequences succeed absolutely. They transcend themselves and become images of our general loneliness and spiritual isolation. Miss Oates avoids senti-mentality by the simple expedient of telling the cold truth.

Maureen's fate is her will to escape the shabbiness of her life. Her career as a prostitute ends when her stepfather discovers her cache of money and beats her severely. She falls into mental illness—that most familiar of all ailments in the Oates canon—recovers, gets a job as a secretary, moves to the same sort of cheerless room that Clara occupies in *A Garden of Earthly Delights*. She enrolls in a night class at the university extension, discovers in her teacher the man she wants to marry and induces him to leave his children and his wife. She gets what she thinks she wants. When we last see Maureen, she is pregnant and worried over money, since so much of what her husband makes must go for alimony and child support. In my judgment, the conclusion of Maureen's story is not written with the depth and complexity that endow so richly the earlier scenes in the book. This may not be totally Miss Oates' fault. Love is at best difficult to write about: there is a sameness to it; lovers everywhere are inclined to think and talk alike. The urge arises. Somehow, somewhere fancy is bred. But how distinguish one urge, one love from all the rest?

The distinction is partially made by the circumstances that surround the development of affection. And by the motivation, which in Maureen's case is firm and sure and one of the best aspects of this part of the narrative. Her desire is not so much an overwhelming passion for the plain professor, but for what he represents in the scheme of her future hopes: she wants a home of her own, a husband, a child. She does not find herself incurably in love with a married man; rather, she chooses him with *sang froid*, feeling no more concern over the fact of his marriage than she feels over the drape of his necktie or the color of his shirt. She captures him simply by going after him, and I suppose we are convinced, if a little surprised by his vulnerability. She, the indifferent student, calls on him in his office and allows him to allow the conversation to repeat itself while beneath the empty, almost silly words, their relationship makes its steady course. This is good work. Only in terms of my earlier comparison does it appear to be inadequate. It seems contrived in relation to the sounder parts of the story.

I think Jules is less successfully drawn than Maureen, which is perhaps a result of the ordinary perils of characterization. Like a good many female writers, Miss Oates may not portray men as well as she portrays women, though I find Carleton in A *Gardon of Earthly Delights* convincing enough. Jules too is believable as a young man, enduring some of the same agonies that Maureen endures, but endowed, because he is a boy, with better opportunities to escape their common fate. He drops out of school, finds a life on the streets, flirts with girls, gets money. But then Miss Oates begins to indulge her taste for the bizarre and Jules becomes not so much unreal as insignificant, unrealized in the ultimate fictional sense. He falls into a relationship with a nervous, mysterious stranger, whose source of livelihood is unknown and whose comings and goings are seemingly without purpose. While Jules works for Bernard Geffen, he meets Nadine.

Or rather, he sees her for the first time when he drives Bernard, who is her uncle, to her parents' home in Grosse Point. At his first glimpse of her, Jules is enchanted with Nadine's beauty—the magic attractiveness of this school girl in knee socks. But he does not meet her until after the strange Bernard has been murdered by gangsters and Jules has a job delivering flowers. Catching sight of her one day on a Detroit street, he hails her, offers her a potted plant, tells her that he loves her. The affair thus begun receives a long development. Jules and Nadine run away together. He supports her by stealing, but he gets sick and she abandons him. Later, when they meet again, she is married and Jules is working for his affluent uncle. Here the decline toward neurosis and violence begins.

Perhaps I have read too much of Miss Oates work in too short a period of time, but I do get a terrible sense of futility, not to mention *deja vu*, watching pair after pair of her characters degenerate into insanity and the shedding of blood. They love and love again, these particular lovers: then on the bright morning after their night of passion, Nadine shoots Jules as they walk together down the street. "The spirit of the Lord departed from Jules," Miss Oates tells us, and I assumed on first reading that Jules was dead. Such is not the case. He survives, and later regains this lost "spirit of the Lord." The end of the book plays itself out: life goes on and Jules drifts through it. He becomes one of the street people around the university, takes in a runaway girl, abuses her and forces her into prostitution. After a race riot, in which Jules kills a policeman, we have one last account of him as an organizer for a leftist group. And the novel is over.

My frustration in trying to deal with *them*, the divisions that cloud my judgment of it are indicative of my view of Miss Oates' fiction taken as a whole. I have already declared how well I think Miss Oates writes. Her best stories are among the very best being written today, and *them* is replete with fully realized scenes and compelling emotional intensity. About life's small defeats and lesser triumphs, Miss Oates almost never fails to tell the truth. It may be that perfection on a small scale is the proper fruit of Miss Oates' talent. The accomplished writer of short fiction who fails when he attempts to work in the larger dimensions of the novel is, as I have said, a familiar figure of our time. But I think there is also a problem of vision involved here, part of it the temper of the age, part of it Miss Oates' own view of the world and time in which she lives.

In *The Edge of Impossibility*, a collection of perceptive and persuasively written essays on modern literature, Miss Oates is concerned with the possibilities for writing modern tragedy. She thinks that tragedy can be written, though it is necessarily circumscribed by our place in history—what I, but probably not Miss Oates, would regard as the deficiencies of our age. She puts her case this way:

> If communal belief in God has diminished so that, as writers, we can no longer presume upon it, then a redefinition of God in terms of the furthest reaches of man's hallucinations can provide us with a new basis for tragedy. The abyss will always open for us, though it begins as a pencil mark, the parody of a crack; the shapes of human beasts—centaurs and satyrs and their remarkable companions—will always be returning with nostalgia to our great cities.

Or to put this another way, the modern hero, placed irrevocably beyond good and evil, must create himself. This necessity for self-creation is at once his doom and his only avenue to freedom; he must transcend his society and in the process he will destroy himself.

This is not the occasion to attempt to trace the ramifications of such a theory, nor do I want to end by saying that Miss Oates' work is a mere demonstration of the perils and the advantages of existentialism. This would be to oversimplify, for writers are not merely the product of what they think: if they were, many of our best ones—Tolstoy, for example—would have been diminished. But what Miss Oates says about Mann and Ionesco and literature in general does suggest that our frantic circumstances inform our frantic art. There can be no question that life as we live it, as Miss Oates describes it, is enough to drive us crazy, but does this mean that we must continue to write the same story over and over—a chronicle where violence is a prelude to total spiritual disintegration and the only freedom is the total loss of self? Perhaps so, if Miss Oates is accurate in her perception of our modern condition. But I can offer no final answer. I wish I knew.

Negative aspects of

"Don't You Know Who I Am?" The Grotesque in Oates's "Where Are You Going, Where Have You Been?"

Joyce M. Wegs*

Joyce Carol Oates's ability to absorb and then to transmit in her fiction the terror which is often a part of living in America today has been frequently noted and admired. For instance, Walter Sullivan praises her skill by noting that "horror resides in the transformation of what we know best, the intimate and comfortable details of our lives made suddenly threatening."[1] Although he does not identify it as such, Sullivan's comment aptly describes a classic instance of a grotesque intrusion: a familiar world suddenly appears alien. Oates frequently evokes the grotesque in her fiction, drawing upon both its tranditional or demonic and its contemporary or psychological manifestations.[2] In the prize-winning short story, "Where Are You Going, Where Have You Been?", Oates utilizes the grotesque in many of its forms to achieve a highly skillful integration of the multiple levels of the story and, in so doing, to suggest a transcendent reality which reaches beyond surface realism to evoke the simultaneous mystery and reality of the contradictions of the human heart. Full of puzzling and perverse longings, the heart persists in mixing lust and love, life and death, good and evil. Oates's teenage protagonist, Connie, discovers that her dream love-god also wears the face of lust, evil and death.

Centering the narrative on the world of popular teenage music and culture, Oates depicts the tawdry world of drive-in restaurants and shopping plazas blaring with music with a careful eye for authentic surface detail. However, her use of popular music as a thematic referent is typical also of her frequent illumination of the illusions and grotesquely false values which may arise from excessive devotion to such aspects of popular culture as rock music, movies, and romance magazines. In all of her fiction as in this story, she frequently employs a debased religious imagery to suggest the gods which modern society has substituted for conventional religion. Oates delineates the moral poverty of Connie, her fifteen-year-old protagonist, by imaging a typical evening Connie spends at a drive-in restaurant as a grotesquely parodied religious pilgrimage. Left by her friend's father to stroll at the shopping center or go to a

*Reprinted with permission from *Journal of Narrative Technique*, 5 (1975), 66–72.

movie, Connie and her girlfriend immediately cross the highway to the restaurant frequented by older teenagers. A grotesque parody of a church, the building is bottle-shaped and has a grinning boy holding a hamburger aloft on top of it. Unconscious of any ludicrousness, Connie and her friend enter it as if going into a "sacred building"[3] which will give them "what haven and blessing they yearned for."(31) It is the music which is "always in the background, like music at a church service" (31) that has invested this "bright-lit, fly-infested" (31) place with such significance. Indeed, throughout the story the music is given an almost mystical character, for it evokes in Connie a mysterious pleasure, a "glow of slow-pulsed joy that seemed to rise mysteriously out of the music itself." (33)

Although the story undoubtedly has a moral dimension,[4] Oates does not take a judgmental attitude toward Connie. In fact, much of the terror of the story comes from the recognition that there must be thousands of Connies. By carefully including telltale phrases, Oates demonstrates in an understated fashion why Connies exist. Connie's parents, who seem quite typical, have disqualified themselves as moral guides for her. At first reading, the reader may believe Connie's mother to be concerned about her daughter's habits, views, and friends; but basically their arguments are little more than a "pretense of exasperation, a sense that they . . . [are] tugging and struggling over something of little value to either of them."(32) Connie herself is uncertain of her mother's motives for constantly picking at her; she alternates between a view that her mother's harping proceeds from jealousy of Connie's good looks now that her own have faded (29) and a feeling that her mother really prefers her over her plain older sister June because she is prettier.(32) In other words, to Connie and her mother, real value lies in beauty. Connie's father plays a small role in her life, but by paralleling repeated phrases, Oates suggests that this is precisely the problem. Because he does not "bother talking much"(30) to his family, he can hardly ask the crucial parental questions, "Where are you going?" or "Where have you been?" The moral indifference of the entire adult society is underscored by Oates' parallel description of the father of Connie's friend, who also "never . . . [bothers] to ask" what they did when he picks up the pair at the end of one of their evenings out. Similarly, on Sunday morning, "none of them bothered with church,"(33) not even that supposed paragon, June.

Since her elders do not bother about her, Connie is left defenseless against the temptations represented by Arnold Friend. A repeated key phrase emphasizes her helplessness. As she walks through the parking lot of the restaurant with Eddie, she can not "help but"(31) look about happily, full of joy in a life characterized by casual pickups and constant music. When she sees Arnold in a nearby car, she looks away, but her instinctive flirtatiousness triumphs and she can not "help but"(31) look back. Later, like Lot's wife leaving Sodom and Gomorrah, she cannot "help but look back"(32) at the plaza and drive-in as her friend's father drives them home. In Connie's case, the consequences of the actions she can not seem to help are less biblically swift to occur and can not be simply labeled divine retribution.

Since music is Connie's religion, its values are hers also. Oates does not include the lyrics to any popular songs here, for any observer of contemporary America could surely discern the obvious link between Connie's high esteem for romantic love and youthful beauty and the lyrics of scores of hit tunes. The superficiality of Connie's values becomes terrifyingly apparent when Arnold Friend, the external embodiment of the teenage ideal celebrated in popular songs, appears at Connie's home in the country one Sunday afternoon when she is home alone, listening to music and drying her hair. It is no accident that Arnold's clothes, car, speech, and taste in music reflect current teenage chic almost exactly, for they constitute part of a careful disguise intended to reflect Arnold's self-image as an accomplished youthful lover.

Suspense mounts in the story as the reader realizes along with Connie that Arnold is not a teenager and is really thirty or more. Each part of his disguise is gradually revealed to be grotesquely distorted in some way. His shaggy black hair, "crazy as a wig,"(34) is evidently really a wig. The mask-like appearance of his face has been created by applying a thick coat of makeup; however, he has carelessly omitted his throat.(41) Even his eyelashes appear to be made-up, but with some tarlike material. In his clothing, his disguise appears more successful, for Connie approves of the way he dresses, as "all of them dressed."(36) in tight jeans, boots, and pullover. When he walks, however, Connie realizes that the runty Arnold, conscious that the ideal teenage dream lover is tall, has stuffed his boots; the result is, however, that he can hardly walk and staggers ludicrously. Attempting to bow, he almost falls. Similarly, the gold jalopy covered with teenage slang phrases seems authentic until Connie notices that one of them is no longer in vogue. Even his speech is not his own, for it recalls lines borrowed from disc jockeys, teenage slang, and lines from popular songs. Arnold's strange companion, Ellie Oscar, is just as grotesque as Arnold. Almost totally absorbed in listening to music and interrupting this activity only to offer threatening assistance to Arnold, Ellie is no youth either; he has the "face of a forty-year-old baby."(39) Although Arnold has worked out his disguise with great care, he soon loses all subtlety in letting Connie know of his evil intentions; he is not simply crazy but a criminal with plans to rape and probably to murder Connie.

However, Arnold is far more than a grotesque portrait of a psychopathic killer masquerading as a teenager; he also has all the traditional sinister traits of that arch-deceiver and source of grotesque terror, the devil. As is usual with Satan, he is in disguise; the distortions in his appearance and behavior suggest not only that his identity is faked but also hint at his real self. Equating Arnold and Satan is not simply a gratuitous connection designed to exploit traditional demonic terror, for the early pages of the story explicitly prepare for this linking by portraying popular music and its values as Connie's perverted version of religion. When Arnold comes up the drive, her first glance makes Connie believe that a teenage boy with his jalopy, the central figure of her religion, has arrived; therefore, she murmurs "Christ, Christ"(34) as she wonders about how her newly-washed hair looks. When the car—a parodied golden chariot?—

stops, a horn sounds "as if this were a signal Connie knew."(34) On one level, the horn honks to announce the "second coming" of Arnold, a demonic Day of Judgment. Although Connie never specifically recognizes Arnold as Satan, her first comment to him both hints at his infernal origins and faithfully reproduces teenage idiom: "Who the *hell* do you think you are?" (emphasis mine, 34) When he introduces himself, his name too hints at his identity, for "friend" is uncomfortably close to "fiend"; his initials could well stand for Arch Fiend. The frightened Connie sees Arnold as "only half real":(39) he "had driven up her driveway all right but had come from nowhere before that and belonged nowhere."(39) Especially supernatural is his mysterious knowledge about her, her family, and her friends. At one point, he even seems to be able to see all the way to the barbecue which Connie's family is attending and to get a clear vision of what all the guests are doing. Typical of his ambiguous roles is his hint that he had something to do with the death of the old woman who lived down the road. It is never clear whether Arnold has killed her, has simply heard of her death, or knows about it in his devil role of having come to take her away to hell. Although Arnold has come to take Connie away, in his traditional role as evil spirit, he may not cross a threshold uninvited; he repeatedly mentions that he is not going to come in after Connie, and he never does. Instead, he lures Connie out to him. Part of his success may be attributed to his black magic in having put his sign on her—X for victim.(37-38) Because the devil is not a mortal being, existing as he does in all ages, it is not surprising that he slips in remembering what slang terms are in vogue. Similarly, his foolish attempt at a bow may result from a mixup in temporal concepts of the ideal lover. In addition, his clumsy bow may be due to the fact that it must be difficult to manipulate boots if one has cloven feet!

Although Oates attempts to explain the existence of Connie, she makes no similar effort to explain the existence of Arnold, for that would constitute an answer to the timeless and insoluble problem of evil in the world. As this story shows, Oates would agree with Pope Paul VI's recent commentary on the "terrible reality" of evil in the world, but she would not, I feel sure, endorse his view of this evil as being literally embodied in a specific being. Pope Paul describes evil as "not merely a lack of something, but an effective agent, a living spiritual being, perverted and perverting. A terrible reality. Mysterious and frightening."[5] Oates' description of her own views on religion is in terms strikingly similar to the language used by Pope Paul. To her, religion is a "kind of psychological manifestation of deep powers, deep imaginative, mysterious powers, which are always with us, and what has in the past been called supernatural. I would prefer simply to call natural. However, though these things are natural, they are still inaccessible and cannot be understood, cannot be controlled."[6] Thus, although Arnold is clearly a symbolic Satan, he also functions on a psychological level.

On this level, Arnold Friend is the incarnation of Connie's unconscious erotic desires and dreams, but in uncontrollable nightmare form. When she first sees Arnold in the drive-in, she instinctively senses his sinister attraction, for she can not "help glancing back"(31) at him. Her "trashy daydreams"(30) are largely filled with blurred recollections of the caresses of the many boys she has dated. That her dreams are a kind of generalized sexual desire—although Connie does not consciously identify them as such—is made evident by Oates' description of Connie's summer dreams: "But all the boys fell back and dissolved into a single face that was not even a face but an idea, a feeling, mixed up with the urgent insistent pounding of the music and the humid night air of July."(32) What is frightening about Arnold is that he voices and makes explicit her own sexual desires; teenage boys more usually project their similar message with "that sleepy dreamy smile that all the boys used to get across ideas they didn't want to put into words."(38) Connie's reaction to his bluntness is one of horror: "People don't talk like that, you're crazy."(40)

Connie's fear drives her into a grotesque separation of mind from body in which her unconscious self takes over and betrays her. Terror-stricken, she cannot even make her weak fingers dial the police; she can only scream into the phone. In the same way that she is Arnold's prisoner, locked inside the house he alternately threatens to knock down or burn down, she is also a prisoner of her own body: "A noisy sorrowful wailing rose all about her and she was locked inside it the way she was locked inside this house."(44) Finally, her conscious mind rejects any connection with her body and its impulses; her heart seems "nothing that was hers" "but just a pounding, living thing inside this body that wasn't really hers either."(45) In a sense, her body with its puzzling desires "decides" to go with Arnold although her rational self is terrified of him: "She watched herself push the door slowly open as if she were back safe somewhere in the other doorway, watching this body and this head of long hair moving out into the sunlight where Arnold Friend waited."(45)

Oates encourages the reader to look for multiple levels in this story and to consider Arnold and Connie at more than face value by her repeated emphasis on the question of identity. The opening of the story introduces the concept to which both Connie and her mother seem to subscribe—being pretty means being someone. In fact, her mother's acid questions as she sees Connie at her favority activity of mirror-gazing—"Who are you? You think you're so pretty?" (29)—also introduce the converse of this idea, namely, that those who lack physical beauty have no identity. As does almost everything in the story, everything about Connie has "two sides to it."(30) However, Connie's nature, one for at home and one for "anywhere that was not home,"(30) is simple in comparison to that of Arnold. Connie's puzzled questions at first query what role Arnold thinks he is playing: "Who the hell do you think you are?"(34) Then she realizes that he sees himself all too literally as the man of her dreams, and she becomes more concerned about knowing his real identity. By the time that Arnold asks, "Don't you know who I am?"(42) Connie realizes that it is no longer a simple question of whether he is a "jerk"(35) or someone worth her attention but of just how crazy he is. By the end she knows him to be a murderer, for she realizes that she will never see her family again.(44) However, only the reader sees Arnold's Satan identity. Connie's gradual realization of

Arnold's identity brings with it a recognition of the actual significance of physical beauty: Arnold is indeed someone to be concerned about, even if he is no handsome youth. At the conclusion Connie has lost all identity except that of victim, for Arnold's half-sung sigh about her blue eyes ignores the reality of her brown ones. In Arnold's view, Connie's personal identity is totally unimportant.

Dedicated to contemporary balladeer Bob Dylan, this story in a sense represents Oates' updated prose version of a ballad in which a demon lover carries away his helpless victim. By adding modern psychological insights, she succeeds in revealing the complex nature of the victim of a grotesque intrusion by an alien force; on one level, the victim actually welcomes and invites this demonic visitation. Like Bob Dylan, she grafts onto the ballad tradition a moral commentary which explores but does not solve the problems of the evils of our contemporary society; an analagous Dylan ballad is his "It's a Hard Rain's a Gonna' Fall." Even the title records not only the ritual parental questions but also suggests that there is a moral connection between the two questions: where Connie goes is related to where she has been. Oates does not judge Connie in making this link, however; Connie is clearly not in complete control over where she has been. The forces of her society, her family, and her self combine to make her fate inescapable.

Notes

1. Walter Sullivan, "The Artificial Demon: Joyce Carol Oates and the Dimensions of the Real," *The Hollins Critic*, 9, No. 4 (Dec., 1972), 2.

2. Joyce Markert Wegs, "The Grotesque in Some American Novels of the Nineteen-Sixties: Ken Kesey, Joyce Carol Oates, Sylvia Plath," Diss., University of Illinois, 1973.

3. Joyce Carol Oates, "Where Are You Going, Where Have You Been?" *The Wheel of Love* (1970; rpt. Greenwich, Conn: Fawcett, 1972), p. 31. All subsequent references to the story appear within parentheses in the text.

4. See Walter Sullivan, "Where Have All the Flowers Gone?: The Short Story in Search of Itself," *Sewanee Review*, 78, No. 3 (Summer, 1970), 537.

5. Andrew M. Greeley, "The Devil, You Say," *The New York Times Magazine*, 4 Feb., 1973, p. 26, quotes an address by Pope Paul on 15 Nov., 1972, as reported in the Vatican newspaper.

6. Linda Kuehl, "An Interview with Joyce Carol Oates," *Commonweal*, 91 (5 Dec., 1969), 308.

Suburban Molesters:
Joyce Carol Oates'
Expensive People

Sanford Pinsker°

Miss Oates' third novel—*Expensive People* (1968)—was a radical departure from the social milieu and gritty realities of her first books. By that I mean, the world of Richard Everett is as much a "fiction" as the fiction he self-consciously tries to write. The result is a parody of the reflexive mode, a book about the making of such books. It is also a Nabokovian romp in the art-and-craft of confessional narration. But, as Miss Oates has suggested, *Expensive People* attempts to out-do the tricksy Master of *Lolita* or *Pale Fire:*

> I would imagine that not even Nabokov could have conceived of the bizarre idea of writing a novel from the point of view of one's own (unborn, unconceived) child, thereby presenting some valid, if comic reasons for it remaining unborn and unconceived . . . (Letter to Steven Paul Rose, 4-18-72)

As in all novels built upon the structural principle of Chinese boxes, the interlocking frames are apparently endless. Richard Everett's highly personal reading of "The Molesters" (a story Miss Oates originally published in *The Quarterly Review of Literature*) reduces it to the level of biographical allegory; Miss Oates' comments about *Expensive People* are an exercise in a similar brand of impressionism. Both imply partial truths, but when "authors" multiply dizzyingly, readers quickly learn the virtues of skepticism.

Let me begin with Richard Everett: As a general rule, narrators who belabor their amateurism, who confess some hideous crime in fits and starts, breed a predictable overcompensation. Less sophisticated and/or self-conscious storytellers plunge directly into the "tale." That is, they collapse the distance between author and audience by invoking such tested formulae as "Once upon a time . . ." or "There were these two Irishmen." Richard, on the other hand, protests too much about the sharp divisions between Truth and "fiction":

> One thing I want to do, my readers, is to minimize the tension between writer and reader. Yes, there is tension. You think I am trying to put something over on you, but that isn't true. It isn't true. I am honest and dogged and eventually the truth will be told; it will just take time because I want to make sure everything gets in. (*Expensive People:* N.Y., 1968, p. 5)

Ironies generate from the considerable gaps between his narrative intention and its fictive result. Put another way: Richard's account of suburban

°Reprinted with permission from *The Midwest Quarterly*, 19 (Autumn 1977), 89–103.

malaise is an exercise in simultaneously calling tensions into existence and then declaring them inoperative. As some recent politicians have discovered, the former is likely to have more credibility than the latter. Telling one's readers *not* to think of white tigers is a perfect way to get such animals bounding through their consciousnesses.

Even the bald statement which opens his confessional narrative—"I was a child murderer"— turns problematic, as if language were a medium which makes precision impossible:

> I don't mean child-murderer, though that's an idea. I mean child murderer, that is, a murderer who happens to be a child, or a child who happens to be a murderer. You can take your choice . . . You would be surprised, normal as you are, to learn how many years, how many months, and how many awful minutes it has taken me just to type that first line, which you read in less than a second: I was a child murderer. (p. 3)

The circular effect places Richard squarely in that camp of writers whose favorite emblem is the snake swallowing its tail. In Miss Oates' case, however, the playfulness is not entirely gratuitous. *Expensive People* is as much a novel about child-murderers as it is about a "child murderer," as much about those who "molest" children as it is about a molested child. The two-hundred-and-fifty-pound Richard Everett epitomizes suburban affluence in its boldest, most grotesque, relief. Moreover, his comic agonies about the exhausting business of memoir-writing (it is "such hard work that I have to stop and wipe myself with a large handkerchief" gives the resulting mirror images a carnival dimension. His artifice stretches the adult world of fat-souled, "expensive people" into curiously distended shapes. Both the teller and his tale become bloated, but even *that* will have little effect upon the comfortable facades of suburban life. As Richard would have it, the problem is "that I don't know what I am doing." To order the events of his life into a coherent memoir is very different from merely *living* them. The past refuses to stand still. The story told next year would differ from the one he is telling now, as *this* version cannot be the same as last year's nonexistent attempt. Even worse:

> . . . it's possible that I'm lying without knowing it. Or telling the truth in some weird, symbolic way without knowing it, so only a few psychoanalytic literary critics (there are no more than three thousand) will have access to the truth, what "it" is. (p. 6)

Later, Hanley Stuart Hingham (an imaginary psychoanalytic critic whose name sounds suspiciously like Stanley Edgar Hyman) suggests the following in an equally "imaginary" review of *Expensive People:*

> Those of us who have read Freud (I have read every book, essay, and scrap of paper written by Freud) will recognize easily the familiar domestic triangle here, of a son's homosexual and incestuous love for his father disguised by a humdrum Oedipal attachment to his mother. Author Everett, obviously an amateur, failed to make the best use of his oral theme by his crudity of material. (pp. 162–63)

Like any Post-Modernist writer worth his dazzle, Miss Oates has fun staying at least one jump ahead of her interpreters. It is not, of course, that Richard Everett's story lacks Oedipal character, but that such reductions contain more parody than conviction in a post-Freudian world. To be sure, *Expensive People* is the story of a matricide, of a son's deisre to revenge himself against the crushing domination represented by his aloof, unappeaseable mother. Unlike the authoritarian father whose brutal, phallic strength presumably terrorizes his offspring, mothers generate a tension which is more insidious, more conducive to literary ambivalence and/or irony.

And *Expensive People* is more a study in comic nihilism, in suburban emptiness, than it is a seriously rendered psycho-drama. As Richard suggests in a revealing "footnote": "My mother had wanted me to call her 'Nadia' but, as a small child, I must have been able to manage only the infantile 'Nada.' Hence Nada—strange name!" Richard's confusion is, of course, a measure of Miss Oates' cunning, for the monicker collapses the distance between two important literary models—namely, Ernest Hemingway and John Barth. In "A Clean, Well-Lighted Place," Hemingway's protagonist bathes himself in the self-conscious despair of a prayer to nothingness, one which insists that "Our *nada*, who art in *nada*," etc. Such is the only wisdom a wastelandish world will support; the rain in Spain falleth mainly *nowhere*. John Barth, on the other hand, inherits a literary milieu in which even *that* futile expression has been used-up, its shock value severely diminished. As the title of Raymond Olderman's study in Post-Modernist literature *(Beyond the Wasteland)* suggests, the postures appropriate to T. S. Eliot are radically modified in the guts of living writers like Thomas Pynchon, Joseph Heller and, of course, John Barth. Interestingly enough, one of Nada's journal entries confirms some of these suspicions. As she speculates about a yet-unwritten story: "in any first-person narrative there can be a lot of freedom. Certain central events—what the hell can they be?—leading up to the death" (p. 139). The description might well apply to a novel like *Expensive People*. Moreover, she even includes one of John Barth's emblematic phrases immediately thereafter: " 'comic nihilism.' " To be sure, Miss Oates is not as reverential about Barthian efforts like *The Floating Opera* or *The End of the Road* as she will be later in short stories modeled upon Joyce's "The Dead" or Henry James' *The Aspern Papers*. Imitation is, indeed, the sincerest form of flattery; parodic echoes—and particularly those which raise the zany to another power—are a very different matter. Like the Ambrose of John Barth's *Lost in the Funhouse*, Richard wears his writer's block on his sleeve. Classical models, earnest advice from how-to-do-it pulps like *Amateur Penman*, Franklinesque lists about what lies in store, all serve to take readers behind the memoir's "plot line" to the comic agonies of its creation.

Yet the gulf between fiction and Reality, between the illusion that is Art and the felt pain that is Life, has its darker, more serious, side. The mobility made possible by affluence becomes as suspect as the itch to exchange one version of suburban life for another. Moreover, Oates is not totally convinced that romantic fulfillments lie just over the next concrete horizon. If Thomas Wolfe could wax lyrical in attempting to prove that *You Can't Go Home Again*, Oates seems just as determined to suggest (albeit, playfully) that in contemporary America one can never *leave:*

Our furniture and belongings were loaded up for us back in our other house (in Brookfield, a suburb of another famous city), and by the time they reached us over the hundreds of miles of winter highways I had already discovered surreptitiously, and Nada announced to us one morning, angrily, that there was a family from Brookfield over on the other street, who had apparently moved at the same time we had: and not one mile away was the same house we had lived in for the last three years in Brookfield, present here in Fernwood like a miracle; and the Hunt Club was the same Hunt Club as Brookfield's except that it had "Valley" prefixed to its name . . . and worst of all, only two houses away from us was Edward Griggs or someone who looked just like Edward Griggs, a man who had been something of a social catch back in Brookfield. (p. 19)

Given the nature of such high-priced realities—that suburban communities stretch, like franchised food chains, from coast to coast, that Edward Griggs is a portable (Protean?) creature rather than a fixed personality—there seems to be little one can do on behalf of individuality. Nadia finds solace in the making of fictions; Richard discovers a similar fulfillment in the rigorous attention to detail a matricide demands and the equally vexing problems which arise when one re-tells the story as "memoir."

But illusion and reality are so ineluctably intertwined, the world of *Expensive People* so reflexively absurd, that confusion threatens to emerge as the only norm possible. Elwood Everett's "career" is a case in point:

Father hadn't graduated from college, but had skipped out after his sophomore year (never to open another book unless it was a paperback left on an airline seat) and joined the Army, did well, was discharged and taken into a small Rhode Island concern that manufactured plastic Christmas tree ornaments, and did so well with sales that he was snapped up by a business that dealt with blotters, paper tubes, and corrugated cardboard. His star rose so rapidly that he hopped about from bolts manufacturers to underwear manufacturers to a brief [pun?] spell with a top-security concern that made, overtly, children's toy bombers; from there to vice-presidencies in seat-belt companies, wastebasket companies, certain curtain companies, and so on to the present. It exhausts me to think of all this. (p. 25)

Even more puzzling, Richard's father "was always happy." Armed with a drink and a philosophical outlook that might be described as resigned pragmatism, Mr. Everett faces the worst that an affluent life can offer with a permanent, almost convincing, good cheer. Mr. Everett takes bad weather, stock-market declines and national emergencies in an unwavering stride. Richard replaces this "happy" father with one more commensurate to his own psychological needs. The result is a Freudian variation of the family romance, with all the usual insistences that one's *real* father will not only return, but will prove to be more satisfying than the imposter currently holding title. Such a father would punish Nadia in ways that the happy (deluded?) Elwood never will. But Richard is a good deal more serious about this than the parodic Miss Oates. The Oedipal triangle Richard constructs has an unconvincing, text-bookish ring. If Elwood's mask always contains an up-turned grin, Richard's is lined with intensity. The former, Richard might insist, is the stuff of which a bland survivorhood is made; the latter is destined for that greatness we call tragedy. Moreover, *Expensive People* insists upon making such divisions along generational lines.

Adults are, at best, unknowing victimizers; their children, on the other hand, are very self-conscious victims indeed:

> You think children are whole, uncomplicated creatures, and if you split them in two with a handy ax there would be all one substance inside, hard candy. But it isn't hard candy so much as a hopeless seething lava of all kinds of things, a turmoil, a mess. (p. 32)

The generalization spreads across Miss Oates' canon. *All* her children are cut from the same bolt of lava-like cloth: Richard Everett is simply more articulate than those who seethe in a befuddled silence. But, ironically enough, the compulsive attempts to tell his story (however representative it might be as archetype) are diminished by the painstaking—and darkly comic—attention to its own self-consciousness. The result is a fiction which "tells," rather than *shows*, its intensity. Which is to say, a playful wit keeps poking through the fabric of Richard's confessional memoir. Genuine turmoil is seldom this calculated.

And yet *Expensive People* makes equations of its own; one does not need to look for *fin de siecle* precedents. As Richard dryly observes, his mother "was so simple in her way that all things ostentatious and expensive seemed emanations of a higher existence . . ." Confident about her own high artistic standards (Nada could become downright embarrassed by the occasional lapses of taste or power in writers like Tolstoi and Mann), she grew shy—indeed, nearly helpless—before anyone who had "the smell of money about them." For her, it is *pecunia* (not *scientia*) which "auctoritas est." Elwood merely provided the means which, as Richard's Faulknernian rhythms speculate, were necessary to make Nada's impersonal vision come all too true:

> She had married Father the way a girl goes on a date with a man she does not at all like, or even know, simply because he will take her to a special event where the very lights and the very sweetness of the flowers set everywhere make up a world— no people are really needed. (p. 43)

It is the costly splendor that matters, not the substance. Or, as Richard soon discovers, it is not one's *intelligence*, but a numerical I.Q. which his mother cares about. The Johns Behemoth School is, in this sense, an aptly named institution. Richard anguishes through a five-part admissions exam both parched and increasingly hungry.

The exam begins with a homonym for *syzygy* (a word which, significantly enough, indicates two opposing points [Richard and his father?] in opposition with a heavenly body [Nadia?] and it ends with "Additudinal Testing" like the following:

> Which would you rather do? (1) Hit your mother (2) Hit your father (3) Burn down your house (4) Eat a worm (p. 55)

Much of the literary humor in *Expensive People* consists of allusions wrinkled, almost unnoticed, through the novel's surface. For example, one of the Everett's departed friends was named Arnold, while a dentist—very much alive—is called Dr. Bellow. And there are even times when the cultural disguises are dropped, when High Brows visit Fernwood under their own steam. Norman Mailer had once given a lecture entitled "The Great American Novel: When is it Due?"—presumably very much like his *Esquire* article on the same subject. Leslie Fiedler, on the other hand, is reduced to an unacknowledged footnote. As Richard browses through an article on "The State of American Fiction," the elegiac tone ("two-thirds of it concerned with the deaths of Faulkner and Hemingway, 'which left a vacuum on our culture,' . . .") is undeniably that of Fiedler's *Waiting for the End,* his funeral rites for the contemporary American novel. Discussions of satiric minor characters like Moe Malinsky and Dr. Muggeridge will come later, but for now it is sufficient to note that the "expensive people" share a passion for with-it intellectuality. Their children wrestle with admissions tests, IQ scores and the competitive, cut-throat style of the Johns Behemoth School; their parents sit through droning lectures.

Unfortunately, empirical data play the cheat in *Expensive People.* As Richard plays out his self-styled role as an avenging (and equally confused) Hamlet, things are decidedly *not* what they seem. Theatre intrudes, until one is no longer certain about what is Life and what is Art. When, for example, Nada notices a small crowd milling around a drive-in bank, she pulls her car into the asphalt drive—"always adventuresome"—and lowers her automatic windows:

> Out of the bank's wide white doors rushed three men, and the men standing outside in trench coats opened fire on them. I saw a blaze of fire from the barrel of a big hip-hugging gun. Two of the three men fell, and the door, which was slowly and automatically closing, was pushed open again; a woman in a white skirt and lavender sweater stood there with her hand to her mouth in an exaggerated gesture of awe. (p. 88)

However, the *exaggeration* is not as deadly as it might appear to be at first glance. Nadia, the trickster, has herself been tricked:

> One of the men who had fallen jumped up and brushed off his clothes. He began to argue with the trench-coated men, and another man joined them from somewhere to the side.
> "Oh, Christ," Nada said faintly, "it's a television show or something. A rehearsal." (p. 88)

The point is not lost upon Richard. By that I mean, his eventual murder of Nada is as much a "rehearsal" as, say, his writing of *Expensive People.* Moreover, the "slain" men—who brush off their clothes and run through the scene until it is perfect—are linked thematically with Richard's surrealistic tale of his dog Spark. When poor Spark is hit by a laundry truck, Elwood insists that the animal "had to go to the doctor":

> "You know, like you did. Dr. Pratt."
> "How come?"
> "Spark needs his measles." (p. 176)

The next day, Spark presumably re-appears—this time with enough shots to be "set for life." To be sure, the confused dog does not recognize Richard-the-participant and Richard-as-narrator remains detached, scrupulously non-evaluative. But the story does not end on such a melodramatic note. Evidently surrogate Sparks are in large supply. A week later, "Spark" is hit once again, this time by a delivery truck. And, once again, a new Spark—"a lot bigger than he was two days ago" and with a coat not so soft—is reunited with his trusting (?) master. In effect, Oates gives the shaggy dog story a darkly comic twist. Asking which Spark is the *real* one becomes a dizzying exercise in perception, rather like trying to establish which time the caterpillar was crushed in Robbe-Grillet's *Jealousy*. But, even here, Oates manages to give such scenarios a disarming quarter-twist. As Richard tells it, the last Spark

> . . . made a puddle right away on the kitchen floor, which the maid had just cleaned, and Nada said something she sometimes said to Father. We fed Spark and spent all day petting him and and trying to make him stop whining. He wouldn't play, and I told Nada I didn't like him any more, and Nada told me that I had better like him if I knew what was good for me.
>
> We had Spark for several years, then when we moved to Charlotte Pointe he had a nervous breakdown and never recovered.
>
> That is the tale of my dog Spark. (p. 178)

The truth about Spark is, finally, that of breakdown, of a special madness which generates from radical interchangeability. Richard watches as the solid contours of his world dissolve into random flow. And, for all his playfulness, Richard cannot accept the terms of such a life. His desire for stability hides just behind the memoirist's reflexive mask. Put another way: Richard is the abandoned and embittered child, as standard a feature in Oates' canon as homicidal hitchhikers or the volcanic eruptions which lie just beneath the surface of banal talk. At one point Richard begins to equate his disappointing performance on an IQ test with the Spark-like condition of the "Two Nadas":

> . . . the one who was free and who abandoned me often and the other who has become fixed irreparably in my brain, an embryonic creature of my own making, my extravagant and deranged imagination . . . And so when Nada said to me that day, "There is nothing personal, never anything personal in freedom," I understood that the free, restless Nada was asserting herself, and that I could not hold her back. *If you leave this time, don't bother to come back. . .* (pp. 118–119)

For Richard, the epiphanic moment comes in darkness, as he descends into the very bowels of Johns Behemoth School—its infamous "Records Room." There he encounters the "official" Richard Everett, an identity made up of medical reports, letters of recommendation and, most significant of all, his IQ scores:

> There were two papers and one said 153 and the other, dated more recently, said 161. I stared from one paper to the other until it dawned upon me what those numbers meant.
>
> Then the not kernel of fire burst in my stomach and I began to sob. I sobbed with rage. What did she want from me then? What more could she want? I couldn't do any better. I had even pushed myself beyond what I could do, and still it wasn't enough for her—I wasn't enough for her—and what else could I do? (p. 130)

The insight both anguishes Richard and, curiously enough, releases all manner of pent-up aggression. As Miss Oates would have it, the opposite of repression is regurgitation. First, Richard literally tears up the room (at one point he even "picked up a stool and sent it crashing into the flickering flourescent tubing overhead" with a dramatic gesture that echoes Stephen Dedalus' "*Nothung!*" at the Nighttown brothel. And after scattering papers and ink everywhere—in a fantasy of revenge against the capital-B Bureaucracy—he stumbles upon "the best and happiest trick of all":

> I was vomiting over everything, summoning up from my depths the most vile streams of fluid that had ever graced any Record Room in history. (p. 131)

Granted, this is not the sort of existential nausea Sartre had in mind, but it is an effective way to end the Johns Behemoth Experience and the first section of *Expensive People*.

Expensive People is divided into sections of roughly equal length. As I have already suggested, Part I is spent in the zig-zagging process of getting Richard Everett, memoirist, untracked. Part II adds an intriguing wrinkle. Much the same way Richard imagines "a mural vast as my imagination, called 'The Abortion that Failed,' " Nadia had projected a short novel about a young man who "leads two lives, one public and the other secret" who buys a gun, frightens people, and ultimately fulfills his destiny as a murderer. Her title— "The Sniper"—is, of course, an apt description of the book one reads as *Expensive People*, especially if the focus narrows to Richard rather than his antagonists. Moreover, Nadia's confusion about motivation—"planned all along though maybe he didn't know it. (Too corny? Should he know it, or not?)"—is matched by Richard's:

> I read this over several times, bent over her desk, surreptitious and impatient in her sacred room. My heart began to pound as if it knew something already that I myself did not know. (p. 140)

Thus, victims unwittingly dream their destroyers into existence; unaborted children return the favor by murdering their parents.

Once Richard's energized dream is released, the dialectic is between a dreamy, narcotic world and one of grimmer, existential outline. Fernwood is "a dream, and everyone in it dreaming the dream; all in conjunction, happy, so long as no one woke up." An introspective moment, however tiny, plunges one headlong into apocalyptical visions, into a universe in which

> ... everything would have been stretched and jerked out of focus, and so ... the end of Fernwood, the end of Western civilization! (p. 171)

Richard consoles himself by making life in *that* sort of world as attractive as possible. Pain is better, after all, than the assorted "messes" Nadia makes. As Richard puts it: ". . . the only truth I know about my mother—a most sorry truth—[is that] she wanted only to live but she didn't know how, that was why she made a mess." By contrast, *he* will hatch elaborate plans, forever escape the role of three-fold victim in his mother's story "The Molesters." He becomes a serio-comic "sniper," an underbush (rather than under*ground*) man shooting into the Cedar Grove night. And, in the process, he also becomes a Minor Character, an identity gradually slipping "out of focus":

> It's difficult for you readers to understand my becoming a Minor Character because 1) you can't imagine anyone except yourself being Major, hence my becoming Minor should be no great shock; 2) you don't believe a genuine Minor Character should exhibit so much anguish, pain, tedium. It's ridiculous, like a vehement pamphlet put out by an organization of white mice. (pp. 271–272)

Moreover, Richard's deadly "game" attracts other players. Art is, after all, *imitation*—and in a novel where illusion has a confusing relationship with reality, unwanted company is hardly surprising:

> . . . on August 2 I was joined by another sniper. That bastard hadn't my Cedar Grove touch. He was obviously lower class, a slob who shot an old man out on the sidewalk and hit him in the knee. As if I, Richard Everett, would have shot an old man in the knee! But while my stomach cringed at the thought of such vulgarity, my heart swelled with unreasonable pride to think that I had a follower, an imitator. The only problem was that the police made no distinction between us. (pp. 285–286)

Thus, the dream maketh villains of us all. Child-molesters (like child *murderers*) surround themselves with high-brow rhetoric and the freighting of twice-told ideas. Richard's existential act—rather like Mailer's insistence in "The White Negro" that the hipster *"Do it"*—brings matricide and his memoir into bold, symmetrical relief. A "baroque X" marks the spot; the newspapers print a photograph (ironically enough, of the Everett's $95,000 house, rather than of Nadia). And, as it turns out, even the exotic Natashya Romanov is really Nancy Romanow, born in, of all places, "a small town in upstate New York with a ludicrous name: North Tonawanda." As Nadia's notebook knew all along:

> . . . the climax will be the death of X, but one must get past. The trouble is getting there . . . and getting past. As in any first-person narrative there can be a lot of freedom. (p. 139)

Expensive People "got there" all right; getting *past*, however, would happen later, in novels which played Oatesian emotions closer to the non-reflexive bone.

The Journey from the "I" to the "Eye":*Wonderland*

Ellen Friedman[*]

Oates's *Wonderland*,like Lewis Carroll's Alice in *Wonderland* is a book about proportions. In fact, Carroll's Alice books strongly influenced the theme, structure and imagery of Oates's *Wonderland*.[1] Oates has expressed great interest in Carroll's work and has taught *Alice in Wonderland* and *Through the Looking Glass* in her classes at Windsor. She considers them very misanthropic works that ask the "valid and terrifying" questions, "Is life really a game?" and "Is everyone cheating but me?" "In Carroll," says Oates, "life is a chess game; you eat one another in order to get to another square."[2] Like Alice, Jesse Harte, the novel's protagonist, undergoes a series of metamorphic transformations in which he grows larger and larger. After he is orphaned—Jesse is the only surviving member of his family after his father murders the entire Harte family and then commits suicide—we see him in succession as an obese adolescent (physically enlarged), as a cold, brilliant, scientist (mentally enlarged), and as a vampirish husband and father (psychically enlarged). In order to escape her father's engulfing domination, Jesse's younger daughter Shelley (her name suggests "shell"), tries to grow smaller and smaller; she attempts to extinguish her selfhood, to free herself of it, by methodically dreaming over her past and "erasing" it. Jesse's narcissistic self-aggrandizement and Shelley's nihilism are deluded attempts to escape the impinging external world by substituting the self for the world.[3] Jesse strives to redeem his personal history and refute a contingent reality by becoming his own world. Shelley, on the other hand, strives to free herself from her personal history, not realizing that her personal history is part of the intricate pattern of time and universal history from which she cannot extricate herself except through death. Jesse and Shelley suffer from a distorted sense of self; they presume the absolute primacy of self. Their refusal to acknowledge the world leads them to opposite routes of narcissism and nihilism.

In Civilization and its Discontents Freud wrote that "a great part of the struggle of mankind centres mainly round the single expedient . . . solution between [the] individual claims and those of the civilized community . . . ."[4] The

[*]This essay is a part of Professor Friedman's book-length manuscript on the writing of Joyce Carol Oates, and is published here with her permission.

question of proportion between self and world is the major question of the book. It is encapsulated in the idea of homeostasis, the controlling metaphor of *Wonderland*. As Alice emerges from the rabbit hole correctly proportioned, the final Jesse shrinks from an *uebermensch* to an ordinary, self-questioning being, who, in the ordeal of rescuing Shelley from death, in the act of expressing love through this rescue, learns that he cannot be self-contained, that the overflow of self to other is an imperative of life. He achieves homeostasis, which, in this novel, signifies the precarious but necessary equilibrium between the self and the world.

In the same way that Alice's voyage through her dream worlds is the voyage of a typical Victorian imagination through a landscape which symbolizes Victorian culture, Jesse's voyage in *Wonderland*, which is in one sense a *bildungsroman*, is the voyage of a representative American through the symbolic landscape of American culture.[5] Jesse's substitution of the self for the world is given an explicitly American context in *Wonderland*. With its emphasis on autonomy and freedom, American culture encourages the distorted sense of self from which he suffers. The anonymous *Times Literary Supplement* reviewer has rightly described Jesse as "the Everyman victim of American history."[6] Like many of Oates's protagonists, Jesse is violently wrenched from family and place, rendered homeless and an orphan by the initial events in the novel. Thereafter, he nurtures his own autonomy rather than depending on the nurture of the world outside. As a result, his becomes a quest for self-creation rather than initiation. Leslie Fiedler writes, "How could one tell where the American dream ended and the Faustian nightmare began; they held in common the hope of breaking through all limits and restraints, of reaching a place of total freedom. . . ."[7] In this American spirit, Jesse follows a Faustian pattern replacing communal life with personal power. However, unlike the European Faust, who has to reject traditions and sympathetic alliances in order to assert the primacy of self, Oates's American counterpart has nothing to reject. Homelessness, the absence of a defining context, is the birthright of every American, a birthright that in Oates's world produces in the individual dreams of self-creation and autonomy, but no means of actualizing them. The consequences of American individualism were well understood by de Tocqueville, who wrote, "Not only does democracy make every man forget his ancestors, but it hides his descendents and separates his contemporaries from him; it throws him back forever upon himself alone, and threatens in the end to confine him entirely within the solitude of his own heart."[8] The violent wrenching of the individual from his identifying context is, in Oates, a symbolic re-enactment of the American Revolution, and the individual who is left orphaned by this act is the symbolic American Adam or Eve who needs to find his way back, if not to Paradise, to some sympathetic, though limited, union.[9]

Both Carroll's and Oates's works are, in one respect, ventures in the pursuit of identity in a capricious universe. In each of Carroll's works, Alice asks, "Who am I?" Alice loses her identity because in stepping into an alien world, she has lost perspective, lost the knowledge of the relationship between herself and her environment. In Oates's work, this lack of a defining perspective is fundamental to the mythos of American culture. Jesse and Alice, aliens in the world in which they find themselves, attempt to discern the rules by which it operates, but on the brink of discovery, the landscape metamorphoses, leaving them continually adrift.

In *Through the Looking Glass*, the landscape alters each time Alice makes a move across the chessboard of her dream world. In Oates's novel, the chessboard is American history from December 14, 1939 to April, 1971, encompassing the Depression, World War II, Kennedy's assassination, the Viet Nam War, the beatniks, the rise in the importance of scientific technology, and the hippie drug culture. With each move her protagonist effects, the landscape shifts into another era of our history which he must confront before proceeding. Jesse's confrontation with his collective history is a condition of his final awakening into an acceptance of his otherness. Like the Alice books, *Wonderland* is episodic, structured by Jesse's encounters with figures who embody the spirit of change undergone by the United States in this time period and perhaps more significantly, who also represent heretical philosophical solutions to the problems of existence. Moreover, each of Jesse's metamorphic transformations is an accommodation to or a rejection of the ideologies of these representative figures. The one element common to all of these figures is that they substitute, in one way or another, the self for the world. In Oates's novel, American history continually repeats the drama of the isolated ego.

The novel's first book, "Variations on an American Hymn," opens with a scene from the Depression, which is the symbol Oates repeatedly employs to portray dislocation.[10] The imagery in this scene conveys a sense of claustrophobia, signifying the economic pressures on the Harte family who are Depression victims, and chaos, signifying the dislocation such pressures cause. Jesse says, "the air looks as if it is coming apart—shredding into molecules of sand or grit" (p. 14).[11] He feels smothered by the crowded quarters of his house, his mother's fifth pregnancy, and his father's financial failure. Later, as his father drives Jesse home from work, his sense of chaos increases, anticipating his father's bloody act and his consequent homelessness: "There is nothing in [the] sky to give a form to the day, nothing permanent, nothing to be outlined with the eye. It is all a blur, shapeless, a dimension of fog and space, like the future itself. Jesse stares at it and as he stares he is being driven into it relentlessly" (p. 41). When he enters his house, he finds it awash with the blood of his family, the result of his crazed father's Depression-motivated acts; the father intends to kill Jesse as well, but he escapes death—although his father succeeds in wounding him before he commits suicide—by jumping out of a bedroom window "into the dark" (p. 44), and into the burden of his freedom. As an orphan, Jesse is the emblem of Oatesian nightmarish freedom, which equates freedom with the loss of identity and with the loss of a sustaining world.[12]

The next phase of American history with which the novel concerns itself is really a glance backward to the time when American life was centered around the farm. When Jesse leaves the hospital, he is in the care of his grandfather, a farmer, who lives alone and shuns human contact. He embodies the American agrarian ideal in which nature is a sufficient provider and companion. He also represents a solipsistic solution to the problem of living. Before the murders, his grandfather is described as moving "in absolute silence, alone, a kind of nullity in the midst of the green corn, moving as if in a trance or a dream, making their [Jesse and his brothers and sister] eyes film over with the starkness of his isolation and his indifference" (p. 52). His creed is "People should leave one another alone" (p. 61). Jesse and his grandfather have a "partnership of silence" (p. 62); "there was a space about them, a dry, holy space that no one else entered" (p. 56). After the murders, Jesse gratefully plunges into his grandfather's life, welcoming the silence and the sense of objectivity the land imparts. Devoted to the rhythm of "sleep, waking, work" (p. 57), Jesse is conscious of himself in this rhythm: "Jesse sleeping. Jesse waking. Jesse at work. He would not have to think about his life because it would pass like this, one day after another, carrying him forward" (p. 57).

However, spring awakens Jesse's memory, and he asks to see his family's furniture, which is stored in his grandfather's barn. Jesse hungers for evidence of his own history, represented by the furniture, but his grandfather refuses to open the barn; he refuses to yield to Jesse's need to come to terms with his past. For the solipsist, this need is a violation of the terms of existence. Betrayed by his grandfather's stubborness, Jesse makes his way back to his father's deserted house, dreaming back over his life as he goes, repeating, "I'm here, I'm here, I'm here. Jesse Harte is a survivor" (p. 64). Oates's homeless protagonists are reduced to viewing mere survival as a triumph, a victory. In order to renew contact with his roots he spends the night in his empty, boarded-up house. The "Closed" sign his father placed on the property on the morning of the murders has been exchanged for a "For Sale" sign, an exchange which represents at the same time Jesse's survival, his orphaned state, and the prospect that he will have to find new connectedness for his selfhood.

After an interval in which Jesse spends a short time in his cousin Fritz's home and in an orphanage, the novel shifts to the time of World War II. Jesse is adopted by Dr. Karl Pedersen, an obese, obsessive, morphine-addicted surgeon and self-proclaimed seer who declares that war is "the very heartbeat of life" (p. 109). A grotesque embodiment of Nietzsche's Superman, Dr. Pedersen is a figure in whom Naziism found its justification. He is one of a series of *ueber-mensch* figures in Oates's fiction, all of whom believe in the self as the final authority. They are gluttonous overreachers portrayed as extremely fat, like Max in *With Shuddering Fall*, outrageously wealthy, like Marvin Howe in *Do With Me What You Will* and power-mad, like Andrew Petrie in *The Assassins: A Book of Hours*. Their obesity, wealth, and spiritual deformity imply the extremest form of individualism, of what Quentin Anderson has termed "secular incarnation."[13] They dominate the landscape in which they appear and, like Black Holes in space that absorb all surrounding energy, they absorb all life in that landscape. They melodramatically suggest the consequences of the cultivation of absolute self.

Perhaps no other figure in Oates's fiction illustrates "secular incarnation" as well as Dr. Pedersen. He declares that his specialty is "correcting defects of nature, modifying certain freakish twists of fate" (p. 98). He states that his fate is to "displace God" (p. 109). "I am straining to be God, to move into that place which is God's place, to take from Him all that He will allow me to take . . ." (p. 109). Concomitant to the idea of the absolute self is the idea of perfection: "Perfection is difficult, but . . . not as difficult as imperfection" (p. 142). In his theology, death is a "surrender," not man's implacable destiny. Dr. Pedersen is less a philosopher than a theologian envisioning his own apotheosis. Jesse becomes his dutiful poselyte, answering Pedersen's question, "How do you, Jesse Harte, intend to confront the riddle of existence?" with "By . . . going as far as I can go, as far as, . . . my abilities will take me . . ." (p. 78). Jesse's answer is the promise each American boy makes for himself, a promise sanctified by the Declaration of Independence, a promise, too, that ignores man's contingency, human finitude, the limitations inherent both in himself and the world in which he seeks to keep it.

In the Pedersen household, the attempt to keep this promise leads to obesity, freakishness, deformity, and the love of war. Every member of the Pedersen household is fat, including Jesse, obesity being the physical correlative of megalomania. All of the Pedersens are crazed by an obsessive hunger, attempting with their expanding waistlines to fill space, to possess the world with their own physical being. As Jesse leafs through the Pedersen's photograph album, "The Book of Fates," he notes that "as the years passed, Dr. Pedersen's face grew wider and merrier, like a balloon being blown up" (p. 119). And he sees Mrs. Pedersen gradually transformed, "heavier hips, arms, a face that grew rounder, that grew almost round, a bosom that suddenly billowed out . . . the whole body thickening, growing outward like the trunk of a giant tree, corseted tight and rigid" (p. 118).

The episode with Dr. Pedersen concerns itself with freaks, which were probably suggested to Oates by the strange characters who populate Carroll's books. But perhaps more to the point, the condition of being a freak, of being deformed, is an extreme form of individualism, implying "a freedom in the very intensity of being."[14] Pedersen is a collector and promoter in his own family, of freaks. He adopts Jesse because of the unusual way in which Jesse was orphaned. He maintains a "Book of Impersonal Fates" that contains clippings from accounts of bizarre accidents. Among his collection of freaks, he numbers his daughter Hilda and his son, Frederick, whose respective skills in mathematics and music do not suggest genius so much as freakishness, deformity. In fact, they cannot manage simple hygienic routines like brushing teeth or changing dirty underwear.

The radical imbalance between self and world, which Dr. Pedersen and his family exemplify, an imbalance serving the grotesque aggrandizement of the self and leading to the exaltation of deformity, is countered with the idea of homeostasis, which is first articulated by Jesse at the Pedersen dinner table:

> The living being is an agency of such sort that each disturbing influence induces by itself the calling forth of compensatory activity to neutralize or repair the disturbance. . . . *The living being is stable. It must be so in order not to be destroyed, dissolved, or disintegrated by the colossal forces, often adverse, which surround it.*

By an apparent contradiction it maintains its stability only if it is excitable and capable of modifying itself according to external stimuli and adjusting its response to the stimulation. It is stable because it is modifiable—the slight instability is the necessary condition of the true stability of the organism. (p. 107)

Equilibrium and modifiability, then, are the key factors in the maintenance of homeostasis, factors conspicuously absent from Dr. Pedersen's ideology.

Although Jesse has memorized the definition of "homeostasis," he does not achieve this condition until the last page of the novel. His willing absorption into the Pedersen household has precluded homeostasis. When Pedersen shows Jesse the headline, "Boy Eludes Gun-Totting Father," he rejects it, feeling that it "had nothing to do with him" (p. 121). Moreover, when he meets his cousin Fritz, who is a soldier about to enter World War II, he speculates that "if [Fritz] dies in the Navy there will be one less person to know me the way I used to be" (p. 106). In denying his past, in not accepting it as part of himself, he has violated the law of homeostasis, which requires that one adjust to pain. He lives severed from his past and thus out of the normal continuum of time.

Irving Malin in his essay, "The Compulsive Design," notes the pattern in which many American protagonists "construct a design—a pattern to master their environment—but it becomes an inflexible measure which eventually destroys the self."[15] These "compulsive designers" are usually the heroes of American fiction according to Malin, but in Oates, they are either the villains, like Pedersen, or the uninitiated, like Jesse. Following the pattern Malin describes, Jesse continually projects himself into the future, compulsively designing his future self, because he, for all practical purposes, has no past with which to substantiate his present self. He has only the projected Jesse of the future to confirm his existence.

However, Oates does not allow Jesse, the novel's hero, to totally capitulate to the imperatives of Pedersen's philosophy. Although he has tried to obey these imperatives because with his obedience has come the protective circle of a home and family, there is something in Jesse that responds to another's helplessness. It is this saving attribute that eventually redeems him. When Mrs. Pedersen tricks him into arranging her escape from her husband, he is reluctant, but he helps her. The attempt, of course, is futile and ends with Dr. Pedersen's declaration that Jesse is "dead" to him.

Oates describes the episode of Mrs. Pedersen's escape with cartoon-like exaggeration, doubtless inspired by Carroll; the cartoons become more and more extravagant as Mrs. Pedersen's and Jesse's predicament becomes more desperate. We see these two distraught, obese figures waddle luggage-less into an elegant hotel. We see a panting Jesse drive back and forth from the hotel to the Pedersen home for more and more of the useless possessions Mrs. Pedersen—who cannot quite sever the umbilical cord that connects her to her home—desperately insists on having. We see them devour bag after bag of "take-out" Chinese food, their hunger the size of their fear. Before Jesse opens the note in whick Pedersen declares him dead, he enters a fast-food place in order to stem the "tears of hunger that dimmed his vision" (p. 183). "Jesse settled himself carefully on one of the stools and ordered six hamburgers with chili sauce on them, three side dishes of French fries, and a Coke. . . . hand trembled as he reached for the first hamburger in its large toasted bun. . . . His insides were buzzing with expectation. . . . He was so hungry; he felt sick with hunger. He would like to explain . . . that he had only wanted to do what was right . . . that there was a shrill hunger in him that rose like a scream. . . ." (p. 182). His hunger is an externalization of his loss. He is hungry for the nourishment of home and family from which he has been orphaned for the second time, once at the age of fourteen and now at the age of seventeen. Jesse's compulsive substitution of food for loss is a paradigm of his future behavior pattern.[16] Although he no longer overeats, he will attempt to fortify his selfhood in other ways, first by expanding mentally—he becomes a brilliant neurosurgeon—and then by expanding psychically—he tries to possess his family. These are attempts to substitute the self for the world in order to become invulnerable to loss and defeat.

When we next encounter Jesse, as a young man, he is a student of medicine at the University of Michigan; the episode opens Book Two, "The Finite Passing of an Infinite Passion." His mentors during his medical studies are Dr. Cady, whose daughter, Helene, he marries, and Dr. Perrault, whose position as head of neurosurgery he acquires. They embody America's obsession in the 1950s and early 1960s with science as the way in which man can control his world. They offer empiricism and behaviorism as the ultimate philosophy and psychology. Dr. Cady compares the human body to a machine. He believes that our senses are our only access to reality, that ultimately, "the world is our own construction" (p. 194). Dr. Perrault instructs Jesse that "the personal self and the soul are sentimental notions" and that "personality is an illusion, a tradition that dies hard" (pp. 339, 337). These theorists who reduce man to a machine, who deny the mysterious and manifold, relegate them to the status of mythology, are asserting their own power over existence. If existence is merely a matter of "mass, substance, no miracle in creation" (p. 312), then as scientists, they are in complete control. As Jesse absorbs these lessons, his sense of control is heightened, a sense that is "pure, impersonal, brute" (p. 312).

As she takes her hero through American history, Oates exposes the various forms in which the self is substituted for the world: Jesse has confronted his nihilistic father, his solipsistic grandfather, the megalomaniac Pedersen, the empirisist Cady, and the behaviorist Perrault; yet the forms are not exhausted. Opposed to the heresies of empiricism and behaviorism are the antithetical heresies of Manicheism, whose avatar is Monk, a one-time medical student turned beat poet, and sensualism, whose avatar is Reva Denk, a kept woman whom Jesse first encounters while treating her lover after he castrated himself. Monk, known to his friends as Trick, believes that "man is a mouth and an anus" (p. 202), and thus the ultimate cure is the "separation of the spirit from the flesh" (p. 208). It is Monk, though, who accurately assesses Jesse's motives in his medical studies, stating that "Jesse aspires to a condition of personal bloodlessness' (p. 237) and that he wants "to raise the dead" (p. 234). Trick correctly gauges Jesse's drive to become a top neurosurgeon as a drive to insulate himself from the rest of humanity by becoming Christ the healer, by raising the (near) dead in removing their cancerous tumors. However, Jesse is a failed Christ because he cannot cure all humanity of its mortality. Medicine is finally dissatisfying; the cancerous tumors are infinitely more prolific than his ability to remove them.

Although, as we shall see, Oates portrays the final Jesse as Christ-like, he has yet to reject sensual love, which the dream woman Reva Denk offers him, as a means of escaping the pluralistic world. His infatuation with Reva releases him from a dependence on science as a means of controlling reality, but in fact, she represents just another guise of the self-enclosed ego. Reva Denk, as her name suggests, represents all "dream-thinking," which must inevitably be relinquished for reality. While he prepares for their reunion with a ritualistic cleansing of his body, he studies his face in a mirror: "It was a curious terrain of slopes and ridges, skin and cartilage and freckles and small veins and hairs, brute dark hairs, pits bumps, hollows" (p. 377). This examination leads to a moment of recognition, an epiphany, reminiscent of a similar moment that Sartre's hero, Roquentin, experiences.[17] Unlike Roquentin, who abandons the world for the self, Jesse abandons self-indulgent sensuality for his responsibilities to his family and patients. With a razor-blade, he hypnotically makes numerous cuts on his body, performing a ritual of purgation, an act that initiates the process that will cleanse him of narcissism and repair the rift between Jesse and the world. "Bleeding," is an image of humanity; the previous Jesse, we recall, aspired to a condition of "bloodlessness." In the final cut, "he drew the blade through the tangle of pubic hair" (p. 378). This gesture of self-castration reminds the reader that the first time Jesse encountered Reva was when he treated Reva's lover after he had castrated himself. Thus Oates, in a curious and telling reversal of our expectations, associates Reva Denk, "dream thinking," with castration, demonstrating Oates's anti-romantic orientation. This act of self-mutilation and, strangely, of self-purification, ends Book Two, in which the "infinite passion" from which Jesse suffers, perhaps for all of us, the passion that the self can control reality or get beyond it or that the self *is* reality, submits to a "finite passing."

With Jesse, Oates has created a Faustian character who makes pacts with modern devil figures—grandfather Vogel, Dr. Pedersen, and Dr. Perrault, and although he has rejected these figures, he must, like Faust, still win salvation, which in Oates does not mean a place in heaven, but rather a place in the world. Although Jesse has left Reva for his family out of an inchoate awareness that his authentic selfhood is substantiated by the bonds and the web of responsibilities inherent in family membership, he wrongfully assumes that he *is* his family, that by possessing them, by absorbing and assimilating them, he can render them and thus himself inviolable. His wife, Helene, complains, "He wants to own us. He wants to be us" (p. 422). This effort to control and dominate indicates that Jesse's consciousness is still clouded by the delusion that the self is the world. Baffled by his failure to establish himself, he compulsively writes the word "homeostasis," as if to achieve this state through incantation (p. 422). Taking a walk, Jesse "circles" his house, "a circle that must have taken him five miles, the house remaining in its center, in the very center of his consciousness, his wife and daughters sleeping in the center" (p. 434). Thirty years after his father orphans him, he is still attempting to re-enter the sanctity of home and family, to re-create those violently severed bonds.

The last episode in American history that the novel treats is that of the hippie drug culture, which takes up Book III, "Dreaming America." It is structured largely by the letters that Jesse's runaway daughter, Shelley, writes to him. She is under the influence of Noel, the last devil figure in the novel. Noel is a figure out of America's 1960's. An apostle of nihilism, he preaches an absolute denial of ego, of history, of existence. He says, "We are all becoming extinct" (p. 400). By becoming Noel's proselyte, Shelley is countering the tyranny of her father's narcissism. Shelley strives for freedom in self-extinction: "I want darkness, the flow of blood without bubbles of oxygen or memory, I want to be free of you [Jesse], I want to be free" (p. 407). Despite her effort to oppose her father with a quest antithetical to his, she is engaged in a similar effort because narcissism and nihilism are alternative quests for autonomy and freedom.

Shelley's rejection of Jesse strikes at the very root of his inadequacy. His myth of control is dissipated by Shelley's flight. As remedy, Jesse applies the only lesson he ever learned from reading fiction, that "love demanded rescue." As he makes his way through the crowded hippie community in Toronto, from which Shelley has written a veiled plea for rescue, Jesse rehearses all of the identities he has taken on and cast off: "Maybe another Jesse here somewhere, hidden by the crowd, on the other side of the street, hunting . . . a perspiring, overweight Jesse, hurrying to keep up with this lean, anxious Jesse, . . . a scrawny, frightened young Jesse hurrying along this confusing tide" (p. 466). Tellingly, Jesse speaks of himself objectively, in the third person.[18] Aware of the futility of pursuing these cast-off selves, he seeks for yet another redeeming self: "Was there, in that shadow-ridden heaven, another form of Jesse too, watching him, yearning to draw up to him Jesse's hollow, radiant, yearning self? Yearning to purify himself at last, after so many years?" (p. 466). However, he tacitly renounces this ephemeral Jesse, renounces all of the objectively created Jesses, with the gesture of throwing his clothes and his wallet, containing all of his identification papers, into a garbage bin in order to proceed with the more urgent task of Shelley's rescue.

The first hardcover edition of the novel (Vanguard, 1971) ends differently from all subsequent hardcover and paperback editions. Although Jesse rescues Shelley from Noel, this edition ends on an ambiguous note, with him still pursuing "the true, pure, undefiled Jesse."[19] The focus is on Jesse rather than on his redeeming act as it is in the subsequent editions. Oates has said that the revised ending, which came to her in a dream, is the one she prefers. We can be grateful for the revision since the closing sequence of the first hardcover edition seems to violate the intrinsic movement of this carefully structured novel.[20]

In the authoritative edition, Jesse brings the gun he purchased in recoil against President Kennedy's assassination to Noel and Shelley's room, but when he arrives, he vows, *"Nobody is going to die tonight. Not on my hands"* (p. 478). Thus, instead of repeating his father's act, he redeems it, and in so doing, he recovers his lost identity. As Jesse leads Shelley away from Noel, she says to her father, "You are the devil . . . come to get me to bring me home . . ." (p. 479). However, Shelley is mistaken. Satan, as Milton saw, deludes man with the promise that he can be equal to God. Paradoxically, by denying his daughter freedom, by forcing her back into the limitations of time and history, to the ironically nourishing restrictions of life lived within the bounds of family and place, Jesse finally becomes the redeeming Christ who acts on the imperative that "love demands rescue." As Alice successfully moves across the chessboard to become the white Queen, Jesse has moved across the chessboard of American history to become kingly.

Oates further associates Jesse with Christ in that in addition to his being a healer whose redeeming act is an act of rescue through love, "Jesse" signifies the genealogical tree that represents Christ's genealogy. However, the novel also contains some perversions of Christian figures. "Dr. Pedersen," for instance, suggests St. Peter, but the church he builds is on the rock of gluttony and megalomania. Further, when Jesse enters the Toronto apartment in search of Shelley, Noel (the name is itself a pun) identifies himself as St. John. Yet the revelation of this ersatz prophet is of a new heaven and new earth in which humanity will be extinct. Thus when Shelley accuses Jesse of being Satan, she is using the vocabulary of this perverted universe, a universe that Jesse redeems.

Jesse answers Shelley with the question, "Am I?" The reply is a Cartesian declaration of existence, a question that reveals his recognition, too, of his contingency; it serves as an answer to his former question, *"Jesse Vogel, who was that,"* and it signifies that Jesse has finally "entered his own history," has achieved the precarious equilibrium between self and world.

The inviting, perhaps inevitable, yet self-deluding American hymn of individualism, of freedom, yields to the more realistic achievement of initiation. What Quentin Anderson has said of Hawthorne may be applied, with modification, to *Wonderland:* "that life is rootedly reciprocal . . . and that the fantasies we try to enact, the aspirations we express . . . are to be praised or dispraised on the ground that they foster or impoverish our relationships with those around us."[21] Anderson underpins his critical statements with moral judgments. Community is good; individualism is bad. Oates's argument, on the other hand, is ontological rather than moral. It is necessity rather than virtue that drives her characters back into communal existence. She, as opposed to Anderson, is sympathetic to the quests of her characters for freedom; she imbues these quests with urgency, if not righteousness. Since in the United States communal alliances and beliefs do not have the force of tradition behind them, the individual cannot depend on a web of nurturing associations. The spotlight glares harshly on the individual in his singleness. This predicament, of course, is not only indigenous to America, but to the modern condition, a situation announced by Nietzsche's declaration that God is dead, reinforced by Einstein's theory of relativity, enlarged by the threat of nuclear war, and hallowed by Existential philosophy. Yet America is undeniably the emblematic place of this condition, although perhaps not its only home. Dreams of freedom and individualism have traditionally centered on America since the eighteenth century.[22] However, in Oates the dream is also the nightmare burden, relieved only through initiation, the social correlative to biological homeostasis. Alice's last question in *Through the Looking Glass* is "Which dreamed it?" Addressing her cat, she says, "Let's consider who it was that dreamed it all. This is a serious question . . . ." Perhaps Oates, who entitled the last section of the novel "Dreaming America," is also asking, "whose dream (or nightmare) are we caught in?"

The novel is organized by a complex structure of iterative imagery that reinforces the movement from narcissistic individualism to homeostasis. Probably inspired by the eating scenes and the fluctuating sizes of characters in Carroll's works, Oates strews the novel with images of mouths—and related images of wombs, sacs, boxes, shells, and cells—and pictures of disproportionate human bodies. Jesse's father is pictured as continually "chewing and grinding" (pp. 24, 26, 37). At the Pedersen's Jesse feels that "tiny pinpricks, tiny sparks, seemed to be rushing from every part of his body toward his mouth, concentrated most fiercely in the moist flesh on the inside of his mouth" (p. 95). In addition, the Pedersens are usually pictured at the dinner table, where Jesse studies their "moving jaws." Jesse feels rage at the sight of Trick's "moving mouth," and Trick writes a poem entitled "Mouth." Helene, studying cell slides through a microscope, describes the cells as "pure mouth" (p. 265). In a gynecologist's office, she describes "the raw reddened gap between her legs" as "a face more powerful than her own face, a raw demanding mouth" (p. 278). Jesse's image of Reva is the "mouth with its perfect smile" (pp. 333, 347).

Through the oral imagery, Oates associates the drive for individualism with the infantile consciousness. The mouth is the organ through which the infant experiences pleasure and through which it expresses pain. The demanding infant depends on the external world for satisfaction, yet has no awareness of it, sees it as an extension of the self. His limited awareness allows recognition only of his own pain and satisfaction. The mouth thus signifies a narcissistic apprehension, the infantile consciousness before it has learned to differentiate between itself and the world, suggesting that extreme individualism arrests the natural maturation of consciousness.[23]

The image of the womb, especially the pregnant womb, has similar reverberations. Moreover, the fetus in the womb imagery is sometimes a doppelganger for the woman herself. For Hilda, Dr. Pedersen's daughter, the womb is a place to which she may retreat from her rapacious father. It is her "secret space"; "In that small sac of a space where a baby might grow, . . . she lived in secret from [her family]" (p. 125). She fears that her father will violate this space, that "he knew about the tiny sac inside her . . ." (p. 131). Helene, too, is obsessed with her womb; she is revolted by the biological process of pregnancy to which she must surrender her body. She sees it as an impersonal process: "It could have been said of any woman, anyone at all" (p. 280). When she passes some pedestrians huddled in their coats against the wind, she is reminded of the fetus' dependency and isolation: "All of them swelling outward in sacs, their lips thirsty and pressd against the walls of sacs, sucking blood" (p. 282). In the image of the fetus she recognizes herself, and belligerent resentment against her dependency and isolation wells up within her. Helene, like all of the characters in *Wonderland*, suffers from a disproportionate sense of self. The pregnancy violates her integrity, intrudes on her singleness, and signifies her victimization by a process outside her control. Shelley, on the other hand, wants to drain herself out of her shell (p. 382); she wants to regress into the cell, expelled by her father, from which she came (p. 384). Characteristically, she imagines her womb as barren, writing to Jesse, "My belly is hollow" (p. 460).[24]

In a demonic perversion of the Eucharist, Trick takes home a uterus, refrigerates, broils, and eats it.[25] Although Trick performs the ritual as a tribute to Helene, for whom he professes love, his real love object is Jesse, who comes to loathe him. His cannibalism is an act of transubstantiation in which the uterus represents Helene's feminity, her power to win Jesse's love. There is a wider significance to Trick's act however. Since the womb is the place of the self in seclusion, before it enters the outside world, his cannibalism is also a grotesque ritual of the religion of individualism. As the womb is the ultimate symbol of insularity, cannibalism is the ultimate symbol of the primacy of self.

The particular distortions of mouth and womb are part of a larger distortion of the entire human body. On the day of the murders, a drawing in the boys' lavatory "catches [Jesse's] eye":

> a woman's body seen from the bottom up, the legs muscular and very long, spread apart, the head at the far end of the body small as a pea, with eyes and eyelashes nevertheless drawn in very carefully so that they look real. Someone has added to the drawing with another, blunter pencil, making the body boxlike, the space between the legs shaded in to a hard black rectangle like a door. The arms have also been changed to walls and even the suggestion of brick added to them. . . . (pp. 30–1)

Jesse, fascinated by the drawing, feels, "It is something you could walk into and lose yourself in, all that empty blackness . . ." (p. 32). A drawing of a closed box is superimposed on the erotic drawing of a woman's body, suggesting that the prisonhouse of self is a kind of auto-eroticism, meaningless ("empty blackness"), but absorbing ("something you could walk into and lose yourself in"). He sees a similar image in Mrs. Pedersen—whose body he compares to a coffin—when he forces the door of the bathroom in which she has locked herself and finds her on the floor, naked. "She was like a ball of warm breathing protoplasm. . . . The head at the far end of the body seemed too small for it, as if it were an afterthought. . . . It was the body that was important, exaggerated, swollen to the shape of a large oblong box, a rectangle like a barn" (p. 157). These distorted images yield to an image of a body correctly proportioned that Jesse sees on another lavatory wall, minutes before he rescues Shelley: "a woman's cadaver, the heart and the lungs exposed, the stomach sac, coils of intestines, the womb carefully drawn. Jesse found himself examining the drawing, surprised that it was so good. The organs were in their proper proportions. At the very center of the little womb was an eye, elaborately inked in" (p. 466). In this drawing everything is exposed, the body free, not imprisoned by walls or a coffin. The fetus in the womb is an "eye," symbolic of Jesse's rebirth into a truer vision, into a delicate balance between self and world in which the narcissistic "I" has yielded to the "eye" whose sight is bifocal, turned inward and outward at the same time.

The poem, "Wonderland"—first published as "Iris Into Eye" in *Poetry Northwest* (Autumn, 1970)—precedes Book One of the novel and is a poetic encapsulation of the novel's movement. It traces the evolution of life from inorganic atoms, "spheres are whirling without sound inside/ spheres," through the beginning of biological life, "the collapsible space begins to breathe/ the vertebrae lengthen into life," to the emergence of consciousness:[26]

> the eye widens
> the iris becomes an eye
> intestines shape themselves fine as silk
> I make my way up through marrow
> through my own heavy blood
> my eyes eager as thumbs
> entering my own history like a tear
> balanced on the outermost edge
> of the eyelid

For Oates, the process of creation culminates in consciousness, in the dual awareness of self and other. She suggests that although it is a precarious and painful condition ("a tear/ balanced on the outermost edge of the eyelid"), it is the only way to enter one's history, to achieve one's own identity. The poem treats in cosmic terms what the novel treats in historical, cultural, and philosophical terms.

Wonderland is perhaps Oates's most ambitious book. Of it, she said, "I couldn't do it again. It might be my last novel, at least my last large, ambitious novel, where I try to re-create a man's soul, absorb myself into his consciousness and co-exist with him."[27] She has taken her protagonist through major events in a thirty-two year period of American history in which he encounters figures who offered violence, solipsism, megalomania, empiricism, behaviorism, Manicheism, sensualism, and nihilism as paths of truth in order to point to the redeeming path of love which requires a recognition that the world is larger than the single ego. The novel's structure—the correlation of the historical, cultural, religious, philosophical, and psychological in the life story of one character—is possibly Oates's attempt to realize what she has called her "laughably Balzacian ambition to get the whole world into a book."[28] The fact that this attempt is worked through the story of a single protagonist is, perhaps, proof of her sympathy with Kierkegaard's statement (though she disagrees with Kierkegaard in other respects), " 'the individual' is the category through which . . . all history, the human race as a whole must pass."[29] Although her fiction leads the individual protagonist away from his individualism, his singleness, he is led to community only after he explores the possibilities of the self and learns his limitations and thus the inevitability of community, of the world.

Notes

1. In an unpublished paper presented at Special Session 505 of the MLA Convention, 1977 on Joyce Carol Oates's *Wonderland,* Joanne Creighton thoroughly explores the specific analogies between Carroll's Alice books and Oates's *Wonderland.*

2. Personal notes from Oates's class in creative writing (New York University, Summer, 1977).

3. In *Civilization and Its Discontents* Freud argues that "the oceanic" feeling, the feeling that the individual is at one with the universe is an attempt "to reinstate" "limitless narcissism." Jesse and Shelley's attempts to substitute the self for the world has, perhaps, a similar source; Joan Riviere, trans., (1930; rpt. London: Hogarth Press, 1957), p. 21.

4. Freud, p. 61.

5. See Horace Gregory's "Foreward" to Lewis Carroll, *Alice's Adventures in Wonderland and Through the Looking Glass* (New York: Signet, 1960), p. vii.

6. *Times Literary Supplement,* July 7, 1972. p. 765.

7. *Love and Death in the American Novel,* (1960; rev. ed. N.Y.: Stein and Day, 1966), p. 143.

8. *Democracy in America,* Phillips Bradley, ed., (New York: Knopf, 1945), I, 99.

9. David Madden in his introduction to *American Dreams, American Nightmares* (Carbondale: Southern Illinois Univ. Press, 1970), which he edited, states that "It appears there are two major American Dream myths: the Old Testament idea of a paradise hopelessly lost, followed by endless nightmare suffering; and the New Testament idea of a paradise that a New American Adam will eventually regain. . . . Hope for clear vision lies in the ambiguous area between Paradise Lost and Paradise Regained" (p. xxxix).

10. See *A Garden of Earthly Delights, them, Childwold.*

11. All references are to the Fawcett, paperback edition (Connecticut, 1971); see discussion of variant endings, p. 20 and n. 20.

12. In a perceptive review, Jan B. Gordon argues that *Wonderland* approaches "the loss of history" through the metaphor of "adopted children and their foster parents" just as the Victorians approached this same loss through the metaphor of the orphan. However, Gordon is making clever rather than accurate distinctions. The three elements common to both the Victorian novel and *Wonderland* (Gordon implies as much) in their approach to the "loss of history" are the orphan, his "quest for Origins," and deceiving, rapacious foster parents. *Commonweal,* Feb. 11, 1972, 449.

13. *The Imperial Self: An Essay in American Literary and Cultural History* (New York: Knopf, 1971), p. 7.

14. Brian David Davis, *Homocide in American Fiction, 1798–1860: A Study in Social Values* (Ithaca: Cornell Univ. Press, 1957), p. 48.

15. *American Dreams, American Nightmares,* p. 58.

16. Calvin Bedient's very wise review entitled "Blind Mouths" makes the point that "To eat others to feed identity, to spew them out to escape it—the novel roils with the futile strain of both." *Partisan Review,* 39 (Winter 1972), 124.

17. Roquentin: "I draw my face closer until it touches the mirror. The eyes, nose and mouth disappear: nothing human is left. Brown wrinkles show on each side of the feverish swelled lips, crevices, mole holes. A silky white down covers the great slopes of the cheeks, two hairs protrude from the nostrils: It is a geological embossed map." Jean Paul Sartre, *Nausea,* Lloyd Alexander, trans. (New York: New Directions, 1964), p. 17.

18. Jesse's self-objectification indicates a schizoid disjunction between self and world. At another point in the novel he asks, *Jesse Vogel: who was that?* (p. 397).

19. p. 512.

20. Oates reports that the Fawcett edition is the one she prefers in *American Journal,* July 3, 1973, pp. 17–21.

21. Anderson, p. 60.

22. Bernard Bailyn offers a convincing account of the origins of these ideas in his book, *The Ideological Origins of the American Revolution* (Cambridge: Harvard Univ. Press, 1967).

23. See Anderson, p. 54. In his study of nineteenth-century writers, Anderson comes to a similar conclusion, associating extreme individualism with an infantile narcissism.

24. Moreover, Jesse is repeatedly pictured as enclosed in box-like rooms. He recurrently dreams of examining a corpse in a "bare white room" with walls of concrete (p. 190). His student quarters is described as a "rectangular box" (p. 213). Shelley describes her father's home as "a perfect tomb" (p. 403). These are images signifying Jesse's self-enclosure and insularity.

25. Trick is one of a series of prophet-trickster figures in Oates's fiction. Some examples are Arnold Friend in "Where Are You Going, Where Have You Been?," Hugh in *The Assassins,* and Bobbie Gotteson in *Triumph of the Spider Monkey.*

26. The poem echoes Professor Kuckuck's description of the emergence of organic life in Thomas Mann's *Confessions of Felix Krull, Confidence Man.* Oates has often expressed her admiration of Mann's art. See, for instance, her interview in Bellamy, p. 27.

27. Bellamy, p. 23.

28. Walter Clemons, "Joyce Carol Oates at Home," *New York Times Book Review,* September 28, 1969, p. 48.

29. *The Point of View for My Work as an Author,* Walter Lowrie, trans. (1859; rpt. New York: Harper and Row, 1962), p. 111.

"Paedomorphic" Art: Joyce Carol Oates' *Childwold*

Eileen T. Bender*

In 1972, Joyce Carol Oates chose the occasion of an appearance on the *New York Times* "Guest Word" page to take stock of the state of modern American literature and issue a ringing manifesto against its gurus and literary "high priests," the self-conscious and self-styled "fabulators." Her essay, "Whose Side Are You On?," begins with criticism of her own previous work as well as that of her contemporaries:

> Two decades of self-consuming, self-nourishing despair will be ending soon, and those among us who have prowled around in the gardens and cemeteries, after dark, will be eager to help with the raking-up, the reclaiming of the vandalized land, because it will occur to us that energies released in the daytime, in the sunlight, can be as exciting and powerful as energies released at night.[1]

Oates goes on to challenge those writers who have produced or are producing a literature of "entropy," of "exhaustion," of "pure" subjectivity, of paranoia, of "black" comedy, of "fragments," of egocentric, autonomist art:

> For many years our most promising writers have lined up obediently behind Nabokov, Beckett and Borges, to file through a doorway marked THIS WAY OUT. How eagerly they have taken their places! If they glance around at the rest of us, who are holding back, they are ready with mechanized scorn. . . .

It may seem a curious statement from a writer one critic has called "The Dark Lady of American Letters,"[2] and many categorize as "gothic" or "grotesque." Indeed, it is for that reason that this essay assumes more importance than its brevity and mocking tone might suggest, reflecting Oates' own transition from the darkness and despair of her earlier work toward new contexts for the groping modern self. As she notes, her more "fashionable" contemporaries reject realism, looking to form itself to provide stasis and order in a treacherously shifting universe. For Joyce Carol Oates, assimilative, eclectic, working through a succession of literary styles and traditions, form is not the issue. Risking charges that she is imitative and even anachronistic, or simply not "interesting," Oates sets up other terms for the artistic quest—searching for an alternative mode of fiction which itself might serve to "reclaim" a fallen world.

---

*This essay was written specifically for this volume and is published here for the first time with permission of the author.

117

Oates' 1972 essay, denouncing the "antiseptic purity" and perverse, "prematurely elderly" attitude of fabulation, opposing the nightside with light, anticipates, and can be read as a fascinating gloss to her 1976 novel, *Childwold*.[3] "So much, such a profusion!" cries one of the narrators of this frequently lyrical and sunlit book. Oates is simultaneously translator, critic, and celebrant of a world of abundance, a "universe of trash, of beauty" (p. 64). She exploits its every sprawl and polyphony in *Childwold* with an ear tuned to the clamor of the landscape, offering a memoir of adolescence and images of an older world through a collage of voices, oddments, and a flood of detail which gives the novel density and substance, as opposed to the "transparent things" of literary fabulation.

In *Childwold*, Oates returns to the scene of her earliest fictions, Eden Valley, an overgrown rural locale once a backdrop for savage human encounters, now reimagined to admit other dimensions of loving possibility. At the center of things is a sensitive fourteen-year-old heroine, Laney Bartlett. The plot involves her abortive relationship with an extravagant grotesque, a half-mad, childless, orphaned, forty-ish writer and recluse, "Fitz-John Kasch." Laney lives amidst a child's souvenirs in a noisy household. Kasch lives alone in untidy confusion in a tiny apartment behind the family museum, the last of his line, longing only for a "voyeur's pleasure" (p. 111). Instead, he is drawn unwillingly into the violent and sordid passions of the world below, lured by Laney's unconscious attraction as well as by the fraudulent mockery of perfume impelled by social and literary models to act out the masculine role of heroic defender and killer. Striving for purity of style, he emerges as a figure of tragicomic proportions, frustrated and condemned.

Woven between the sequential monologues of these unlikely lovers are the narrative perspectives of the other members of Laney's family. Most vocal is her mother Arlene, lazy, promiscuous, requiring a man to complete her story whether it be Kasch, or the man he kills (a former drunken lover), or the policeman who comes to investigate the crime. Unreflective, earthy, and tenacious, Arlene is appropriately the only character to survive the rush of events fundamentally unchanged.

Laney's grandfather Joseph is another of the novel's voices. He lives half in and half out of a vivid world of memory peopled by ghosts of old friends and lovers. Throughout *Childwold*, Joseph is pursued by menacing spectres; finally, he surrenders to black-winged death. A fifth narrator is Laney's brother Vale, a mutilated Vietnam casualty, a brutal rapist. Disfigured, he cannot find his way back to "Childwold"; yet he expresses his frustrated love and longing by anonymously shipping his family a truckload of Christmas gifts purchased with stolen money. His violent experience has radically reordered his perception; he has lost his capacity to see "chronological sequence" (p. 117) in the chaos of modern events. The voices blur and overlap and clash, confusing the narrative threads.

In contrast, Kasch attempts to impose a fabulator's order on existence: "If you doubt me," he cries defiantly to his off-stage love, "you will cease to exist. . . . There are no things but in words" (p. 109). Language indeed seems the most vivid reality to Kasch, the "glue" that holds personality together.

> How real the world strikes us, the world of the present moment, the world of daylight! Tactile, it is; palpable. Demonstrable. . . . Yet once the world slips into the past tense, once it shifts into "history," it is revealed to have been insubstantial, illusory; deceptive. And we, caught in it, are we not insubstantial as images in a film . . .? A certain force, perhaps no more than linguistic habit, connects me with the Fitz John of those years, a boy in his mid-teens, but I have no true memory of him. . . . (p. 128)

Like so many of Oates' heroes, Kasch is desperate to slow the film, to stop the menacing slippage, to correct the fatal "error of the body" (p. 225); he longs for love, for human relationship. Yet when he does retreat from the physical world, he becomes the vehicle of errant ideas, a vessel for mysterious thought-waves:

> The interior life constitutes the authentic life, and actions performed in the exterior world are peripheral. Reality is what I am thinking, what is thinking through me, using me as a means, a vessel, a reed, even, streaming through me with or without my consent; the interior life is continuous, unhurried, almost undirected, unheralded . . . . (p. 138)

"Enchanted, enchained, inchanting" (p. 265), Kasch attempts to embrace the world of the Bartletts, to transform them into fiction, to deny time and change. Yet he is caught in a monstrous double bind: he finds himself a character in their murderous family scenario, a victim of forces they have set into motion. Recognizing the absurdity of his existence, he muses near the novel's end, "If only we had had the grace to break into laughter . . ." (p. 290). Occasions for outright laughter are rare in Oates' novels. But *Childwold* does offer the occasion for Oates to demonstrate her own fabulist skills, as well as the playfulness of art. That play includes word-play, the weaving of multiple narrative voices, "cinematic" flashbacks, and bursts of light and shade.

It also involves a fabulator's game. That cagey fauulator, Nabokov, and his *Lolita* are the incongruous "parents" of *Childwold*, creating an imaginative counterpoint to Oates' characters and themes. Oates has called Nabokov's work a masterpiece, "one of our finest American novels, a triumph of style and vision . . . a wedding of Swiftian satirical vigor with the kind of minute, loving patience that belongs to a man infatuated With the visual mysteries of the worlds."[4] Tbe Nabokovian "infatuation" with things is mirrored in the profusion of *Childwold:* the eccentric Fitz-John Kasch is a version of another grotesque voyeur, Humbert Humbert. Both are melancholiac, aging intellectuals, without issue except for their esoteric, unread manuscripts; both have unslakable sensual appetites; both are in panting pursuit of the virginal, the evanescent, the metamorphic, the pre-mature. Both are arch-fabulators.

But Oates' novel is not simply a playful imitation. It has also been generated by antithetical energies, her continuing disapproval of the fabulator's stance. While Oates appreciates *Lolita* she declares that Nabokov's "purposes" are "to deceive, to conceal, to mock, to reduce Nature to an egoistic and mechanical arrangement of words"[5] she finds he has "a genius for dehumanizing" character; "obsessively conscious," he denies the divinity of the world in favor of the divinity of his own personality.[6] Oates thus has set herself the task of raking-up and reclamation in *Childwold*. Nabokov's novel is a self-conscious monologue controlled by Humbert Humbert's singular perspective; his nymphet is elusive, cool, almost maddeningly insouciant. In contrast, Oates offers us a composite tale, allowing for multiple perspectives. Finally, although Kasch may seem to dominate the novel through the seductive attractions of his ingenious and self-aggrandizing performance, Oates subtly shifts her primary focus from the decadent solipsist-voyeur to the responsive, youthful object of his desire. It is a critical "re-vision."

Again like Humbert Humbert, Kasch plays the role of Pygmalion and introduces his child-love to the world of art, "deliberately . . . created" in contrast to *Childwold*'s messy, antic scene. Laney is momentarily intoxicated, even stunned, by the symmetry and order in a gallery of photographs. Later, however, she begins to understand the cost of such artifice, the loss of human value, the "lie" and "exaggeration" of inorganic, static art. Beyond the world of Kasch's intellect, Laney glimpses another realm of human possibility, joining her physical and spiritual selves:

> The air rings with life. The light is so living everything is alive. . . . Your vision goes out of focus. You are not dizzy, you are not lightheaded, you see the coin-sized splashes of sunlight, you hear them, you feel them burst in your blood . . . . it's lovely, it won't hurt, nothing will hurt for long, it's what you must accept, it's normal, it's beautiful, it's alive, it's living, you don't own your body, you don't own the creek, you can't control it, you mustn't try, you must float with the current, the plunge of the rapids, you must close your eyes and move with it. . . . (p. 197)

Through nature's agency, Laney feels herself transformed. It is another of Oates' recent attempts to articulate the mystic's oceanic, higher consciousness, a dimension of life forever closed to the crafty, egoistic fabulator.

But in moving toward the edge of "impossibility," Oates does not deny the excitement of the life of the mind. Laney seems able not only to feel herself transformed through nature and sensual possession, but through intellectual adventure as well; Kasch and his tutelage indeed have changed her life:

> You read and reread, you underline passages, you make notations in the margins; sometimes you try to decipher Kasch's notes, but his handwriting is too small. . . . The subject is life: life itself. You will never come to the end of it. . . . Life is a flow, a powerful directed flow, not to be stopped, not to be stopped for long. You read, absorbed, shivering with excitement. You forget everything else. (p. 238–9)

Laney Bartlett indeed outpaces her "author," and thus he must set her free: "Where are you, why have you gone so far? The books you read are not my books, the language you use is not my language. You are no longer recognizable! You are no longer mine!" (p. 290).

Kasch—eccentric artist, lover, murderer—labels this new form of fiction

"Paedomorphism," suggesting it as a means of salvation in a decadent, intellectual society: he advocates renewal of the race through cultivation and exploitation of the infantile. For him, it is a mad joke, one of his portmanteau words. But *Childwold* has more serious intent for Oates; clearly, it is meant to exemplify her own idea of "paedomorphic" art, embracing primary data and sense impressions, suspending the autocratic and perverse reign of the intellect to admit the chaotic, profuse, and unfinished; evolving toward a vision of self-renewal.

For this reason, then, the last words of *Childwold* are not the words of Kasch, but the child's words. Released from one prison, Kasch has entombed himself in another enclosure of his own choice—the literal ruin of the Bartlett house, a figurative, ramshackle house of fiction. Laney Bartlett stands outside in the field of "insect-ridden blossoms," glimpsing the shadow of Kasch behind the windowpane, calling up at him: "Kasch? Is it really you? Here? After so long? By why? Am I here, calling you? Waiting for you? Kasch? My Love?" (p. 295). Attuned to the throbbing landscape, she feels her own power to restore Kasch to life through her own imagination; in a surge of love and hope, she waits breathlessly for "a sign, a sign."

Open-ended, *Childwold* thus represents another stage in Joyce Carol Oates' continuing search for style and fable to offset the vandal's scenario, to open the possibility of individuation and transcendence. Tony Tanner seems to articulate Oates' position and the predicament of other contemporary writers in his *City of Words:*

> . . . the dilemma and quest of the hero are often analogous to those of the author. Can he find a stylistic freedom which is not simply a meaningless incoherence, and can he find a stylistic form which will not trap him inside the existing forms of previous literature?[7]

For Oates, the problems of character and the self in the modern world are indeed analogous to the problem of the contemporary artist; the drive for autonomy in the personal and political sphere is mirrored by the drive for artistic "freedom" and originality. Yet these struggles engender a climate of anxiety, a sense of paranoia, laments for an "exhausted" convention. Sensible of the risks of ontological dissolution and doubt, Oates does not question the need for artistic control; but for her, the goal is not autonomy but an integrity of vision which can accommodate a universe of trash, of beauty—the given, the sacred, the collective legacy. She celebrates the artist's special power and authority to recreate and honor that realm. At the same time, she also questions the myth of the artist as hero—an authoritarian rather than an authoritative figure, an imperial self who imposes his will on a pliant and bewildered audience.

From her own point of view, Oates sees the literary tradition not as a "trap" to be skirted but as a realm of reality open to infinite revision and counter-statement, a realm of play and illusion. Her imitations are thus not the parodic acts of a fabulator; they are serious and even passionate responses to other fictive worlds. Thus, the fiction of Joyce Carol Oates offers a corrective to those contemporary authors who assert their own isolate identity as they "dehumanize" art.

In her formally-inventive eighth novel, Oates plays with several layers of theme and image. *Childwold* can be read as a lyrical memoir of adolescence. It can also be viewed as the most ambitious of her literary "imitations"; taking on the arch-fabulator Nobokov at his own game, she resists the seductions of *Lolita* and writes her own version of the self's possible trajectory. But it is imitation raised to another power: an act of restoration; "recreation" in a double sense. Turning Nabokov's plot back upon itself, reimagining the nymphet first as a bewildered child and then as a wondering, even triumphant heroine, Oates offers a moving counterstatement to *Lolita*'s final dark grimace. Ultimately *Childwold* is most interesting as an example of Joyce Carol Oates' own "paedomorphic" art—filtered through a child's expanding consciousness, remedial rather than self-serving, embracing primary data and sense impressions, recording a profusion of images and a play of tongues. Something of a fabulator herself as she plays with considerable subtlety on Nabokov's "prematurely elderly" themes, Joyce Carol Oates moves through that world of intellectual forms and symmetrical enclosures into a scene which beggars the autonomist's imagination—profuse, unhurried, continuous, sensual, *almost* undirected, teeming with felt life, offering the promise of radiance and regeneration.

Notes

1. Joyce Carol Oates, "Whose Side Are You On?" *New York Times Book Review,* June 4, 1972, p. 63.

2. Joe David Bellamy, "The Dark Lady of American Letters: An Interview with Joyce Carol Oates," *Atlantic Monthly,* Feb. 1972, pp. 63–67.

3. Joyce Carol Oates, *Childwold* (New York: Vanguard, 1976). All further references to this work appear in the text.

4. Joyce Carol Oates, "A Personal View of Nabokov," *Saturday Review,* Jan. 6, 1973, p. 37.

5. Joyce Carol Oates, "Updike's American Comedies," *Modern Fiction Studies,* 21 (1975), 460.

6. Joyce Carol Oates, "A Personal View of Nabokov," p. 37.

7. Tony Tanner, *City of Words* (New York: Harper & Row, 1971), p. 19.

The Poetry of
Joyce Carol Oates

Peter Stevens[*]

Too many readers pay scant attention to poetry written by novelists. Thomas Hardy's poetry went under-appreciated for many years, even though he spent the last thirty years of his career writing it. In the world of contemporary literature only Robert Penn Warren has been given due respect for both prose and poetry. In a sense, Joyce Carol Oates' prolific production of fiction has operated against her because critics have concentrated on her novels to the almost total exclusion of her poetry, which now forms a substantial body of work published in five volumes.

Those critics who have tackled the poetry in reviews tend to assume that Oates is primarily a novelist, and that her poetry will necessarily be inferior to her fiction. They surmise that the themes of her poetry only repeat those of her fiction, and that nothing new is being said, although they generally make no attempt to relate the poetry as poetry to those fictional themes. In fact, using the fiction as an entry point often blinds the insight. Helen Vendler, reviewing *Angel Fire*, complains that the poetry has two problems: "the problem of untruth of situation and the problem of abstraction in situation."[1] Vendler's subsequent remarks indicate that she wants to find the strengths of Oates' fiction in her poetry: "Oates, who can create whole landscapes peopled with dramatis personae almost overnight, banishes detail, in any luxuriant supply, from her poems. They are short, sparse and unattached, mostly, in space and time. They take place in some nebulous region with a speaker uttering over-wrought words about some agitation of love or family."[2] Such a criticism fails to recognize that the poet is exploring a nebulous region, a region beyond the realism of her fictional world. Oates' probing of states of consciousness does not necessarily require a narrative context.

Readers of Oates' poetry should not overlook what Jerome Mazzaro describes as her technique of separating, and thereby emphasizing, single images: "Abandoning the unified central symbol or image that poets have used since the New Criticism, she realizes each particular separately."[3] Technically, Oates' difference from other contemporary poets is striking. So too is her vision. Her admiration, as she insists in *New Heaven, New Earth*, is for the *visionary* writers, those who are "attempting to locate images adequate to the unshaped,

[*]This essay was written especially for this collection, and is used with the permission of the author.

unconscious horrors they sense." Seeing life clearly, they yet manage to affirm even facing "the most perverse and terrifying possibilities of the epoch," using their art "to somehow transform what is given," the "unshaped, unconscious horrors"[4] of our time. Oates' aim seems to be to move from the scattered and seemingly unrelated details of those horrors (the technical method of her poetry, as well, often, as of her fiction) to some plane of affirmation: art as transforming agent is surely not a new concept to modern letters.

In her long essay about Lawrence, Oates responds to the overall ambiance of his poetry, its expression of "the protean nature of reality" and of a "deep, unshakable faith in the transformable quality of all life."[5] She suggests that Lawrence's notion of "the beauty and mystery of flux" makes him "exactly contemporary with us: at last, men whose training has been scientific and positivistic and clinical and 'rational' are beginning to say the same thing."[6] We should therefore look into her poetry for some expression of 'Becoming,' not 'Being,' for those heightened moments which transcend reality even as they pass, rather than for some overall scheme of unchanging value. This, in itself, also suggests why the conventional techniques of modern poetry are the ones she will find inadequate to her needs.

What we will find, I think, is what she establishes as the conflict within Kafka's work, a division "both negative (in terms of history) and positive (in terms of the human spirit)," for Kafka believed in the "individual's ability to detach himself from history and to achieve a transcendence of the merely historical."[7] These ideas emerge again in different terms in her comments on the poetry of James Dickey who, she states, in one particular poem "tells of the poet's need to prove that life is still possible."[8]

For Oates, both Lawrence and Dickey riddle their work with questions, even if they provide few answers. And both poets use animals as metaphoric subjects for the analysis of humanity, and in Dickey the process of hunting and extensions into warfare provide an atmosphere of primitivism, with physical risk-taking as a test of one's full humanity. Risks may bring about those breathtaking moments that enlighten, that transform, and at those times life is indeed more than possible; it is fulfilled.

It is in these critical ideas rather than in the novels that one will find guidance into the poetry, though I do not wish to suggest that her poetry is as schematic as this brief and generalized summary of her reading of certain writers suggests. Furthermore, it does not take into account her own sense of feminism that surfaces in some of the poetry, although she relates the poetry of Sylvia Plath to the ideas she finds in both Lawrence and Dickey. It may seem strange to link Plath with the life-affirming visions of the other two poets, but Oates explains that although Sylvia Plath is the most despairing of these writers, she sees in her "a furious impatience with the limitations of the ego (which she called the 'mind'), a raging selfdisgust that, had it not ended in suicide, might have cleansed her of those impurities of her era she had absorbed, and allowed her the visionary experience she sensed was a human possibility."[9]

In approaching the first volume of poetry, *Anonymous Sins*, then, we might expect to find some expression of moments of personal intensity often sliding away into the morass of the historical process, ideas of seeking out risk (with violence as a metaphor, perhaps, of risk-taking), of living in a darkness that reveals layers of primitivism which cannot emerge for long in our common lives, even though we may sense some capability for transformation, could we follow these urges and desires within our living. And indeed this volume introduces many of these topics, for it is a poetry that raises these fundamental questions about the quality of life, so much so that the reader becomes impatient with the statement of these questions within the poems as the question looms large as a syntactical and structural device. Nonetheless, the whole volume, while it suffers from the faults of many first volumes in its packing in all manner of methods, images, structures, themes in a bewildering kaleidoscope, still establishes in embryo what one might call the Oatesian poetic ambiance.

Perhaps nowhere is that ambiance with both its stark reality and its mysterious surrealism, its question-raising and its question-begging, its assumption of vision and its inability to find an exact form for that vision, more conspicuously expressed than in the title poem itself. The poem turns around a couplet at the poem's centre, a couplet left deliberately vague. One of its lines expresses a central theme with all its ambiguities and ambivalences: "they are history." The 'they' of this poem encompasses many people: the mass of humans, the ritual heroes, the individual trapped within his own obscure destiny. This last-named may indeed be so obscure that his sense of wrong-doing, his removal from meaningful ceremony, his lack of knowledge about the forces he must fight against all lead him to a sense of anonymous sins, so that all his actions lose meaning.

This seems to me to be the gist of the poem which, although it is in a sense organized around a parallel structuring, flickers uneasily and rapidly from scene to scene, from long-shot to close-up, unsettling the reader's orientation. It starts by presenting a panorama of history so distanced as to be "beyond the imagination/of pain." This scene contains heroic duelling, the conflicts of life elevated to ritualistic pattern, the violence and battling instinct with meaning beyond articulation, even to the rising of a leader—prophet, king, sacrificial hero. But, placed against all this is the meagreness and meaninglessness of contemporary life, a vague continuance with no significant end, continuing yet with no permanence, no solidity. Even love disintegrates into violence: the heroic figure of the first part raises his hand and the crowd sees flowing from his palm "surprising blood in a vow," whereas the 'I' of the poem, "seeing that my love/is endless" gazes down on "a mangled body." Life now has no power within it of ceremony or transcendence; it goes on simply being "used/used up" and the stately motions of the first part of the poem within "a flower-decked arena" with "clouted beasts and young men/charging together," where it "is spring/ and blood and music join" are now transformed to empty movement "too abrupt at any pace." Yet there may be a kind of minimal and stoic vision implicit at the close, for the voice of the poem introduces the bleak view of man-woman relationships by the phrase, "I understand . . .".

Despite its double structure (parallelism and a sudden shifting of scene), despite its echoing effects, despite its seeming directness of statement, the poem is still hedged by questions. The two main stanzas are formed as questions, and the answers to them are in part images which do not offer enough specificity: the vow the leader makes is unclear, the connection between a woman's feeling of being used and used up and a man's movement being too abrupt at any pace is not sufficiently pulled together. And yet in the context of the book itself it is understandable why this poem would serve for its title, for the collection attempts to pack in various expressions of the loss of some overall vision of life within contemporary man, even though hovering around him somewhere may be the means for him to transcend his emptiness, to transform his life, a kind of equivalent of what the poet sees as an aspect of Kafka's conception of history and modern man's relation to it in the note on his work from which I quoted earlier:

> Kafka certainly believed in the individual's ability to detach himself from history and to achieve a transcendence of the merely historical. Though the individual is always *in* paradise, he is not always aware of the fact, and this failure to be aware of his own participation in the divine, this failure to *see* the illusory nature of his own ego, constitutes the only hell (its highlights sensationally recorded as history!) possible.[10]

The context of the duality of existence, the possibility of a paradise surrounding the individual with his unawareness of it is presented in the opening poem of the book, "The Dark." Here again the larger historical life, that is a mythic, ritualistic, essentially transcendent life is set against our mundane reality. The poem sets up a Jungian atmosphere, the dream world with its mythic personality within its darkness contains the ceremonial Figures, "fragrant faces" and "special animals," which move to an accusation of our lives. The wood with its immense flowers becomes a picnic area with a crowd of people. As the dreamer awakens, he is puzzled by questions about the other life. The poet suggests that there is meaning for us to grasp in the darkness of sleep. It is a dark knowledge but we can immerse ourselves in that large expansive world, which is different from the normal historical process:

> In sleep the hand creates its weapon; swift as thought the bullet finds its magic mark. Concentrate. Civilizations' declines are discoveries of books, and are never real as the warm dark of dreams, Egypt's dark warmth, the cry of horses' deaths in battle, the dark.

Much of the rest of the book deals with that mundane reality in which men and women search for an explanation of the events of their lives. The very next poem's title, "Lines For Those To Whom Tragedy Is Denied," indicates that absence of tragic destiny which the critic George Steiner has lamented, the reason being that we have lost our sense of human destiny in the larger context of religion, for now God is dead. But that is a view Oates has answered in *The Edge Of Possibility*. The women in this poem have lives of tremendous events in their personal lives reduced to boring or trivial meaning, so that life remains for them unfulfilled, locked in reality. Their love collapses inside the ordinariness of their marriages, their childbirths, their displacements, their loss of relationships through endless movements.

These relationships which should be based on love reach no level of density. This volume contains a variety of poems about approaches to love, the attempts to reach heightened and intense moments, sometimes destroyed by external reality. Two lovers who dream of "a holy/Love" seem to miss it, even though those intense moments exist for them: "We should use this moment but the moment streams through us." The whole atmosphere of their love militates against moments of transcendence, but the possibilities perhaps persist: "Is there a mysterious sight in here/We know nothing of, a delight to be seen?"

This poem, "A Nap Without Sleep" is the first of a series, "Five Confessions," which all focus on love and its viability within ordinary life. "Marriage" suggests transcendence but it is only momentary; the partners remain "puzzled in the dark" at the end of the poem but at least they do "draw together." In "Women In Love" a woman sinks under the pressure of love even as she feels an extraordinary vibration in love. Always, the phrasing implies, she is victim, an animal hunted: "Love in me/ uses me/running its way/ to earth." In "Cupid And Psyche" love may transcend but "We fall backward into love/ and into time." "Like This . . . So This," the poem which immediately precedes the title poem, in its closing section brings together the transcendent world achievable by human love and the ordinary world the individuals inhabit: "improbable beasts/ . . . wander listless among/ barns and coops and pens."

Some of the situations of human love in the book suggest adulterous relations, so that the humans involved participate in that sexual life which can be meaningful only if an element of guilt exists, the atmosphere Oates sees in both Dickey and Mailer. This in turn relates to risk-taking as a way of transcending the demands of the history in which we live. Such a poem as "The Ride" while on its surface seeming to be a rather breathless detailing of a fast auto ride in the memory of an eight-year-old becomes in these terms an experience of transformation and transcendence. The children cling to the seat, and the father changes as he rushes the car through the landscape. He becomes a "strange father," his hair becomes plumage, and the children look through the car windows "at the zoom of air outside/in the new dawning dark." Such a rushing and wild journey removes them from ordinary life into that transcendent darkness with which the volume opened.

A similar poem is "On being Borne Reluctantly To New York State By Train," though here the journey is taking the persona back into an unwanted past. Perhaps the rush of motion is important, not the destination, which will root the travellers in time, for the train's movement flows into them: "The rumbling sleepy rage/ of wheels on tracks/ drifts upwards into/our marrow and tissue/ but somehow cannot live."

Such risk, such decision to recognize the urgency within life, even though this leads to death, even to a choice of death, as in "Of The Violence Of Self-Death," will be a brave, even heroic act, "demanding/that an ordinary house's walls not impede the/strange passage of death, fought with hammer/ and crowbar, alone, fought bravely/ and mysteriously as others/fight for life." In similar terms, then, the search for intrinsic personality rather than the one grafted on by mundane history—suburbia, peer pressure, social convention—even if it leads ultimately to violence, is perhaps a life-affirming act. The title "And So I Grew Up To Be Nineteen And To Murder" contains the only reference to murder in the poem, which examines the process by which a personality is moulded, even though it is invented or untrue to the dreams and ideas of the speaker. Her frustrations at being unable to transcend the social world of her parents will erupt into violence, the title tells us, but the poem is a nagging search for the true human.

Anonymous Sins sets up many of the thematic concerns of Joyce Carol Oates—which is not to say that her later poetry merely repeats and extends these themes. The emphases of each individual volume change; new images surface and fresh approaches emerge, so that though her next volume, *Love And Its Derangements*, takes up obviously the ambivalences of human love in relation to the ordinariness of human existence and the larger context of history and the transcendence of history, all of which have been introduced in *Anonymous Sins*, the poems take hold more specifically, elaborating in different ways what was tumbled out almost too kaleidoscopically and perhaps too incohesively in the first volume. Jerome Mazzaro expresses the difference between the two volumes in this way:

> If one theme of *Anonymous Sins and Other Poems* was the inability to get out of oneself except through the stereotypes of society, the theme of Joyce Carol Oates's second book of poems, *Love and Its Derangements*, is the difficulty of Sartrean intersubjectivity—of getting others to accept an individual as he conceives of himself.

Mazzaro goes on to suggest that this central theme is expressed in poems which examine "the uneasiness, struggles, and readjustments that lovers make to compensate for the changes in themselves and their lives."[11] And again it is the title poem which announces the dualities of love, together with its place in ordinary life (the ongoing process of history), here cohering around images and notions of public and private.

The surface of "Love And Its Derangements" obviously presents a female voice detailing her sense of an oppressive male power: the phrase "they want" echoes through the poem. The persona is subjected to violent manipulation, often in terms which recur in other poems in this volume but which themselves go through unique metamorphoses, just as lovers in the poems often have to arrange, re-arrange, derange themselves. Terms of the body—skin and bone—are here, as are water and a sense of "flat white walls/ of the rooms we use," as well as the idea of spring and growth.

Undoubtedly this poem states the dehumanizing and vicious force that serves as communication across the line that "is abrupt between male and female." There is "a code of male conspiracy," men are constantly trying to drag the persona by the hair in order to somehow sully the idea of feminine purity: "they want the river's white sails/ to collapse into the dirty water." And the poem concludes with the female's sense of an eroded self: a body subject to biological rhythms is further manipulated, "all the inches of its skin/rubbed raw with the skin/of men."

However, in spite of this powerful running statement of female subjugation which Mazzaro tends to establish as a kind of negative tone throughout the volume, together with the usual bleak vision of history, the title can be read as an expression of the essential duality. Love is not always deranged, and the poems offer alternative visions, There are poems about love in a positive sense as well as poems about the manipulative distortions love can force upon people. The title poem certainly suggests that negative view of love. The phrase "they want" is totally selfish, the notion of male power over the female. Yet the epigraph of the book is from Byron: "Passion is the element in which we live; without it, we hardly even vegetate." So "want" is also related to desire and passion. The changes and derangements brought about by love are not always distorting and crippling. Thus, some poems partake of the ambivalences and ambiguities already obvious in *Anonymous Sins*. "Turning To Another Person" in its title suggests the reaching out to someone else as well as the demands made upon a person within a relationship to fit into the dimension imposed by the other person, and indeed the poem is full of words like "stronger," "authority," "overcome" and hard violent words of breaking and noise. But at the close, after the reverberations of an imposed change, the poem settles into a calmer language, and while there may be hints of irony clinging to these lines (an ironic comment on the romanticism of two-becoming-one through love), yet the tone is also direct and open:

> we have the look
> of living
> of beginning again
> in a new latitude
>
> we have the look
> of being complete.

Indeed, the volume is framed by poems which express the idea of love as some shattering experience which moves to a calm, the passion itself being the equivalent of those intense moments in the flux of living that were a part of the poetry in the first volume. The opening poem, "Parachuting," describes the height and the fall through passion, release and then the grasp of gravity, the orgasmic splendour rushing down to earth. The rush of language here is reminiscent of the moment streaming through the lovers in "A Nap Without Sleep," just as its central qualifying stanza repeats the idea of love in mundane reality: "dirty and loving in air." This line is embodied in a section which begins "we are public here," and other poems in this volume take up the discrepancies between the public and the private faces of love, another example of the centrality of duality, caught in the simile in "Parachuting," "like cindered stars." Such transcendence falling back to rootedness and reality, such violent disruption containing both ecstasy and mortality, with the controlling device of parachuting, is perhaps somewhat akin to Dickey's "Falling," a poem whose central persona Oates describes as "a kind of mortal goddess."[12]

The central image of falling in the opening poem is transformed into one of rising in the last poem in the book, "How Gentle." Here the calm induced by love is at the centre of the poem, a kind of passivity partially undermined by a language that manages to merge images of hardness with the softness: the hardness of "jaw/upon jaw" and "your weight is/the sky lowered suddenly" is set against the lightness of "turning to silk, texture of flashy/airy surfaces scant as breaths."

That calmness also appears immediately after "Parachuting" in "Sleeping Together," though it contains an adumbration of the idea of the loss of individuality in love, this loss being linked to the remorseless power of one person over another. The privacy of sleep is complete loss, so the privacy of love by implication may mean too much loss as well. And this poem has a mirror-image in "What I Fear. . . ." Sleeplessness after love forces the presence of reality on the lovers, though the poem still presents the dimensions of love as something opening into fresh existences: "we are newly derailed and newly/awakened." Somehow, though, such radiance "is only for others to see." Love is public in the sense that it cannot be divorced from the accretions of the past, and in "Public Love" such an idea moves ambiguously, though finally ironically, because the speaker is held in love by all the shadowy predecessors who exist in the outer historical process, the public eye. The lovers cannot exist in their own individualities; they "are loving in pantomime."

These layers of outer, other lives force love into cages. There is no room for development and growth. The fate of love is a deliberately planned movement from which lovers cannot escape. They are public symbols; they are expected to behave in orthodox ways. They become "lovers, inspired/to an infinite love/ in a series of boxes." The growth of love, however, can move to "a completion like the exhaling/of a single breath."

But there are also perils in the privacy of love, for it erects a membrane against the outer world, a membrane in "Loving" that becomes the living process itself, a membrane that obliterates. Thus, this skin needs to be peeled off in order to reveal another form, either by the individual him-/herself or by an external force (a lover or the public image of love) as in "Wounds" which echoes the phrasing of the title poem:

> my skin is rubbed raw . . .
> I am a wound nursed open
> germless in the hot sun . . .
> an ordinary violence
> girls strain from windowsills
> to achieve.

The revelation of true individuality is perhaps best achieved, according to the poet, not through love, not through the process of public life, but through the total perception of self, and this is presented in "Portrait" which uses the image of a painter engaged in painting a self-portrait revealing her real self beneath the superficial (public? historical?) self: "the surface of myself peeled from me,/the facial skin reclaimed for that canvas." However, that act of discovery entails finding a self that is outside the living self, so again the poem is really examining those dualities of private and public, dream and reality, immortality and history, that is at the heart of the previous volume, the dualities that can be transcended through moments of intensity, which in *Love And Its Derangements* may be achieved in moments of love, even though these are transitory, and the lovers must return to earth and ordinariness. Or, as "Portrait" puts it in its last lines:

> I see how the fact of myself is a puzzle of parts
> forced into a certain shape
> a tiny void filling an ordinary canvas.

Running through the volume are notions of speed and journeying, a sense of the flashing scenes of historical process in which everything blurs together and no moments stand out with significance. All language is reduced to the inane messages of radio; all motion distanced by being the mere indication of a speedometer. But at times these appear in the poems as obvious clichés, working against the overall concept of love in its distorting and transcending forms throughout the book. Some poems present scenes which collapse either because the narrative element is too undeveloped or because the details of the scene move too explicitly into symbol without being embodied as real situations. At such times the book seems to justify in part the kind of criticism levelled at the poetry by Helen Vendler quoted earlier but this kind of writing does not appear often enough to justify the criticism being levelled at it as a sweeping comment.

In fact, the book closes with a sequence immediately before the last poem (already quoted and discussed), a sequence entitled "Landscapes" and in its three parts it emphasizes the various facets of love presented within the volume's opening and closing poems. "A Landscape of Back Yards" presents a viewing of life from the outside, a viewer peering through a window into another life's privacy but in a sense making it public. To the viewer such love between man and woman is too ordinary, too obvious, too trapped to have meaning; like the back yard it is "a patch of frozen domestic muck." The irony of the poem resides in the fact that although the viewer is on a moving train outside that stasis, the viewer and her lover are also trapped inside the motion of the train within the accumulations of history (symbolized here, as it often is in Oates, particularly in her later poetry, by a newspaper). Although they believe their love "will be articulate," this poem closes with them in stasis: "our feet on the *New York Times*/our faces frozen to this time."

The second poem of this sequence, "A Landscape of Forms," is too vague in its scenic presentation but attempts to suggest an almost platonic sense of ideal form residing within structures. Past events remain within a room, and so people partake of that past, a reminder of the dualities of the past effects on the present love, as in "Public Love." Even if a room becomes a place for private love (and here the poet uses "holy" as she did in "A Nap Without Sleep" which describes a similar situation) it reaches to others' love:

> Being holy we come upon in the darkness
> of any room the remains of someone's joy
> a holy flowering in someone's brain
> we think *These doors will not be our true exits.*

The last poem in the sequence expresses an ideal of love that contains an orgasmic expression and expansion, a denial of the individual, a transcendence, and yet love must still reside in language to give it true form, another of the dualities of love in that it moves beyond expression and yet can be defined only in terms outside itself. And of course this volume is attempting to do that, which make the closing lines doubly ironic, and yet an essential statement about love, given that the last poem of the book, which follows immediately, repeats two images from this poem. The last couplet in the book contains the phrase, "I am Loved." And as mentioned earlier, the transcendent love of "How Gentle" has "the texture of flashy airy surfaces," language which echoes the last three lines of "A Landscape Of Love":

> Love is a matter of words being aired
> it is a matter of the choice of words
> that, being aerated, shape a world.

Although "Lovers' Bodies," the title of the opening section of Joyce Carol Oates' third volume of poetry, *Angel Fire*, would seem to suggest that the poems in it continue the examination of love that is certainly central to the second volume and is introduced in *Anonymous Sins*, several new developments in the poetry and in the structuring of the book make this book different from the others. Because of this new alignment, the poetry demonstrates some uncertainty but not specifically along the lines of Helen Vendler's criticism discussed earlier. It is rather because the poetry is pushing the ideas into a different direction, hinted at in the earlier volumes but here teased out in various ways, reaching in its third section to an attempt to simplify the complex nature of the other two sections.

This sectioning of the book, each with its own title, a structuring into named parts that the poet uses from now on, indicates a more positive desire to see the poetry as a unity, each part adding its weight to the whole concept. Her first two books work within a kind of framework as I have tried to indicate, but *Angel Fire* is more substantially organized than the other books of poetry.

The title poem is at the almost exact centre of the book and points both backwards and forwards, though there are other considerations of structure besides this use of one poem as a focal point. This poem leads immediately into another section which opens with a further poem about fire, dedicated to the memory of Flannery O'Connor. This dedication is a clue to the atmosphere of *Angel Fire*.

At a surface level there are similarities between the fictions of these two writers: both are Catholic in upbringing, both can be loosely termed Gothic writers. Oates shows her great admiration for O'Connor in her essay about her fiction, calling her "one of the greatest religious writers of modern times."[13] The use of the word "religious" cannot in any strict sense be applied to Oates' work but the general aura of ritual, psychic spirituality, the search for meaning beyond history are all present in Oates' first two volumes of poetry, and the poem dedicated to O'Connor, "Firing The Field," does circle around belief and beyond, with ideas of purgation through violence, and the central image of the poem stems from a vision of the main character in O'Connor's "Revelation," a passage Oates quotes with approval in her essay. Furthermore, the poem opens the third section of her book, entitled "Revelations."

Her view of O'Connor's writing going beyond naturalism into a kind of surrealism is also an answer (when it occurs in her own writing) to such critics as Helen Vendler who persist in seeing an untruth of situation in Oates' poetry, particularly in *Angel Fire*.

It is difficult to isolate ideas in a general sense from her essay about O'Connor, as she connects them to their working out in the fiction. She insists that O'Connor sees "the necessity of succumbing to the divine through violence that is immediate and irreparable. There is no mysticism in her work that is only spiritual; it is physical as well."[14] O'Connor's stories initiate the protagonist "into a vision of reality. This is accomplished through ceremonial, almost ritualistic devices: the gathering together of the unfaithful in order to witness a 'miracle.' "[15] Similar notions are woven into the texture of Oates' first two volumes of poetry: the expression of ritual, the search for some reality beyond ordinary history, the references to violence as a means to this.

Perhaps Oates secularizes the struggle of the individual to find the meaning of self in his sense of isolation in and alienation from the modern world, sometimes using the classic definition of that conflict in Freudian terms, as she explains it in this essay: "a dynamic struggle of the conscious ego or self to maintain its individuality against the raging forces of the primitive unconscious and the highly repressive reservoir of civilization."[16] Thus, contemporary man must go through physical transformation in order to gain spiritual transcendence, so in Oates, and particularly in *Angel Fire*, as in O'Connor, disease is symbolic of that connection between body and soul, mind and spirit: "the diseased body is not only an affirmation or a symbolic intensification of the spiritual 'disease' that attends physical processes; it becomes a matter of one's personal salvation . . . to interpret the accidents of the flesh in terms of the larger, unfathomable, but ultimately *no more abstract* pattern that links the self to the cosmos."[17] Man may be burned up by a fever. In spiritual terms this may mean destruction even of his ethical life. "It is not simply our 'virtues' that will be burned away, but our rational faculties as well, and perhaps even the illusion of our separate, isolated egos."[18]

The title poem of *Angel Fire* deals with the notion of the physical reaching to the spiritual. The experience inside the car in the poem while the world burns in the heat outside is "better than marriage!" The heat burns the two in the car, melds them and opens them to new transforming experience:

> every pore breathes in this fire
> spasm of light radiant
> as pain
> so bright you can't feel it.

The spiritual embodied in the image of angels, perhaps messengers from that larger ceremonial (or divine, primitive) world "direct their fire/ . . . to penetrate the old selfish tightness." Everything burns:

> more vicious
> their fire original and clean as music without words
> killing the old selves of us
> the old shadows
> in one radiance.

This poem is the closing poem of the second section called "Domestic Miracles," and the emphasis in most of these poems in this group is on the miraculous developing within the ordinary, the marvellous embodied within the self, the yearning for the prodigious in ordinary reality. The title poem is a simple series of imagist-like descriptions of happenings transformed beyond their ordinary causes: bruised thighs (from love-making?) are caused by "a stampede of hooves" and earthly love makes the beloved "permanent/as old unlovely busts of clay/unearthed in the Mideast/of forgotten people." Selfhood here is transformed, just as love blossoms beyond itself in "Our Common Past." In another poem a young wife, trapped inside sordid domesticity, still becomes fearful as things impinge from outside and she still senses the "beast crouched beneath a bed," even though it is a recent marriage, "this new bedstead." Hallowe'en creates symbols to keep the spirits at bay but the whole outer cosmos of the dead reaches into our lives. Our dark dreams on the other "side of the eyelid" are adapted into our waking lives, not banished but somehow "shaped to fit the contour of a hand"; those dark visions have to be "relearned/rewon." Those two worlds of self and the larger world, the ceremonial, perhaps divine, primitivism and ordinary reality are seen in terms of landscape in "Leaving The Mountain" and "Mile-High Monday."

The opening section of the book concentrates on human love but in larger terms than in the previous volume. The title poem of this section sees a large, public love as a genuine pulse beating behind the ordinary pulse of history. The poem closes with the idea that "all visible things/repeat themselves/into permanence," an idea somewhat akin to the view of human love in "Domestic Miracles." Many of the poems in this section express a sense of something prodigious behind the ordinary motions of life, prodigies that the personae of the poems search for and perhaps find at intense moments that pass as they return to present reality. Yet such extraordinary perceptions are vested in human reality; the spiritual is reached through the physical:

> I was pierced only by something human
> wanting to die in an explosion of dust and rock
> I died only in moods
> and ascended again
> humanly.

The dualities of love are included in these poems as well as the barriers that prevent the merging and melding that figure in "Angel Fire," though the experience of love still reaches towards transcendence, "a groping in immense light." Women through menstrual tensions and releases are involved in larger, unlived, unborn life, and in "Structures" the concept of boxed-in life which seemed negative in *Love And Its Derangements* is more ambivalent. Man yearns to be infinite but can express his spirituality through love only within the physical demands of his body, so that love may transform and release—"I have no weight/gravity eludes me"—but always there is a return to the finite. Love, because of its limitations, encompasses hate, even though it may reach beyond the finite:

> you will hate me after
> your loving concludes
> you will pass finitely through me
> through the structures we inhabit . . .

This poem is a prelude to the strange poem, "Hate," which attempts to make connections between saintliness, human love, and hate. Saintliness seems too pure, too dry, whereas "love is prodigious." Hate is structured, like the hate in the previous poem, and sometimes reached after love, for the lover comes to a consciousness of limitations, falling back into time, perhaps seething with his inability to find his constant transformation. Everything becomes "readable and ordinary/ the needle rests at zero/in a sanctity/of hate." This paradoxical conclusion is the nearest statement in Oates' poetry to what she sees in those grotesque, violent but saintly protagonists in O'Connor's work.

Towards the end of this opening section is a sequence called "Several Embraces," which repeats ideas of those larger external lives taking over ordinary lives, or at least, if not taking over, being present, almost tangible to us in our waking lives. One of this sequence, "Fever," is especially relevant to the concept of the diseased body as somehow part of a physical process towards spiritual salvation. The fever becomes the fever of love, a physical passion that transcends itself, as the embrace of the lovers is entwined within the embrace of some other:

> his figure darkly transparent
> his breath unfevered and unshrill
> his dark cool hands caressing our flesh in a mock prayer
> a net of his arms outside the net of ours.

But the embrace is ambivalent. The other will deliver them, 'save' them, but also cure them of their fever, pull them down "to cerebral stone."

This section is followed by another already mentioned containing poems about the miraculous embedded in or sought for in the ordinary and domestic, closing with the title poem, already discussed. And this is turn leads to the final section, "Revelations," occupying one half of the book, and introduced by the poem in memory of Flannery O'Connor, "Firing The Field."

The poem is about that idea that is in O'Connor's work about the burning of everything. The fire is a purifying agent, destroying all life. The field is "stubbled with black weeds." Perhaps this is the meanness we must all be reduced to (part of that recognition of our inner darkness that Jung insists we face in our process of individuation), perhaps it is the meanness of the true believers (the poem begins with an apostrophe to the readers: "Unbelievers, look!") who are the leaders of the procession in O'Connor's story, perhaps it is simply the meanness of violence and destruction. But out of that, our revenge falls from us, may indeed be a fertilizing agent that falls "mightily/upon all creation."

The revelations which follow this purging act—a poem which invites the reader to follow it into meanness, a poem which closes with the phrase "all creation"—inhabit a range of human life, although some of them fall short of what they are seeking, that is, their images and structures are not clear and strong enough to convince the reader as revelations. One or two revert to the old habit of cataloguing questions, as in "Family." Sometimes the landscape of a poem does not establish itself as reality or symbol, there are some repetitions which do not add or expand, particularly those poems about dream states, one or two refuse to give up any specifically clear meaning either as single poems or as parts of a general sequence of revelations. I find "Prophecies," "Becoming Garbage," and "Elegy Of The Letter 'I' " so dense in texture, so jagged and shifting in structure that they give nothing but cloudy hints, drifting off into obscurity. And yet there are a sufficient number of poems here to substantiate that principal theme of two worlds physically experienced or sensed, whether as outer vision or inner feeling. "A Midwestern Song" depicts a housewife stranded in a landscape but with intuitions, echoes, quick, flickering visions of something beyond her alienated life washing into her like the sounds of an ocean which conjures up for her some other life, richer, more ceremonial, more mythic, but which transforms the immediate landscape of her life.

A similar poem which embodies that cosmic life in landscape is "Entering The Desert," in which the landscape promises unity and balance, but the vast continent is "too raw to absorb you" and so you turn back to the human self (as the housewife does in "A Midwestern Song"), somehow finding an inner calmness, for the landscape has invaded that selfhood: "entering the desert, you are yourself/entered and shaken and relearned."

These poems are not without irony, of course; that inner self may in fact be a desert, the motions of the sea the housewife hears within may be delusion or mere memory. In another poem the transformation may not be possible or the person involved unwilling, the body turned into a fiction that people deal with without any sense of its identity. That outer force may be reductive. But there is a life outside us, not simply ordinariness or history, the body overtaken by fevers, memories, dreams, 'other' personalities, which we want to recognize, which we want to embrace and merge with:

> I am begging you for the imprint
> of your face upon mine
> hot enough to give me a face
> to press upon me the features of a face
> already proven to be human.

That point of contact, that bridge between two worlds, two states of consciousness is best exemplified by two poems towards the end of the book. "City Of Locks" with its punning title presents a dismal picture of urban decay and collapse. Water is hemmed in, flowing in man-made canals. It is sludgy, foamed with pollution, stagnant. Nothing can rise from this reality. The persona stares across the canal waiting for some revelation but "nothing happens . . . nothing is declared." Perhaps residing behind that word "declared" is a sense of a border to be crossed where we are asked to declare ourselves and our belongings, our true identity. But here there is no bridge to cross that border, whereas in the following poem, which in a sense is the title poem of this section, "Revelations In Small Sunbaked Squares," the view is of clustering houses clinging to the natural landscape even within "a great American city." This is a "finite map/of human streets" which is preferable to our longing "for a dull infinity," for this finite world contains human life "beyond our imaginations/urgent and finite in mysteries/beyond our judgment." Suddenly, then, this physical world releases a vision from within us:

> The city in our heads
> breaks from us
> suddenly
> swings from us   free
> unconfined   unjudged
> unwhole
> unpossessed.

This poem with its simple language, its direct statement, its description which is also left somehow unsubstantial is as near an expression of that mystical bridge between micro- and macrocosmic worlds, the release of the ordinary self from selfhood into a transformed self as occurs in Oates' poetry. The spiritual release is achieved through physical vision, so it is fitting that the volume closes with a poem about the physical means of vision but expressed in terms of evolution and growth. The eye may be personal vision but it may also be what Henry Miller calls "the cosmological eye" (and with the insistence on selfhood perhaps with a pun around the sound 'I'). Our finite lives may see but may also be seen through. One is reminded that as an epigraph to her essay on Flannery O'Connor, Oates uses a quotation from Teilhard de Chardin: "something is developing in the world by means of us, perhaps at our expense."

In spite of its title, the next volume of poetry, *The Fabulous Beasts*, concentrates perhaps more than any of the previous volumes on the immediacy of the physical world, although the last section, which has the same title as the

book, moves to a more affirmative statement after the poetry's bleakly deter-
ministic view in the earlier sections, the poems gradually modifying the bleakness through the book. The title poem itself is a frightening depiction of the
terrors of life, the emergence of history in everyday events reported in newspapers. The newsprint clings to fingers, it dirties our lives, the newspapers come
out each day filled with these ordinary and violent facts of our existence, so that
it becomes an image of our destiny reborn each day, swallowing us into itself:
"A huge creature, its outer membrane not yet congealed, stirs no more than a
flame as you enter."

And yet Oates' view of the piling-up of historical realities, which tumble
out in ironic juxtapositions of the trivial and the profound, the commercial and
the horrendous, in this title poem states the view that the reports of these
historical events are only dubiously valid. At the end of the first section of the
book newspapers are seen as providing "clarity in our time," though at the same
time, just a few lines later, they negate the effects of tremendous happenings by
summarizing and by limiting them inside the digest format of a newspaper:
"any tragedy that can be explained in ten inches of type cannot be a profound
one." This notion of the validity of an event and its distortion, so that responses
to its immediacy are numbed, is a central theme of this book, which is filled
with poems structured around images and phrases expressing speed and lack of
permanence, the gaps between people and between a specific event and its
symbolic abstraction, the search for clarity and the blur of destiny around
individuals, the lack of communication and the search for meaning within the
physical world and its connection with a larger, cosmic universe. As such, *The
Fabulous Beasts* obviously picks up themes, though in different ways and with
different emphases, established in the first two volumes and worked out in
larger terms in *Angel Fire*. This book, then, concentrates on immediate things
and it may be the book of poetry which most nearly corresponds to the novels in
that it presents these ideas in a recognizably realistic world, particularly in its
third section, though it would still be mistaken to read the poems in novelistic
terms, as the narrative elements are left muted, often unfinished, simply because the thematic concerns focus on the evident enigma of mundane reality.
Such expression of bewilderment leads to some puzzling poems and it is difficult
in some cases to know whether the bewilderment is an end in itself within a
poem or whether it is a deliberate effect to establish a muddy environment
through which the poet works to a clarity towards the end of the third section
and in the closing group of poems. It is certainly true that Section II, "Forbidden Testimonies," promises in its title to expound in some poems happenings,
even narratives, but they remain somehow unresolved and finally
impenetrable.

Another connection with the novels, although it is better to see the connection with some of the short stories, particularly with those strangely distanced
tales in *The Poisoned Kiss*, rather than with the novels, is the inclusion of two
long prose poems. Both are parabolic in intention and the longer one, "A
Posthumous Sketch," is a key not only to the thematic urge of the volume but
also to its images.

Its surface narrative concerns the narrator's attempts to reach to the truth of the experience of a drowned friend; as the epigraph puts it, the challenge is "to conquer the element that had drowned my friend." Perhaps this is Conrad's destructive element, reminiscent also of that view of the two elements, the larger, ceremonial one and the nearer everyday one of "Anonymous Sins." The friend has constantly tested himself in that element, lacking the essentials to cope with it, yet daring his fate with it, "to the very point of breaking." It is in this parable that the tragedy of his death is reduced by the newspaper to a digest of ten inches. The narrator himself has lost contact with himself, and with both his immediate world and the larger universe, symbolized by his isolation at the beginning and by the depersonalized messages and noises on his telephone (an image that occurs in the opening poem of the volume).

He is called to identify his friend's body and though he does, he has no certainty because his friend's features have been obliterated. The lifeless, face-less body is a mirror-image of himself, an expression of his own loss of identity. Later, the waves falling on the shore whisper to him, "Acedia," though even-tually their sound becomes more robust, enticing him out to his own testing, in order to go beyond his friend's youthfulness, his own personal past (he has a mirage of swimming alongside himself as a boy). He sees himself swimming over the drowned body of his friend so that he senses a kind of triumph at having conquered the element and having over-reached his friend. Then he feels he can turn and swim to shore, but that is not enough. His friend had really triumphed by giving himself to the sea (here is the notion of risk-taking as fulfilment that has always hovered inside Oates' poetry). The narrator can feel the triumph only when he is swimming, symbolic of that idea of Becoming in the face of spiritual deadness, the urge for a continuing process of life rather than the dead weight of ordinariness, of being reduced to ten inches in a newspaper. So he returns to swim out again into the sea. It is a kind of conquest, even though the title tells us he suffers the same fate as his friend.

This parable summarizes that attempt to bridge the gaps between worlds, to go beyond the immediate, even though the significance of one's life may be achieved through a totally experienced personal life, not the distanced histor-ical process of events in the world of reality. This may be Oates' expression of what she finds in both Kafka and O'Connor, an essentialist, rather than an existential view of existence:

> man does not create his soul through free acts but is instead given a soul with which he must live, however unsuitable it may be. . . (Man's) anxiety is expressed only in terms of a higher, invisible, possibly malignant Being, while the heroes of a typical existential novel create their own values completely.[19]

Here one is reminded of the fabulous beast, and in "A Posthumous Sketch," the narrator ponders the mysterious nature of the oceanic element: "It gave no sign of me to myself. I might never have entered it, might never have been born, for all its rough noisy Being acknowledged of me."

This parable closes the first section, "Broken Connections," the opening poem's title as well, a poem which states the impossibility of meaning without plunging into the process. The experience is there; it may be incomprehensible, the distance between the individual and any outer significance may be "snow-maddened miles" but the world is lived and living, so it becomes recognizable, even if all that is recognized is "the snow, the silence/of broken connections." In "After Terror . . ." some overwhelming but in the poem unexplained experience allows us at least to cautiously "decipher the code that surrounds us." And the other two poems of this section suggest both the sudden gaps and the inexplicable stases of existence as well as a sense of the wonders within our immediate world, and "If you are not wonder-working/ Who will have you?"

This section is followed by "Forbidden Testimonies," a section I have already suggested is densely enigmatic, though its surface is full of unexplained narratives, states of mind and case histories, as if the poet is presenting evidence about various events, searches, personalities, which may reveal something if the people involved in these violences and mysterious happenings could only discover them. The section mirrors the gaps between event and meaning, and so is full of ordinary details, perhaps the equivalents of those news items indicated in "The Fabulous Beast." There are poems about rape, suicidal fears, robbery, fear of blindness, a river rescue, the breakdown of love, appearance and disappearance of friends through travel and death, storms and upheavals, journeys leading to no destination, partings, creating a wasteland of meaninglessness. This is the reality within which modern man has to live:

> Sinners may be cleansed pure as snow,
> by snow.
> No God abides in this landscape but the landscape:
> Brittle the crust, perfection in every footprint.

The following section is titled after the prose poem which opens it, another parable, this time about the meanings imposed on the portrait of a martyred child in a window, and the child's own sense of the variety of meanings invested in him by other people, the gaps between the Real and the Ideal, the search for meaning which may obliterate the original and real experience. But nonetheless, such reading of his existence is life, may indeed be his fate. The poems which follow clarify this response to life, for they raise questions about the meanings of events, but unlike the previous section, they move towards a kind of clarity, even though there may be an acknowledgement that the gaps between our lives and our sense of the mysteries of a life beyond can never be wholly bridged. Even violent events can be contained within an immediate vision, can be accepted at a local level, even if the larger destiny is still questionable. That immediate life may seem mundane and repetitious, but through the experience of life those intense moments may be reached, as in "Being Faithful," where this idea is expressed in terms of journeys along the highways of America:

> Drivers must prepare all their lives
> for certain short lunges
> past darkened farmhouses, where a girl watches,
> faithful to them.

They appear, they gain speed, they rush transformed
into the rush of wheels, the scan of headlights,
the wind.
Then the sudden fading-away
the highway empty again
abstract
unimagined.

This poem occurs about midpoint in the third section and from then on the poems attempt to express an acceptance of the patternless motivations of life within which man must search for his self in a continuous Becoming and Being: "We persist in our Being./We are never known." Each segment of our living offers new dangers but also opportunities for new beginnings. We can acknowledge our pasts but build on them and eventually slough them. Those who are dying know "ordinary facts"; their lives and their dying offer us instruction.

Two poems rework the experience of the storm in Section II. At this point, however, the upheaval is lived through to move in the end to "noon in a planet of debris." After a snowstorm in which the snow has piled up in a blanketing silence overnight, voices shout No against it, "there are birds in the evergreen bushes" and daylight comes with its own kind of wisdom. A journey through a storm at sea is survived as "someone engineers us rockily/ through the original sea." A November storm is destructive, yet life persists as it has done for long eons, and the section closes with "A Vision." Out of the enormous wasteland, violence and destruction of contemporary life comes a moment of vision which may diminish to "dull-gleaming metal" but it once existed intensely: "a junk-yard vast as a kingdom/tossed up light."

Then there is the final short section beginning with the fabulous beast of modern horror and triviality. But that newsprint which smears our fingers and our vision is made from trees which in the next poem leap "through history/in one place/singular/multiplied endlessly." They have achieved their continually growing forms while man desperately seeks to find his essence, trying to reach out, invent, imagine, see himself. This is followed by two poems in which the wasteland impinges again, the rootedness of existence is obliterated, and the gaps stretch across generations.

But in both the closing poems a key word is "waiting": indeed, that is the title of the last poem. There is somewhere a "curious unity," though "The pattern shrieks, breaks," but the persona of this poem closes with a defiant, if muted statement: "I am patient/I am waiting/I will triumph," perhaps the ambivalent triumph of the swimmer/narrator of "A Posthumous Sketch," for the last poem repeats the image of the waves which for that narrator changed from whispering "acedia" to shouting more robustly. In "Waiting" the life of the water, as the persona watches it, goes on, unaccountable, unpredictable, both immense and shallow. The observer is in the middle of this seething but undefinable life. "Is this perfection?" he asks. But if it is, it is ungraspable. "He waits for the next wave to change everything," as we must all wait, both watching and involved, accepting the innumerable happenings around us, involved in the changes, waiting in our living for the moments to stream through us; even if "the coil of harmony eludes us/defies us," it still "streams through us."

The next volume, *Women Whose Lives Are Food, Men Whose Lives Are Money*, extends the interests of *The Fabulous Beasts* in its use of external, realistic details and its ideas of two worlds crossing each into the other at moments of intensity in spite of the massive mundaneness of ordinary reality. But the poetry is not merely repetitive. Indeed, this volume can be seen as completing a circle of themes first announced in *Anonymous Sins* and elaborated in the other books. The sub-titles of each section neatly rehearse the ideas which have been developing in the poetry: the first section carries the same title as the book, and the others are titled respectively, "Metamorphoses," "The Resurrection Of The Dead," "Public Outcry," and "Many Are Called."

The structures of the poems are recognizably the same as those in previous books, but this last collection has a calmer, more definitive note to it. The poet has moved from the continual questioning of her first volume to a much more declarative mode. Many of the poems here are expressed in assertively straightforward sentences, often simple in structure, or if complex, the clausal construction is direct. Often the lining corresponds to the grammatical arrangement, so in general the tone is one of assurance and strength. Added to this is the persuasive clarity in the expression of the details of external reality, and this definition is given further bite because the poet injects some satiric humour into some poems, particularly in the "Public Outcry" section.

Many of these characteristics are evident in the title poem. The repetitive dullness of suburban life is established by the details as well as by the repetition of phrasing itself. Satiric thrust is here, but its comedy is muted because the poet is endeavouring to suggest that in some way modern man must break out of these routines to seek a life beyond his own narrow borders, beyond the silly mirroring, trivializing and romanticizing he may find in the media. For women, life is a dreary life of consuming and being consumed, of collecting and discarding. For men, life is earning and spending. There may have been some vague hints that something exists outside this routine but nothing has been fulfilled. The younger generations repeat the old search for new frontiers but the journey is inconclusive. They return to find nothing has changed. The poem closes on the isolation of women, finding a bleak peace in "the relief of emptiness."

This opening sets up surely a picture of modern meaninglessness but the mood is tempered throughout the volume with flashes of hope, especially in its references to children who have an innocence that is ignorant of what will be grown into, so implicit irony resides in these references, even though a poem in the opening section is called "The Eternal Children." Oates does not have even this muted belief in adolescents, presumably because they have grown into some knowledge and because their searches have led them back to what existed before. Later in the volume a poem summarizes the aimlessness of young adolescents, who feel they can expect nothing from this world: "Every holiday has arrived every package torn open" but they have achieved that bleak and empty peace of the housewives of the opening poem.

The book is riddled with details of this remorseless insignificance of life. There is an emphasis on the physical decay of the body, the cheerless mechanization of survival in medical terms, the sense of loss, and dying. Survival often seems to be achieved only through reaching a plateau of numbness, and yet finally the tone of the volume is not entirely bleak. Two sections of the book have titles that indicate the possibilities for change and rebirth. Some poems focus on the idea of man affirming his life beyond himself. Such a poem as "Lovers Asleep" opening the second section coheres around the notion of lovers reaching across half a continent. They overlap even if their stretching is "the impulse of the abyss." The closing poem of that same section, "Abandoned Airfield, 1977," while it centres on details of decay, still has memories of flight in frail structures, some notion of escape from gravity, even if that reality of flight has collapsed. Yet the poem closes with a flight of birds, though man can no longer follow them.

Human love is still the duality it has always been in the poetry, for it is a means both of transcendence and of limitation. Lovers "locked in love" become somehow obsessive, trapped inside a monumental concern for love: "they are immortal/they are writhing in pain." It is very much an embodied mutuality that frees them from the ordinary and because it is achieved through and beyond the body, "Mere death would canonoze them," so they fear the loss of love, the death of love itself. That locking inside love, then, can also be a terrible romanticism.

But in the last section the poet proffers an alternate view of love, one that suggests a reaching into real physical stretching, a kind of risk-taking in its commitment, which will offer a crystallization of oneness:

> Taking the curve of the road too fast
> the car swerves, the tires hit gravel,
> fence posts never seen before lurch crazily
> then are righted again.
> A miracle.
> Our pulses now race in a single spasm:
> other curves lie ahead.
> If we die today we die together.

That is the equivalent of those intense moments of passion she has included in earlier poems but the transcendence of flesh is specifically linked with its shadow side in this volume. Those streaming moments of earlier poems are here lightning strokes which shed light, send the commandment, "Live as if you were immortal." But there are "counter-signs," "every pore is a betrayal," for the lightning strokes cause shadows. It is as if the idea of love continues in ordinary weather, the merging in love is stormily transcendent but impossible to retain, both as intensity and as unity beyond the self: "We quarrel to regain our souls."

This theme of the shadow side of existence recurs throughout the book, linked to other themes in the previous poetry. In that first section a woman's body hauled out of the river is seen as a betrayal of the dream of love which in its beauty may attract violence and is therefore consumed, just as in another poem "last summer's pets abandoned" are changed to wild creatures "over-leaping the love/of (their) masters." A poem about an old movie queen, dying of cancer, sways between her being consumed by the disease as she watches her earlier self in movies, and her realization that the movie self is an invention, not her real self. Such a dream of her self is "a miracle," full of "raw glowing life." She escapes from herself, yet the movie plays within reality, always returns to the theatre. In spite of the miracle, "the theatre's floor is deep in mud," so that plateau of dullness experienced by the housewife can become a balance that smooths out everything, the intensity at both the ecstatic and the painful level: "No dancing, no raging, no hurt."

In the closing poem of the first section the poet imagines another woman talking to her from the dark side of the earth, now becoming aware of what she is, of what she has been denied, of what she has been offered as help, so her hatred is perhaps being eroded, boiled away. She sees what she has become, and she now can see the woman she is addressing. Both are now part of her hatred but inextricably held as part of her existence: "I hate you both/but would not lose you." Here again the poem elaborates that ambivalence within love, hate, and saintliness first expressed in "Hate" in *Angel Fire*.

The metamorphoses of the second section are equally ambivalent. This section's title poem wavers between an uncertainly fulfilled life of seven decades withering to death within an hour, an individual life but one also common and ordinary, and the question of a life filled with screams and motiveless changes, a life that questions the value of living. The close again reaches to a kind of peace, though perhaps again an ironic one.

Most of the changes involve facing a doubleness. To be addicted is to suffer "this hunger/this perfect thirst," seemingly always living on an edge in a ceaseless quest which can be fulfilled for a time, even though the grasping may be illusory, may be momentary, but again the poem seems to express some hovering around a possibility of waiting for the transcendence. Man must face his fears, his own demons, his unlived lives, another Jungian concept, till a living balance is achieved. It is better to welcome those demons: "Your weight balances the weight of those terrible limbs eager to spring into yours." Possibilities can open for man, maybe opening out into death but also perhaps opening out into survival. Here again man is "waiting for something," though things around him are constantly in the process of flux and change.

The idea of waiting opens the third section in a poem in which the environment is "glacial," reduced to "an absolute zero," perhaps one of those numb plateaus, for by means of it, panic can be outwaited (is there an echo of "outwit-ted" here?), in this place which contains no rituals. But the poem ends: "wait-ing/surviving." This middle section is a kind of turning point, with poems centering on death but including also stratagems for survival, except that the poet casts doubt on whether the mere expression of those ways of survival are sufficient. In one poem she may even be suggesting that recording ideas of love and survival is a treason against the pure desire of living, the classic confronta-tion between life and art, for the moments of intensity, either of ecstasy or danger, go beyond the forms the poet (or in a larger sense, mankind in general) tries to hold life in: "Emergencies are savage poems that elude the rhythms/we have devised." At this point in the volume it is almost as if the poet wants to go beyond words. The confines of a rumpled bed become the spaciousness that the two lovers reach across in an earlier poem in this volume. Indeed, the bed goes beyond language, encompasses all human life, opens out into the cosmos:

> No words no words no words
> a beginning and a probable end
> a bassinet   a death-bed
> shadow-soiled, fold upon fold of worn sheets
> waves washing eternal
> a planet's slumbrous play.

This poem immediately precedes the title poem of the section in which the dead rise to reclaim the earth, to reclaim us, and as if to repeat the notion of going beyond the ordinary means of language, this is the only poem which splits open with abnormal typography, with the final lines surrounding a framed slab (a concretization of a headstone to be overturned at the resurrection and re-turned to life?) which expresses that recurrent theme of finding significance for our lives in earthly existence. We can only be transfigured by living within our physical beings: "I am here/I have returned/I want my place again/on earth," the framed portion of the poem reads.

As if to remind the reader that this earthly life is still full of the dullness, the ordinariness, the violence, the triviality, the ambiguities, the sordidness, the consumerism, expressed in the first section and running as a continuing theme of ongoing history in the present, the fourth section is a "Public Outcry," poems about national holidays, the jumbled items in newspapers, city life disarranged through power failure, parties, endless travel, before the book moves into its final section.

For the most part the poems that close the book concentrate on those moments which transfigure. Included here are those poems already discussed about the intense moments of love, structured around the image of a lightning-stroke and a fast ride almost out of control. The consumerism and the shadow sides of life of the opening section are narrowed here to the focus of a single pear which glows with the fulness of its own existence, accepting its flaws. That ripe pear contains the wonder of life within its single identity:

> that first pear's weight
> exceeds the season's tonnage
> costly beyond estimation
> a prize, a riddle
> a feast

In "In Medias Res" man may often be caught within narrow limits or in mundane existence. Perhaps he will suddenly discover that the midpoint of his life, a time for a real assessment of himself, has arrived in "a cafe in West Virginia—/drafty, smelling of grease, with mudstained floor." Man then should look at that environment closely, even focus it more narrowly and severely, examine it, as others have examined it, assessing himself as individual and in relation to the common lot. The possibilities are open, the self and the shadow, the reality and the dream can overlap: "Rituals seek to enter us/as if the body were a sacred event." And the final poem denies the idea that transcendence belongs only to the elect, for it is called "Many Are Called," a poem which deliberately refuses to complete that phrase with the normal conclusion, "but few are chosen." Instead, the last line reads, "It seems that all are chosen."

There the poetry of Joyce Carol Oates rests at the moment, a statement of man living within the possibility of survival and growth beyond the ordinariness of existence, within a state of suspended animation, torn between moments of flight and rising and the pull of gravity and drowning. But even the negative experiences have their place within our lives, for we must search for wholeness now that we can no longer rely on a belief in divine powers outside. Yet such outer worlds exist, a larger History beyond the terrifying nullity of historical process, so that we can live no longer aimlessly but searching for connections through the past, encountered in a large cosmos of ritual and ceremonial mythology.

Such ideas are abstract, and the poetry does not always manage to cope with the abstractions. At its worst it falls into prosiness with lines that display flabby rhythms, with images that remain vague, with structures too jagged to reveal the ideas. But at its best, particularly in those poems which establish a core of realistic detail, even if placed in surreal contexts, the poetry expresses itself as a consistent vision, repeating ideas from the fiction but demanding to be read on its own terms. Constantly the poetry returns to the idea of transcendence, stating that intensity of experience is possible even in the midst of the overwhelming triviality and horror of the contemporary world. The form of poetry enables Joyce Carol Oates to intensify her vision of human possibility by freeing herself from the demands of narrative and realistic plausibility. It is an expression in poetic terms of what she herself calls the "sense of the mystery and the sanctity of the human predicament."[20]

Notes

1. *New York Times Book Review*, April 1, 1973, as quoted in Carolyn Riley, ed., *Contemporary Literary Criticism*, (Detroit: 1975), III, 361.

2. Vendler in Riley, p. 361.

3. "Feeling One's Oates," *Modern Poetry Studies*, 2, No. 3 (1971), as quoted in Riley, p. 360.

4. All the quotations in this paragraph are taken from "Preface," *New Heaven, New Earth* (New York: 1974), p. 7.

5. "The Hostile Sun: The Poetry of D. H. Lawrence," in *New Heaven, New Earth*, p. 45.

6. "The Hostile Sun," pp. 47–48.

7. Note to "Kafka's Paradise," in *New Heaven, New Earth*, p. 307.

8. "Out of Stone, Into Flesh: The Imagination of James Dickey," in *New Heaven, New Earth*, p. 242.

9. "Preface," in *New Heaven, New Earth*, p. 7.

10. "Kafka's Paradise," in *New Heaven, New Earth*, p. 307.

11. Both quotations are from Mazzaro, "Feeling One's Oates," in Riley, p. 359.

12. "Out of Stone, Into Flesh," in *New Heaven, New Earth*, p. 242.

13. "The Visionary Art of Flannery O'Connor," in *New Heaven, New Earth*, p. 145.

14. "The Visionary Art of Flannery O'Connor," in *New Heaven, New Earth*, p. 144.

15. "The Visionary Art of Flannery O'Connor," in *New Heaven, New Earth*, p. 149.

16. "The Visionary Art of Flannery O'Connor," in *New Heaven, New Earth*, pp. 150–51.

17. "The Visionary Art of Flannery O'Connor," in *New Heaven, New Earth*, pp. 165–66.

18. "The Visionary Art of Flannery O'Connor," in *New Heaven, New Earth*, pp. 174–75.

19. "The Visionary Art of Flannery O'Connor," in *New Heaven, New Earth*, pp. 147–48.

20. Joyce Carol Oates, "An American Tragedy," *New York Times Book Review*, Jan. 24, 1971, p. 2, as quoted in Mary Kathryn Grant, *The Tragic Vision of Joyce Carol Oates* (Durham: 1978), p. 4.

Unliberated Women in Joyce Carol Oates's Fiction

Joanne V. Creighton*

Joyce Carol Oates is not usually thought of as a feminist writer. Although women play an important role throughout her fiction, she does not call attention to herself as an articulate woman thinking and writing about women. Nor does she for the most part present women who can articulate their own distress. While often her subjects are intelligent women, intellect is inadequate as a vehicle of self-understanding and equilibrium. All of Oates's characters—men and women—are buffeted about on the vicissitudes of emotion, and liberation, if it is to come, must first be emotional release. Characteristically, her central male characters seek emotional release through violence and her central women characters seek protection from emotion in passive withdrawal. Potential liberation through healthy sexuality is a possibility. But very few of Oates's characters—especially very few women—achieve this liberation. The quote from John Donne which prefaces *The Goddess and Other Women*, "Things naturall to the Species are not always so for the individual,"[1] is fittingly descriptive of the unnatural adjustments that most of Oates's women make to their unliberated selves.

In her novels Oates creates recurrent female types, Mothers and Daughters. The Mothers—Clara of *A Garden of Earthly Delights*, Nada of *Expensive People*, Loretta of *them*, and Ardis of *Do With Me What You Will*—have all perfected the art of survival but at a cost to the people around them, their lovers and husbands and maladjusted children. They are cheerful and adjustable, egotistical and self-sufficient, feline and attractive, opportunistic and pragmatic, manipulative and amoral. All are ambitious materially and socially, and all, except Loretta, have jettisoned themselves into a higher social and economic position. All experience little self-doubt or sexual inhibition. But their cold self-sufficiency closes them off from genuine feeling and denies them the emotional release so basic to true liberation in Oates's fiction. The Mothers engage Oates's attention less fully than the other type, the Daughters.

Karen of *With Shuddering Fall*, Maureen and Nadine of *them*, Helene and Shelley of *Wonderland*, and Elena of *Do With Me What You Will*, all daughters of a strong mother or father, share a selfless sisterhood. All are fragile, quiet, insecure, introspective, and above all, vacuous. Opposed to the catlike

*Reprinted with permission from *World Literature Written in English*, 17 (April 1978), 165–75.

agility of the Mothers, the Daughters have little resilience and are incapable of dealing with the unexpected. All are skirting the edges of severe psychological disorder. Karen spends time in a mental institution; Maureen's catatonic state and Elena's somnolent trance are expressions of extreme anxiety neuroses; Helen has an hysterical fit in a gynecologist's office; Shelly attempts to obliterate reality through drugs, and Nadine attempts to kill her lover Jules and herself. Concerned obsessively with orderliness and containment, sexually frigid or inhibited, they yet risk sexual involvement. Karen runs away from home with Shar because she hopes to fulfill her father's command to destroy Shar and thereby to reestablish the comfort of the filial bond. In contrast, Shelley runs away with Noel because she hopes to free herself from her father's smothering love and protection. Maureen first resorts to prostitution to provide the money that seems to be necessary for security and then sets out to get married and thereby find security and identity in the stereotypical role of American wife. Nadine, Helene, and Elena, married women who have not found identity through marriage, risk love affairs, but Helene and Nadine—locked in frigidity—are unrelieved of the burden of nonbeing; only Elena, the central character of *Do With Me What You Will*, is finally awakened to selfhood through love.

Elena, emotionally scarred by a childhood kidnapping by her crazed father, retains throughout her adolescence and young adulthood an exaggerated passivity and fearful withdrawal from experience. At first afraid to speak, fearful of the dark, and cautious in even the most mundane details of living, she morbidly identifies with the victims of accidental deaths. Even after she regains a semblance of normalcy, she remains excessively moldable and obedient to her shrewd and opportunistic mother, Ardis. Ardis tells Elena that she is as peaceful as a statue, divorced from the aggression of ordinary people, and Elena acquiesces readily to this soporific state. Indeed, Elena's husband Marvin Howe, as he later explains to her, is attracted to her otherworldly quality: "you're someone in a vacuum, you're from the outside of everything that's physical and degrading."[2] Of course, the problem with being so peacefully outside of the world is that Elena has no connection to it. She has a hand at the usual activities of a normal suburban matron: she entertains, attends charitable functions, takes classes, even receives letters from her husband's mistress, but none of this creates in Elena any stirring of life. As Part One ends she is stuck in time and place, a self without a selfhood, imitating the perfection and permanence of the statue before her:

> She feels very well now, very happy. Yes, yes, everything has come to rest, in perfection it comes to rest, permanent.
>
> 1:45.
> Stopped.
> Permanent.
> 1:45.
> Stuck. She does not move.   (pp. 164–65)

Jack, a stranger, awakens Elena from her trance, and both are aware of a powerful attraction at the first meeting, but Elena resists his initial overture.

One day while in California, however, acting on impulse she phones him and he flies from Detroit to be with her. At first she retains her state of nonfeeling. But months later, after experiencing orgasm for the first time, a permanent change comes over her. Home in her bedroom she "thought with sudden elation: *This is the last time I will sleep here . . .*" (p. 373). Although not literally true, she will not return to that deathly sleep of Sleeping Beauty. She feels the stirring of new life within her, the equivalent of a pregnancy she cannot control or deny. She realizes that she has to leave her husband to affirm her own life. Taking on a self-determinism that she was incapable of before, she becomes the aggressor in the love relationship with Jack. She goes to his apartment and waits for him outside. At the end of the novel they embark on their new life together.

This uncharacteristically happy ending is the first successful liberation through love in Oates's novelistic world. Perhaps the book is dedicated to Patricia Hill Burnett, a prominent feminist, because Oates wants us to view Elena's awakening as an emblem for all women's liberation. While the orgasmic awakening of Sleeping Beauty has its witty dimension, it may evoke no humor in a dedicated feminist, who believes that women can find selfhood without male assistance. But Oates views the libidinal drive as dominant for all human beings—women and men—no matter how they may seek to suppress it. Fulfillment in Oates's works, as in D. H. Lawrence's, can only come when a man and a woman can open themselves up to the emotional and biological drives within themselves; only when they risk loss of control, loss of conscious self, do they have a chance of liberating the true self within. Such a risk is frightening, and many people are incapable of it. Women in particular— biologically receptive rather than aggressive, schooled in passivity—frequently perfect a state of withdrawal, in which they do not risk the frightening loss of control, but in which they perpetuate a selfless void. Elena, Oates's most extreme portrayal of immobility and vacuousness, is awakened initially through her relationship with Jack, but subsequently through her own determined effort to find herself and to live aggressively. Oates takes care to show that Elena's growing consciousness does not depend upon Jack for its completion. Elena views her new aggression as usurping the traditional male prerogative and it offends her feminine sensibilities somewhat; yet she delights in the experimental nature of her impending activities. No longer seeking to freeze into permanence, she welcomes the unpredictability of life, "the possibility of getting him, even the possibility of not getting him" (p. 525). With Elena, Oates is showing that women can break out of stultifying sexual stereotypes and can approach life with zestful independence.

Elena's success story offers the pattern of self-realization which usually eludes Oatesian women of the short stories as well as the novels. Although stories about women are prevalent throughout Oates's canon, *The Goddess and Other Women* focuses exclusively upon them. Jointly these twenty-five stories offer a composite view of women that is probing but disturbing because nearly all are images of Kali, the dark half of female totality. Kali, the unnamed Hindu Goddess specified in the title,[3] appears in the volume as the garish red-and-yellow statuette in the story "The Goddess," "standing with her legs apart, pot-bellied, naked, her breasts long and pointed, her savage fat-cheeked face fixed in a grin, her many arms outspread, and around her neck what looked like a necklace of skulls" (pp. 407–08). The skulls are symbolic of Kali's destructiveness; she is often depicted as feeding on the entralis of her lovers. But for all her terribleness, Kali is yet looked upon not as evil but as part of nature's totality: life feeds on life; destruction is an intrinsic part of nature's procreative process. So, rather than portraying women as our literary myths would have them, which, as Leslie Fiedler and others have pointed out, almost invariably depict women as either good or evil, Oates presents them as locked into the destructive form of Kali, unliberated into the totality of female selfhood.

Some of the stories in *Goddess* depict pre-teens toying exploitatively and dangerously with a sexuality which they don't really understand. Betsy of "Blindfold" and Nancy of "Small Avalanches" are young girls who sexually taunt considerably older men. To be sure, the men are culpable. Betsy's uncle has devised the perverse little game of blindfold, and sexual molestation is the aim of the pursuer in "Small Avalanches." But Betsy and Nancy adopt with facility the mask of feigned innocence and deliberate naïveté. Betsy accepts the private game of blindfold in exchange for her privileged position as favored niece until their game is discovered by a stranger. Then she totally abnegates all responsibility. She cruelly relishes her uncle's death and exposes his weakness to her mother. At a very young age Betsy is learning the exploitative possibilities of sexual attraction. Similarly, Nancy of "Small Avalanches" also enjoys her superior role in the sexual game she finds herself engaged in with the man who follows her in a car and then on foot. Interpreting his pursuit as a childlike game of chase, she giggles and pretends to be ignorant of his aim. When he is overcome by fatigue and heart palpitations, she, like Betsy, cruelly denies any responsibility: "This will teach you a lesson, I thought" (p. 239). She is a young girl learning that sex is an exciting and dangerous game where "winning" is leading on the male and then frustrating him.

A number of Oates's stories in *Goddess* and elsewhere depict a teenage girl on the brink of existential self-definition, as a "good" girl or "bad," as mother's and father's daughter or as an anonymous pick-up. Oates captures so well that point in adolescence when a girl begins to be aware of herself sexually, when she makes tentative gropings out to the world beyond childhood. "The Voyage to Rosewood," for example, depicts a sixteen-year-old, Marsha, who, bored with high school, decides to take a bus ride to another town, anywhere different. Her adventure ends with a beating by a wierd young man, Ike, who had picked her up. At the end of the story her father comes to the police station to take her home. This time she is returned to the parents whom she loves and the world that is familiar, but life is experimental and identity fluid for a young girl like Marsha who out of boredom half-consciously wills her own molestation.

Resilient, daring, and increasingly self-sufficient, Betsy, Nancy, and Marsha approach life experimentally and men exploitatively. In some ways more distressing are the many portrayals in this volume of girls and women who are passive, frightened, withdrawn and unfree. In spite of their inhibition, they are yet capable of unpredictable, violent behavior. They are sometimes the perpetrators, more often the victims of brutal assault.

Sarah of "In the Warehouse" is a small, skinny, insecure twelve-year-old who is totally dominated by her taller, bigger, and extremely abrasive girlfriend, Ronnie. Here Oates is depicting one of those inseparable adolescent relationships, but Sarah is suffering in her unwilling bondage to Ronnie. She plans and executes a brutal escape: she pushes her friend down the stairs of an abandoned warehouse, closing off the cries for help of the dying Ronnie. In murdering Ronnie, Sarah is killing off the frightening and unwanted part of herself and the world. Twenty years later, married with two children, living in a colonial house in a comfortable suburban neighborhood, she tries but is unable to feel guilt for what she did. In destroying Ronnie, Sarah has destroyed her own emotional life. Through her desperate act she has secured a kind of liberation and security, but at a permanent cost to herself as a person. She has made a typical bargain of an Oatesian woman. Like Maureen Wendall of *them*, she has paid dearly for immunity.

Frequently, however, these vacuous Oatesian women become disenchanted with their emptiness and reach out for some confirmation of their being. The girl of "The Girl" is a case in point. Beautiful and bland, the girl eagerly plays The Girl in the makeshift movie of The Director. Even though the action includes a brutal and unannounced assault and rape and the girl is as a result hospitalized, she holds no resentment towards the sadistic director. Seeing him several months later, her only concern is to be assured that there was film in the camera. Pathetically she needs the film to confirm her identity as The Girl since she has no selfhood as a girl.

Oates is aware of the unlimited capacity for self-abnegation and dedication to men of some women. In "A Premature Autobiography" a young girl who is a gifted composer has a brief affair with her one-time mentor, the famous composer Bruer, and then settles for the unchallenging and mundane life of a piano teacher in a teacher's college. Yet when Bruer's autobiography comes out and she is mentioned in one paragraph as a now faceless and nameless girl who Bruer says was talented and devoted to him and to whom "in a way he owes all the work he accomplished at this time (and after this time)" (p. 382), she feels completed and confirmed as a person. Feeling no need now for any further living, she happily embraces her fixed identity as the anonymous woman-behind-the-man.

Often the frustration of women is turned inward in a conscious or unconscious quest for death. So often for Oates's women freedom seems to lie in the deadening of emotion, in the deliberate quest for nothingness. The woman of "& Answers" has such a low self-esteem and so completely disparages women as people that she has unwittingly attempted to kill her daughter and herself. The story consists entirely of answers to apparent questions put to her by a psychiatrist in therapy following her car accident in which her daughter Linda was killed. High school tests indicate that she is an extraordinarily intelligent individual, but she insists that she is perfectly ordinary, average, and uninteresting. Having mastered the art of female self-deprication, she is embarrassed by the psychiatrist's attention and theories. She has an exaggerated respect for men's opinions—all men: "I believe anything men tell me and I always did" (p. 160). But she thinks that "men expect too much" of women, expect "something like God," and women are doomed to disappoint them because they simply are not equal to these expectations. Unknowingly, this mother tried to undo her motherhood because her daughter reminded her too much of herself and she could not bear the thought that her daughter would endure similar emptiness, fearfulness, and anxiety. Oates presents here an extraordinarily painful yet credible portrait of a woman whose wholehearted acceptance of male superiority carries with it a total denigration of herself as a woman.

Not all of Oates's women sit on the brink of suicide or madness, listlessly waiting for something to happen. Some of her most effective stories depict women with successful careers whose professional competence unfortunately is not matched by a similar facility to relate comfortably and wholesomely to men. For example, Jenny, the bright psychiatric intern of "Psychiatric Services," manipulated by her clever patient, becomes entangled in various sexual roles and loses control of therapy. By taking away the gun of her patient she unwittingly plays the role of virgin castrator and confirms his suicidal tendencies, and by listening to his late-night telephone conversations she falls into a pattern of love-play detrimental to their professional relationship. Meanwhile, she plays the dependent daughter to the father-like authority of her superior, Dr. Culloch, who belittles her by sarcastically pointing out how Jenny's feminine responses undermine her role as a professional.

The professionalism of Katherine, the social worker of "Waiting," increases as her emotional responsiveness wanes. She evolves from the eager, concerned girl who takes home the files of her welfare clients and cries over them at night to the efficient casework supervisor who noses out fraud and coldbloodedly enforces welfare regulations. Katherine's personal life undergoes a corresponding change. Pleading that she must care for her invalid mother, she postpones her wedding until her engagement disintegrates and gradually her life settles into an empty routine. Oates incisively yet sympathetically portrays the encroaching narrowness of the life of this woman who closes off her emotions without ever consciously making a decision to do so. The climax of the story comes when Mr. Mott, a former welfare client, encounters her on the street and gives her a ride home. After she invites him in and makes an awkward attempt to play the role of a woman hosting a male visitor, he slaps and lambasts her for her castrating professionalism in her handling of clients and pours out all his resentment against the welfare system. After he leaves, Katherine cries for the first time in years and realizes "there was a lifetime of weeping before her but she did not know why" (p. 282). Oates understands, as Katherine does not, that she has let her professional self engulf her identity as a woman, that professional competence often extracts a high price in a woman's emotional health, that many men carry an inevitable resentment against any woman who has authority over them, and that many women are hopelessly dependent upon male approval to sanction their self-esteem.

Another professional woman who finds herself in a similar situation is Nora, the university professor of "Magna Mater." Nora is a highly respected scholar who is puritanically dedicated to the view that art grows not "out of ordinary, routine, emotional life" but "from a higher consciousness altogether" (p. 205) and who is most happy when emersed in her work: "When she spoke of her work she seemed to move into another dimension entirely—she was not the overweight, perspiring, rather too anxious hostess, but a consciousness entirely freed of the body, of all temporal limitations" (p. 204). But Nora's personal life intrudes upon her professional detachment. Plagued with disquieting relationships with all the males in her life, she yet needs male approval. Her husband has left her for a younger, more attractive woman, and her father, also a famous scholar, is ill and seems to have lost interest in Nora and her work. She finds her precocious, unstable son irrationally demanding and accusing, and his male psychiatrist disrespectfully probing and insinuating. To complete the medley of unhappy relationships, one of her colleagues, Mason Colebrook, nastily tells her of a poem written about her by a former male student entitled "How Leda Got the Swan." Later in a drunken release of inhibition, he pours out all his contempt for her as a scholar and woman. When his wife attempts to apologize for the scene, he yells: "Nora's the same ugly old selfish sadistic bitch she's always been, she won't give a damn, will you Nora?" (p. 208). But Nora feels "again betrayed by a man she had somehow believed . . . might admire her" (p. 209).

Mason's cruel accusation that Nora is an "ugly old selfish sadistic bitch" has some measure of truth. Nora is guilty of being "ugly" and "old"—or at least plain and middle-aged—and women are still most frequently valued or devalued as women on standards of youth and beauty. Indeed, Nora has been attempting to keep her feminine ego intact after her husband's desertion for a twenty-four-year-old woman. Secondly, Nora has been "selfishly" dedicated to her work throughout her life. The "decade of research, teaching, and motherhood madly combined" angered her husband, "not liking the hurried meals, her distraction when he spoke of his work." He is also annoyed that *she* should make the "name *Drexler* known in the Cambridge-Boston-New York area, as if it were truly her name and not his" (p. 187). It is also implied that her father lost interest in her when his daughter's success and fame threatened to outstrip his own. Her son resents her selfish appropriation of a part of her time for her work and for friends, whereas he demands the rights of a son, her undivided attention. Finally, Nora is a "sadistic bitch." In the name of standards of academic excellence, she writes devastating reviews: "she had truly *hated* to say such blunt, irrefutable things about the intelligence that had written it—but unfortunately 'Someone had to do it,' she said" (p. 206). Obviously, she is deceiving herself. She does not hate to do such work, but positively relishes it. She takes a delight akin to the sadistic in destroying her opponent and in the process affirming her own superiority as a brilliant thinker, graceful writer of "loving cadences," and undaunted protectress of excellence Nora's critical reviews are the sublimated expression of her resentment against men. Intellectually if not sexually she has the upper hand, and it wields the castrating knife.

Yet Nora cannot be so easily dismissed with a disparaging diagnosis. She exemplifies the dilemma of the professional woman in Oates's fictional world— if not, indeed, in life. The qualities which make for Nora's success as a scholar— her lucid intelligence, uncompromising standards, aggressive arguments and refutations, cool self-assurance, unstinting dedication to her work—all serve to undermine her image as a woman in the eyes of her family, friends, colleagues, and acquaintances. It is not only Mason Colebrook who accuses Nora of sadistic dominion over men. Her former student sees her as Leda getting the Swan. Her son fantasizes that Nora murdered his father, and he has a recurrent dream where she deliberately drowns him. But Oates offers a balanced view of Nora. She is intellectually arrogant yet highly competent, sadistic in her reviews yet dedicated to her research and to the upholding of academic standards, self-deceived by others, dependent upon the acceptance and praise of others yet capable of carrying on alone. A "magna mater" she is not, however, except in the most destructive sense of the term. Deeply ambivalent about the messy and distracting role of mother, she is excessively impatient with her son, demanding from him a maturity and rationality which this severely unstable child is incapable of. One of Dennis's recurrent nightmares is that a devouring mouth is in the room with him, a fantasy which—along with his compulsive eating—seems to express his regression to the oral phase of libidinal development, a frequent Oatesian pattern. Overcome with separation anxiety, Dennis's infantile response is to fantasize being devoured, drowned, or abandoned, and he attempts to overcome his fears in part through oral gratification, stuffing his overweight body with Ritz crackers. He is a whiny, obnoxious, cruel child largely because Nora's unconscious rejection and her guilty compensations for it create out of their relationship a sick little society of two, increasingly cut off from other human beings.

Nora has juggled her various roles as daughter, woman, mother, wife, scholar, and professor with uneven success. Despite her professional stature, she will never be a liberated woman. Emotionally insecure, she is too entangled in unsatisfactory relationships with men and too vulnerable to their demands and taunts, praise and criticism, attention and inattention.

With Jenny, Katherine, and Nora, Oates is showing that women's professional successes compound their problems in dealing with female sexuality. There is no such thing as neuter ground in Oates's stories, no professional equality for men and women. Women are different biologically, emotionally, psychically, and socially, and their sexuality necessarily enters into all facets of their lives, complicating their relationships with colleagues, clients, and students. The tensions and adjustments demanded by their professional selves, in turn, rebound back on their personal relationships with lovers, husbands, and children. Women are intruders in the male world of professionalism. The violence and aggression which for men is often a healthy release of emotion, for women—when channelled into the competitive drive for success—effects an unhealthy inhibiting and hardening of emotion. Competent women are often seen by the men with whom they work as usurpers of the male role and by the men with whom they deal professionally as castrators of male sexuality. But the most damaging repercussions of a woman's professionalism exist not in the way that others view her, but in the way she feels about herself as a woman. Sexuality is the ultimate reality for men and women in Oates's world, and women pay for their professional success with precious coin, their stifled sexual identities, and in so doing, they assure their perpetual nonliberation.

But the vast majority of Oates's women do not have careers. Their problem is not in reconciling a variety of selves but in coping with selflessness. They are not desexed by their aggressive intrusion into the male world but devitalized by their acquiescence to female vacuousness. Women are victims of an inadequate model of female selfhood. Those very qualities which are considered to be prototypically feminine—passivity, fragility, beauty, sensitivity, and dependence—make many women vulnerable to the harshness of modern life, insufficiently resilient to cope with life's unpredictability. The characteristic Oatesian woman sits around waiting for something to happen, or builds an impenetrable wall around the self so that nothing can happen, or consciously or unconsciously seeks her own death. Oates's work offers a disturbing view of women's incapacity as a group to deal successfully with their sexuality and as a result with experience. It would be simplistic to conclude that all that is necessary is an orgasmic release equivalent to Elena's in *Do With Me What You Will*. Most of Oates's women are so emotionally withdrawn that they are incapable of any degree of healthy sexuality. Oates does not offer any ready solutions. Of course, she has not encompassed the full range of female possibility in her fiction. Instead, she is exploring, more intensively than any other writer, the sexual roots of female nonliberation.

Notes

1. Joyce Carol Oates, *The Goddess and Other Women* (New York: Vanguard, 1974). Hereafter cited by page number in the text.

2. Joyce Carol Oates, *Do With Me What You Will* (1973; rpt. New York: Fawcett, 1974), p. 532. Hereafter cited by page number in the text.

3. In a letter to the author, 22 October 1975, Oates confirms that Kali is the goddess implied in the title: "Kali is the specific 'goddess' of the title, but the collection deals with other manifestations of the 'goddess'—that is, the image of women in both men's and women's imaginations. Most of the stories turn upon the unconscious or partly-conscious manifestations of the feminine archetype in the character; in a story like 'Magna Mater,' the dominant psychic content isn't realized by the character but by the reader. . . . Our lives are largely guided by unconscious contents and when those contents were given clear, definable titles—the 'gods' and the 'goddesses' of antiquity—it was at least easier to know when one was under their enchantment. Today in a secularized world, we fall under the power of various psychic contents and fail to realize that they are altering our lives, or even that they exist. This is the price we pay for our 'rationality.' "

[On Joyce Carol Oates]

Alfred Kazin*

> So the days pass, and I ask myself whether one is not hypnotised, as a child by a silver globe, by life; and whether this is living.
>
> Virginia Woolf
> *Diary*, 28 November 1928

A "sense of fright, of something deeply wrong." In Joyce Carol Oates's most notable novel, *them*, this seemed to express itself as a particular sensitivity to individual lives helplessly flying off the wheel of American gigantism. While writing *them* (a novel which ends with the 1967 eruption of Detroit's Blacks) she said that Detroit was "all melodrama." There a man can get shot by the brother of the woman he is lying next to in bed, and the body will be disposed of by a friendly policeman. The brother himself pops up later in the sister's life not as a "murderer," but as a genially obtuse and merely wistful fellow. Nothing of this is satirized or moralized as once it would have been. It is what happens every day now; there are too many people for murders to count. There are too many murderers about for the murderer to take murder that seriously.

Joyce Carol Oates seemed, more than most women writers, entirely open to *social* turmoil, to the frighteningly undirected and misapplied force of the American powerhouse. She plainly had an instinct for the social menace packed up in Detroit, waiting to explode, that at the end of the nineteenth century Dreiser felt about Chicago and Stephen Crane about New York. The sheer rich chaos of American life, to say nothing of its staggering armies of poor, outraged, by no means peaceful people, pressed upon her. It is rare to find a woman writer so externally unconcerned with form. After teaching at the University of Detroit from 1962 to 1967, she remarked that Detroit is a city "so transparent, you can hear it ticking." What one woman critic, in a general attack on Oates, called "Violence in the Head," could also be taken as her inability to blink social violence as the language in which a great many "lower-class" Americans naturally deal with each other.

Joyce Carol Oates is however, a "social novelist" of a peculiar kind. She is concerned not with demonstrating power relationships, but with the struggle of people nowadays to express their fate in terms that are cruelly changeable.

*Reprinted with permission from "Cassandras," *Bright Book of Life* (New York: Little, Brown, 1971), pp. 198–205.

Reading her, one sees the real tragedy of so many Americans today, unable to find a language for what is happening to them. The drama of society was once seen by American social novelists as the shifting line between the individual and the mass into which he was helplessly falling. It has now become the free-floating mythology about "them" which each person carries around with him, an idea of causation unconnected to cause. There is no longer a fixed point within people's thinking. In the American social novels earlier in the century, the novelist was a pathfinder and the characters were betrayed as blind helpless victims of their fate, like Hurstwood in *Sister Carrie* or virtually everybody in Dos Passos's *U.S.A.* Joyce Carol Oates is not particularly ahead of the people she writes about. Since her prime concern is to see people in the terms they present to themselves, she is able to present consciousness as a person, a crazily unaccountable thing. The human mind, as she says in the title of a recent novel, is simply "wonderland." And the significance of that "wonderland" to the social melodrama that is America today is that they collide but do not connect.

Praising Harriette Arnow's strong, little-known novel about Southern mountain folk, *The Dollmaker*, Joyce Oates said:

> It seems to me that the greatest works of literature deal with the human soul caught in the stampede of time, unable to gauge the profundity of what passes over it, like the characters of Yeats who live through terrifying events but who cannot understand them; in this way history passes over most of us. Society is caught in a convulsion, whether of growth or of death, and ordinary people are destroyed. They do not, however, understand that they are "destroyed."

This view of literature as silent tragedy is a central descripttion of what interests Joyce Oates in the writing of fiction. Her own characters move through a world that seems to be wholly physical and even full of global eruption, yet the violence, as Elizabeth Dalton said is in their own heads—and is no less real for that. They touch us by frightening us, like disembodied souls calling to us from the other world. They live through terrifying events but cannot understand them. This is what makes Oates a new element in our fiction, involuntarily distrubing.

She does not understand why she is disturbing. She takes the convulsion of society for granted, and so a writer born in 1938 regularly "returns" to the 1930s in her work. *A Garden of Earthly Delights* begins with the birth on the highway of a migrant worker's child after the truck transporting the workers has been in a collision. Obviously she is unlike many women writers in her feeling for the pressure, mass, density of violence in American experience not always shared by the professional middle class. "The greatest realities," she has said, "are physical and economic; all the subtleties of life come afterward." Yet the central thing in her work is the teeming private consciousness, a "wonderland" that to her is reality in action—but without definition and without boundary.

Joyce Oates is peculiarly and painfully open to other minds, so possessed by them that in an author's note to *them* she says of the student who became the "Maureen Wendall" of the novel, "Her various problems and complexities overwhelmed me. . . . My initial feeling about her life was, 'This must be fiction, this can't be real!' My more permanent feeling was, 'This is the only kind of fiction that is real.' " Her ability to get occupied by another consciousness makes even *them*, her best novel to date, a sometimes impenetrably voluminous history of emotions, emotions, emotions. You feel that you are turning thousands of pages, that her world is as harshly overpopulated as a sleepless mind, that you cannot make out the individual features of anyone within this clamor of everyone's existence.

This is obviously related to the ease with which Joyce Oates transfers the many situations in her head straight onto paper. I sense an extraordinary and tumultuous amount of purely mental existence locked up behind her schoolgirl's face. She once told an interviewer that she is always writing about "love . . . and it takes many different forms, many different social levels. . . . I think I write about love in an unconscious way. I look back upon the novels I've written, and I say, yes, this was my subject. But at the time I'm writing I'm not really conscious of that. I'm writing about a certain person who does this and that and comes to a certain end." She herself is the most unyielding lover in her books, as witness the force with which she follows so many people through every trace of their feeling, thinking, moving. She is obsessive in her patience with the sheer factuality of contemporary existence. This evident love for the scene we Americans make, for the incredible profusion of life in America, also troubles Joyce Carol Oates. Every writer knows himself to be a little crazy, but her feeling of her own absurdity is probably intensified by the dreamlike ease with which her works are produced. It must indeed trouble her that this looks like glibness, when in point of fact her dogged feeling that she writes out of love is based on the fact that she is utterly hypnotized, positively drugged, by other people's experiences. The social violence so marked in her work is like the sheer density of detail—this and this and this is what is happening to people. She is attached to life by well-founded apprehension that nothing lasts, nothing is safe, nothing is all around us. In *them* Maureen Wendall thinks:

> Maybe the book with her money in it, and the money so greedily saved, and the idea of the money, maybe these things weren't real either. What would happen if everything broke into pieces? It was queer how you felt, instinctively, that a certain space of time was real and not a dream, and you gave your life to it, all your energy and faith, believing it to be real. But how could you tell what would last and what wouldn't? Marriages ended. Love ended. Money could be stolen, found out and taken . . . or it might disappear by itself, like that secretary's notebook. Objects disappeared, slipped through cracks, devoured, kicked aside, knocked under the bed or into the trash, lost. Her clearest memory of the men she'd been with was their moving away from her. They were all body then, completed.

The details in Oates's fiction follow each other with a humble truthfulness that make you wonder where she is taking you, that is sometimes disorienting, for she is all attention to the unconscious reactions of her characters. She needs a lot of space, which is why her short stories tend to read like scenarios for novels. The amount of *listening* this involves is certainly singular. My deepest feeling about her is that her mind is unbelievably crowded with psychic existences, with such a mass of stories that she lives by being wholly submissive to "them." She is too attentive to their mysterious clamor to *want* to be an artist, to make the right and well-fitting structure. Much of her fiction seems written to relieve her mind of the people who haunt it, not to create something that will live.

So many inroads on the suddenly frightening American situation is indeed a problem in our fiction just now; the age of high and proud art has yielded to the climate of crisis. Joyce Oates's many stories resemble a card index of situations; they are not the deeply plotted stories that we return to as perfect little dramas; her novels, though they involve the reader through the author's intense connection with her material, tend as incident to fade out of our minds. Too much happens. Indeed, hers are altogether strange books, haunting rather than "successful," because the mind behind them is primarily concerned with a kind of Darwinian struggle for existence between minds, with the truth of some limitless human struggle. We miss the perfectly suggestive shapes that modern art and fiction have taught us to venerate. Oates is another Cassandra bewitched by her private oracle. But it is not disaster that is most on her mind; it is the recognition of each person as the center of the coming disturbance. And this disturbance, as Pascal said of his God, has its center everywhere and its circumference nowhere.

So her characters are opaque, ungiving, uncharming; they have the taciturn qualities that come with the kind of people they are—heavy, hallucinated, outside the chatty middle class. Society speaks in them, but *they* are not articulate. They do not yet feel themselves to be emancipated persons. They are caught up in the social convulsion and move unheedingly, compulsively, blindly, through the paces assigned to them by the power god.

That is exactly what Oates's work expresses just now: a sense that American life is taking some of us by the throat. "Too much" is happening; many will disappear. Above all, and most ominously, hers is a world in which our own people, and not just peasants in Vietnam, get "wasted." There is a constant sense of drift, deterioration, the end of things, that contrasts violently with the era of "high art" and the once-fond belief in immortality through art. Oates is someone plainly caught up in this "avalanche" of time.

Through Obsession to Transcendence: The Lawrentian Mode of Oates's Recent Fiction

G. F. Waller*

Situated somewhere near the center of the frenetic fictional activity of our time, "celebrating darkly the traditional pieties of the novel,"[1] as Ihab Hassan puts it somewhat disapprovingly, lie the novels of Joyce Carol Oates. Since 1963, she has published prolifically and while it is still perhaps too soon to speak of major developments in her fictional mode, in her work since 1975 and 1978—five volumes of stories, three novels, a novella, and two collections of poems, not to mention the uncollected essays, poems, and stories which have appeared in a variety of journals from *Southern Review* to *Redbook*—we can perhaps sense a gradual and perhaps major change.[2]

As a Canadian resident since 1968, Oates enjoys an unusual perspective in North American fiction. From Windsor, Ontario, she looks across the Detroit River into what she sees as the "transparent" heart of an America which emerges from her fiction as a felt experience rather than a perceived place. "The border between two nations," she writes in one of her stories about American immigrants to Canada, "is always indicated by broken but definite lines" (*CB*, p. 13): thus boundaries enable us to enter into relationships, to understand as well as to separate. For Oates "Canada" becomes as much a state of mind as "America"—"Canada" is the perspective of a writer compelled to write about what she senses to exist both within and outside her, and "crossing the border" into Canada affords her a fictional or prophetic perspective, not merely a political refuge. It allows her to focus on the obsessions of a civilization without being overwhelmed by them. Indeed, "obsession" is a key concept in understanding Oates's recent development. Her approach to fiction has always been obsessive. More than most novelists, and akin to D. H. Lawrence, her fictional mode has developed a distinct state of feeling thrust at her reader. Some of the most compelling writing in comtemporary fiction forces upon readers an often frightening sense of our own fears, obsessions, and drives. Indeed, her work operates in terms best described by that increasingly fashionable motif in the

*This essay was written especially for this collection, and is used with the permission of the author.

161

contemporary fictional theory, the notion of the "implied reader." The "convergence of text and reader brings the literary work into existence,"[3] argues Wolfgang Iser, and in Oates's fiction we have a vivid example of how a writer must rely heavily on the emotional cooperation of the reader. Her geographical landscapes evoke our own emotional or moral dilemmas and allegiances and in reading her we attend not so much to the shifts of plot or scene but to our own changing emotional reactions.

Indeed, in its insistence upon its readers' involvement, Oates's fiction is an excellent test case for the increasingly fashionable phenomenological emphasis on text-as-experience. It has been argued—for instance on the philosophical level by such writers as Maurice Merleau-Ponty and Paul Ricoeur—that our reading of a text is never divorced from a context of feeling. As opposed to a response of a text as an object-in-the-world, in the manner of New Criticism, for instance, reading is described by phenomenological critics as a process in which we are engaged or confronted by a level of feeling, what Merleau-Ponty calls *sens emotionnel*, or Heidegger terms *Stimmung. Stimmung bestimmt*: mood determines, argues the sociologist-playwright-theologian Werner Pelz, paraphrasing Heidegger. Without plunging into the middle of this whole critical debate, which seems bound to dominate Anglo-American critical theory for the next decade or more, we might note how well Oates's work fits into such categories. In Heidegger's words, "it is we ourselves" who are "the entities . . . analysed." It is from the midst of our own "throwness" that we respond to the text before us, and it is our awareness of our felt contingency that opens up Oates's fictional mode to our experience.[4]

"Feeling," writes Paul Ricoeur—arguably the most suggestive theorist of the new criticism—"is the manifestation of a relation to the world which constantly restores our complicity with it." In order for her novels, to use D. H. Lawrence's phrase, to "inform and lead into new places the flow of our sympathetic consciousness," Oates's fiction plunges us into a distinctively felt atmosphere. She is attempting to evoke peoples' struggles to "order their fantasies, their doubts, even their certainties, into an external structure that celebrates the life force itself, the energy of life." As well, she writes, "The use of language is all we have to put against death and silence." The form, or formlessness, of her work, then, is deliberately perspectival as we, her readers, are driven to create the form, or formlessness, or our own lives and our own private fictions.[5]

Along with the overriding apprehension that, as Alfred Kazin observes, "nothing lasts, nothing is safe, nothing is all around us," there is also in Oates's fictional world something of what she perceives in Lawrence's poetry, where one finds "literally everything: beauty, waste, 'flocculent ash,' the ego in a state of rapture and in a state of nausea, a diverse streaming of chaos and cunning." In Oates's work such chaos is invariably situated in the emotions, in the convulsive eruption of obsessive feeling, in the pain, anguish, distraught embarrassment, and violence of the personality.

"I sometimes write as if to relieve my mind of things that haunt it," Oates has said, but one outcome of her therapeutic approach to art is to face her readers with their own disturbances, just as D. H. Lawrence, in shedding his own sickness in his novels, moves his readers (often violently) to an awareness of their own psychic and spiritual health or destructiveness. Indeed, Oates's fiction can be tellingly approached through a Lawrentian perspective. Her brilliant account of Lawrence's poetry—surely, despite its brevity, one of the most suggestive pieces of Lawrence criticism in recent decades—speaks of him in terms that strangely reverberate upon her own approach to the artist's role. Lawrence, she writes, "is one of our true prophets," especially in his "moody and unpredictable and unreliable" contemporaneity, speaking from the total engagement of his art to the chaos and disorder and the hope of our era. "He is fascinated by the protean nature of reality, the various possibilities of the ego," and in that openness lies his prophetic relevance, his "deep, unshakeable faith in the transformable quality of all life." Interestingly, Lawrence's art may often seem, like Oates's own, slapdash, urgent, repetitive. He "seems to be writing, always writing, out of the abrupt, ungovernable impulses of his soul," which he refuses to shape into perfected, and so completed, art. In the prophetic flux of Lawrence's art, "aesthetic standards of perfection . . . are soon left behind by the spontaneous flow of life." Lawrence himself wrote of *Women in Love*: "This novel pretends only to be a record of the writer's own desires, aspirations, struggles; in a word, a record of the profoundest experiences in the self."[6] Fascination with flux, with art as prophecy, with the therapeutic exposure of the self—these central Lawrentian motifs are fused and re-created in Oates's work.

Another central Lawrentian motif in Oates's work has been what Lawrence called the "spirit of place." It emerges as an obsession with the spirit or structure of feelings, of a setting, not with its surface or geographical details. Even the most factual descriptions of highways, gas stations, or motels are part of a mythopoeic rather than a naturalistic world. The smallest details of domestic life may be loaded with threat; seemingly innocent traits of personality or small incidents will open up fearful significance. Oates's America is an experience, not a place; it is what our personalities create as well as what we are thrown into. Oates draws her readers into a world simultaneously jarring, gross, violent, and yet metaphysically whole. There is a vastness of metaphorical suggestion that points through surface details of setting, character, and story to a consistently organized, complex pattern of feeling. She has an awesome ability to show the interpenetration of material or personal detail with significance. She seems, at times, as one reviewer noted, "an inspired medium in contact with characters already formed in the dreamscape of her imagination."[7] She reveals an awesome ability to immerse herself in the phenomenology of the contemporary and to convey the morphology of searching for meaning in a dream-haunted America—writing not only about the search for meaning itself, but what it feels like to feel that search as a constant, infinitely detailed and surprising experience. Reading the best of her fiction we are struck again and again by how she conveys the mythic significance of the most common or materialistic aspects of America, not in the classic Puritan manner of allegory, spelling out a meaning as Hawthorne, say, does with the garden in "Rappac-cinni's Daughter," but through rendering the surface detail symbolically trans-parent through constant psychological or emotional intensity, most especially by means of the felt pressure of obsession.

From her most recent work, that of the late seventies, we can see emerging the outlines of a fictional mode that uses this obsessiveness she sees as so central to the American experience and which is so integral a part of her own aesthetic, but seeks a transcendence of that obsessiveness. One of her recent collections of stories, *The Poisoned Kiss*, speaks of Oates herself being "possessed" by an imaginary author, one Fernandes de Briao. Although "he has no existence," she writes, without his guidance "I would not have had access to the mystical 'Portugal' of the stories—nor would I have been compelled to recognize the authority of a world-view guide antithetical to my own" (*PK*, p. 15). "Posses-sion" is an explanation for the intensity—what I have called the obsessiveness—with which she experiences and by which she is forced to articulate her vision. The stories collected in *Night-Side* show a similar fascination with the irrational invasion of the personality by alien, unpredictable forces. "Famine Country" evokes the impact of strange dreams which highlight the banality of the person-ality's everyday, material life and a strange, neglected area of the personality traditionally represented by religious or mystical experience. Ronnie, the cen-tral character, is invaded by two dreams: one, a "student-dream," concerned with incomprehensible examinations and buildings, the other, the terrifying, alienating "God-dream" which confronts him with a radical and unprepared-for invasion of his life. In "Further Confessions" a Portuguese nobleman (re-lated to the persona of the Fernandes stories) is similarly disturbed by dreams and visions. Starting as a man "far more than most, *attuned* to the world," he is horrified by the intensity and alienation of his dreams—of his own death, of his father—so much that he is cut off from all his former life, and made to face the primacy of the nonhuman, "the vast indifferent spaces of the world itself—the 'world' as it exists emptied of the human and of all human values" (*NS*, pp. 310, 311). These stories remind one of Borges, and while there is a genuine con-tinuity with Oates's earlier work—violence, dream, and vision have always been means of shock or recognition in her work—it seems that, like Borges, Lawrence, and in some ways like Doris Lessing, she is pushing her work toward the mystical and prophetic, grappling with areas of experience traditionally regarded as beyond fiction-making.

As if to highlight her sense of her own transition as a novelist, Oates has written of our civilization as "approaching a kind of manic stage," preparing itself for "a transformation of 'being' similar to that of individuals as they approach the end of one segment of their lives." "We are approaching," she argues, "the end of a traditional ego-centered consciousness," and she discusses with a fascinating mixture of hostility and homage the poetry of Sylvia Plath as exemplifying how the West's "very masculine, combative" spirit has become pathological so that "whoever clings to its outmoded concepts will die."[8] Her long novel, *The Assassins*, is a grim evocation of this pathological consciousness.

It depicts the reactions of the Petrie family, close-knit, upper-crust, "famous for the transactions viciousness can make with civilization," to the assassination of one of its members, a right-wing politician and philosopher. His death is a reminder of the ego's inability to transcend the sheer brutality of the world of grasping egotism, status, and violence, in which no object can possibly satisfy our needs. Even sexual love is an unreality, merely a "blur of motion" (*ASS*, pp. 45, 53), and its exaltation of the personality a delusion. Individually, we are obsessive seekers of meaning, but we inevitably find that meaning comes to us as a gift: it cannot be willed into existence.

In *Wonderland* the mystery of the individual personality in its fragility was constantly bombarded by the crude materialism of time and space and yet remained the final realm of human meaning. In *The Assassins* Oates suggests, more radically that the Western emphasis on the reality of the personality is an illusion, as much a material snare as roles imposed by the world of medicine, law, politics, or even art. Whereas in *Do With Me As You Will*, the lovers' struggle toward authenticity, however painful a process, was made possible because romantic love contained the seeds of its own transcendence, in *The Assassins*, no activity, however temporarily fulfilling, can do anything but fragment us. Even the contemplative Stephen Petrie, of all the family the least dragged down by a preoccupation with ego, panics before the possibility of total self-surrender. As a child, he has pored over an old map and sensed the impermanence of anything recognizably personal and historical. He sees the seemingly unchanged natural features of an apparently familiar world—rivers, lakes, mountains—but "everything that belonged to a specific moment in history, everything specifically human" is impermanent and unreal. He struggles to learn to abandon such reliance on the idea of a permanent, fixed self. He alone knows, even if fitfully, of the terrible unreality of the material world and the grasping egos which inhabit it. What alone seems real are the fleeting experiences of escaping the entrapment in the flesh, in the ego, in any kind of connection with the world: "Not existing, not wishing to exist, he lived a life of constant surveillance; his host was *Stephen Petrie* and he was forced to dwell within that host, sharing a common bloodstream, common organs, a skeleton, a dim reservoir of memories" (*ASS*, p. 446).

What vision of the universe is Oates offering us in *The Assassins*? Initially, we are faced with a paradox. The world the Petries have inhabited through their history is a world of fact, materialism, cause and effect. And yet, beneath this hard, rational, competitive world we are forced to sense that somehow another level of reality operates. Events occur without apparent reason or cause; the world seems locked together by "certain patterns, certain non-casual events" (*ASS*, p. 160), where the concept of the "cause" of a violent death may be irrelevant to the real spiritual reverberations that surround an individual's death. A sense of premonition, a sudden emptiness of personality, may be truer reflections of the ultimate reality of things than the usual account by cause and effect. The "assassins" are, in the everyday world of fact, causality, and material reality, an unknown group of murderers; the real assassins may equally be those grasping, destructive egos with which we are burdened and with which we collide. On the spiritual level, we are all assassins. Andrew Petrie "provoked someone into killing him" (ASS, p. 4), broods his brother, and we sense that Yvonne, too, is a victim of her own as well as her husband's spiritual destructiveness. We are in a world of accumulated spiritual violence, distorted energy, and thirsting egos so that violence, even apparently random, becomes seemingly the inevitable outcome. The gruesome death of Yvonne, hacked to pieces by some unknown assailants, possibly those who killed her husband, seems to be a manifestation, causeless and yet at the same time determined, of the distortion of a universe from which she cannot escape and which she is both a victim and a willing participant. Oates eerily draws us into a view of the world which, it should be noted, has been implicit in her fiction from the beginning, but which only in *The Assassins* is given what almost amounts to an explicit philosophical backing. The world, Hugh's psychiatrist suggests, is "so constructed . . . that there is a network of relationships invisible" unless one is enabled to wave aside "the mists of what is known as 'common sense' "—and so discover "certain patterns, certain noncausal events" (ASS, p. 160). The events of *The Assassins* provide us with such a pattern, "a rent in the cosmic fabric through which all sorts of ugly things poured" as Andrew's cousin Pamela puts it.

How do we find meaning in such a universe? At one point Hugh broods that "when there is no meaning to events, we are surly, dissatisfied, deathly," and then immediately balances his feeling by the observation that "when there is too much meaning, we are terrified" (ASS, p. 100). Does the world have a given meaning? Are our grasping egos so frightened by the possibility of meaninglessness that we must find or impose a meaning to justify our uniqueness? The possibility that Andrew's death had *"No meaning to it"* terrifies his brother: "merely things that happened, to him and to others bound closely to him. Stray formless events—whispers that never rise to coherence—repugnant to me" (ASS, p. 112). For the Western mind, trained and guided by rationality and causality, there must be "a reason for everything. Nothing without its reason." Otherwise, we panic: "Causality: sanity. Chaos: unsanity" (ASS, p. 238).

In her book on Lawrence, Oates comments on the revolutionary implications of Lawrence's poem "Fish":

> . . . my heart accused itself
> *Thinking: I am not the measure of creation.*
> *This is beyond me, this fish.*
> *His God stands outside my God.*

Oates argues that "calm and matter-of-fact as this statement is . . . it is a total rejection of that dogma of the West that declares *Man is the measure of all things*" (NHNE, p. 79). Only the personality-bound ego must project its own need for justification upon the universe. We may be seekers of meaning, but we inevitably find that meaning comes to us; it cannot be created or willed into existence. "The universe," wrote Lawrence, "is like Father Ocean, a stream of all things slowly moving," with "each other, living or unliving" streaming "in its own, odd, intertwining flux." "Nothing," he goes on, "not even man . . . nor anything that man has thought or felt or known is fixed and abiding." Our life consists not in desiring to be everything, not in conquering and achieving power over the material world. The power over the world such as that sought by the Petries is, in Lawrence's words, "a platitudinous bubble." The true way of discovering meaning is "not to *have* all . . . not to *grasp* everything into a supreme possession," but to achieve a pure relationship of acceptance and change with the circumambient universe.[9]

How paradoxical it is, in both Lawrence and Oates, that a passionate concern with personality, singleness of being, and commitment, should lead to a no less passionate celebration of a mystery beyond personality! Lawrence, says Oates, "allows this experience—whatever it is—to take possession of him; he does not attempt a false possession of it." But in the world of this novel, none of the characters escapes the endless circles of the world. Andrew Petrie is dead, Hugh prostrate with brain damage, Yvonne dead: everyone is doomed. Even Stephen, with his vision which allows him to accept the world as unreal and deceptive, can find no way of relating that vision to the world into which he is thrown.

The Assassins is Oates's most forbidding novel to date and seems to mark a crossroad in her vision of America. She has progressed from observing and evoking the tragic irony of the dislocation between dream and materialism in America; here, the dream is not only deceptive but unreal. The only reality is renunciation, and yet modern America cannot escape the bondage of its history. *The Assassins* seems to reach this despairing conclusion: we are bound to a world into which we have been thrown, a world measured by the "hours" of the novel's subtitle, and from which there apparently is no escape.

Many of the stories written about the same time have concentrated on the similar struggle of the personality to define itself in a world where dream, ideal, and striving are constantly and brutally materialized. Neurosis may be, paradoxically, healthy in such a world. "The impulse to 'make well' may be the most sinister of Western civilization's goals," Oates suggests. Violence, too, may be a means of cleansing and affirmation. Her novella, *The Trimph of the Spider Monkey*, is a super-realist evocation of Bobbie Goteson, a maniac killer and suicide. His insanity is a multiplicity of survival techniques, "forms of sanity that keep moving and eluding definition." The acts and articulations which society regards as "the graphic workings of a sick mind" are radical challenges to the cloying, material, stereotyped judgments of that society. "Love," Bobbie broods, "does us all in . . . We falter, stumble, stoop over, steal fire . . . and are punished, mocked, picked to death by tiny painted nails, ooooh'd and aaaah'd over by tiny button-like lips" (*TSM* pp. 13, 45). His rapes, muggings and brutal killings are therefore assertions of his self, the more fearful because they are the microcosmic manifestation of a whole society. This novella deepens Oates's fascination with obsessive violence as a means of transcendence—in the figure of Jules in *them*, for example. Pain, fear, and vulnerability are experiences by which we are challenged to reach beyond ourselves; anguish, "passion and its necessary violence" may become our route to transcendence.[10] The stories in *The Seduction*, for instance, grow from Oates's concern with the vulnerability and unpredictability of the personality in its struggles with sexual roles and stereotypes. Contemporary men and women too often experience their sexuality as either derangement or fate. Love and terror, ecstasy and dislocation of the personality seem inevitably interwoven. "What is the connection between men and women?" "What does it feel like to be a woman?" "I—I want—I need . . ." are typical of the obsessive questions and ejaculations that form the psychic landscape of her stories. Her characters are overwhelmingly manipulated by their obsessions, caught in patterns of biological, social and emotional determinism they barely understand. Her women characters especially are rigidly encased in their mental concepts of the self, hypersensitive to their ego's fragility, fearful of their bodies' darker urges, buffeted by and largely formed by others' reactions and desires. The stories overwhelmingly point to the deep-rooted and fearful determinism of contemporary women. The stereotypes we have inherited are seemingly bound into our deepest demands; even when they are demonstrably social in origin, they seem to become inexplicably rooted in our chemistry. With few exceptions, the greatest achievement of Oates's women is just to survive.

Some of the stories in this and other recent collections focus on the myth, so widespread in our culture's history, of the greater body-consciousness of women. Oates treats it as a fearful source of psychic confusion, frustration, and violence and, only very occasionally, of liberation. Her women are victims: they are obsessively used, exploited, often virtually invented "to explain the humiliating chaos" of a man's life, or else victimized by their own half-understood drives or desires. However indignantly they (and we) may reject such stifling roles, too often we are driven by barely understood forces that constantly re-create the sexual roles we try to destroy. Oates passionately asserts that "the mechanical fact of possessing a certain body" should not "determine the role of the spirit" since "to have the spirit trapped in an unchosen physical predicament . . . is a kind of death."[11] Yet too rarely can sexual love offer the possibility of transcendence. Occasionally, she evokes the possibility that love may be a surprising rediscovery of our deepest hopes and that through the terror and vulnerability it offers, we may be given the gift of transcendence.

Increasingly, however, these recent novels and stories are pointing, as Lawrence did, beyond sex, beyond personality. For the western mind, the personality's fulfilment has traditionally been an individual one. Oates seems to be moving closer to an Eastern doctrine of *annatta* or *nirātina* (non-ego) where negation becomes the means to overcoming the bondage of desire and ego-centricity. Only by self-abandonment, letting be, can the endless material circles and our culture's stifling roles and stereotypes be overcome. Both *The Assassins* and the next novel, *Childwold*, articulate this viewpoint. *Childwold* focuses on the love between a middle-aged recluse and a fourteen year old hillbilly girl. It alternates between fearful evocations of a frenzied, obsessive passion and a lyrical search for transcendence. We sense the surprise of love and fear of its final unreality; we are caught, as the book's hero Kasch is, between individual fulfilment and the entrapment of life in the flesh. And finally, we sense the terror of a world where we may pursue our deepest obsessions and find them defeated not by their inherent good or evil but by the arbitrariness and, paradoxically, the determinism of the material universe.

More than any of Oates's earlier novels, *Childwold* relies on fragments of interior narrative and revelation, on partial and dislocated understanding held together largely by an atmosphere of intensity. All the major characters have their own narrative voices: an objectified "you" for Laney as if a narrator were providing the confused, semiliterate girl with an articulate voice as she looks back at the events; the direct and obsessive "I" of Kasch, also remembering what he announces in the book's first paragraph to be "that final year of my life"; and a host of voices that swirl around—confusing, violent, voices of the present or the familial past, all of which seem to bear down upon the central actions. We are given glimpses of people and events in the lives and ancestry of both Kasch and Laney—Irish and German immigrants, Laney's grandfather and her brother Vale, a violent, predatory Vietnam veteran, rural superstitions, Kasch's parents and family. Overwhelmingly we sense that every incident in the present is subtly and unconsciously determined by people and actions of our pasts—our ancestors live through our apparently autonomous actions and dimly grope and battle within us. The book's overall atmosphere is therefore one where motives and intentions dissolve under the pressure of a multiplicity of intangible or unknowable factors, where obsessive leaps at freedom are at once the only authentic human actions and yet those most rigidly predetermined.

Like *The Assassins*, *Childwold* is a book of hours, thrusting at us the eerie fear of the ultimate unreality of time, the body, the personality itself. Kasch apprehends himself as "pure consciousness trapped in time, in a body" (*CW*, p. 126), and he is torn between the enjoyment and surprise of the present that his love for Laney opens to him and his fear of its final unreality. "How real the world strikes us, the world of the present moment. . . . Tactile, it is; palpable. Demonstrable (Aquinas: Knowledge begins with the senses.)" (*CW*, p. 128). Kasch knows, intellectually, that *"existence involves changes and happenings"* (*CW*, p. 129) and yet he is deeply aware too that "the body must be an error. . . . Nothing can explain it, that we are trapped for a certain period of time in a fleshly vehicle. Cruel, cruel. Capricious" (*CW*, p. 225).

Although it clearly continues many of Oates's typical themes and the obsessional drives of her early novels, *Childwold* is also a moving and powerful indication of her growing technical skills. It is probably the most skilfully constructed of her novels since *them*. It evokes with care and power the obsessive desire for transcendence, but it does so by seizing upon the moments and fragments in our lives when we are threatened or invaded. While *Childwold* recapitulates familiar themes from her work—the emphasis on the falsity of fixing the self, the awareness that "the interior life constitutes the authentic life," and that "reality is what I am thinking, what is thinking through me"

(*CW*, p. 138), the tragic arbitrariness of the physical universe. But alongside *A Garden of Earthly Delights*, or even *Wonderland*, the novel is amazingly sophisticated and complex in its narrative form, continually forcing us to make connections, puzzle over motives, and participate in the obscure surges of powerful feeling that are both the book's subject and its most impressive technique. It takes us into areas of desire and terror we recognize, from which we are glad to escape, as we are glad to escape from the concentration of tragic intensity of *Macbeth* or *King Lear*. To live by obsession totally is to go mad, but—at least as Oates articulates it in her novels—except through facing and, through fiction, reliving our obsessions, we will hardly be able to face the possibility of transcendence that those obsessions yearn for.

Son of the Morning (1978) extends Oates's thematic interests into a familiar yet rarely explored area of contemporary experience, evangelical religion. Yet it seems to mark a technical regression in her work. It is the autobiographical calling-to-account of Nathan Vickery, an evangelist who emerges from the Eden Valley (a setting reminiscent of *Childwold* and returning, of course, to the milieu of the early fiction) to preach a gospel of radical spiritualism and of the absolute Otherness of God. The novel has the familiar emotional landscape of violence, obsession and what Oates has consistently seen as the tragic yet (given the dynamics of our history) inevitable striving towards a dualistic repulsion towards the world, the body, sexuality and the self. The novel contains passages of fearsome intensity but, as well, a great deal of flat narrative padding. It is as if Oates is fumbling, not quite finding the right fictional vehicle to articulate her evident fascination with religious experience. The novel's dedication is addressed to "One Whose absence is palpable as any presence-" and, unquestionably, it contains extended passages of intensely focussed obsessive narrative equal to those in, say, *Childwold* in which the *deus absconditus* Oates so clearly feels as part of contemporary experience is evoked in clarity and compelling terror. But alongside Coover's *The Origins of the Brunists* it lacks narrative and, thereby, intellectual coherence. Yet as with much of Oates's writing (her poetry comes most immediately to mind) where the obsessive vision is frustrated by its inadequate articulation, the reader nonetheless is gripped and fascinated by the seriousness of the vision and by the underlying restless search for a breakthrough in form which will be adequate to that vision.

As with any artist growing through a major transition, Oates's recent work is frequently uneven and unpredictably regressive or experimental. Such formal unevenness can be easily explained by her conception of the novelist's role. Like Lawrence, she has always conceived of the novelist as a prophet, with technique often (perhaps too often) coming, as Lawrence himself put it, from the end of the pen. Her vision, too, has consistently relied on evocation to an unusual degree. Above all she tries to shock and disturb her readers by the intensity of what she observes and senses about our lives. Much as Lawrence did, she is forcing us to confront ourselves at the boundaries of experience. As well, she makes us aware, perhaps uncomfortably, of the role of the reader, critic and, especially, the teacher of her work—to struggle with her, helping through dialogue to make other readers sense the importance of their own, subjective wrestling with the issues the writer thrusts before us. I have frequently used Lawrence as a companion through this essay because, of all major modern writers, he can remind us most powerfully of the way the novelist meditates not on abstract ideas but on the age's changing structures of lived feeling—and also because, above all else, Lawrence's vision is thrust before us in particularities. Like Lawrence, Oates's work articulates for us both our ideological dynamics and the more complex structures of feeling which lie deeper than the surface of our age. Around the words and the structures of our idioms and patterns of thought accrete subtly, often contradictory, implications, which the great artist—a Shakespeare, a Hawthorne, a Lawrence—struggles uneasily to verbalize, knowing uneasily the problem of articulating the movement of an age while living through it. As Oates's skills as a novelist have developed, her work has increasingly evoked the confusing experience of our time and, more importantly, related our chaotic and imperfectly apprehended experiences to wider patterns of significance. Her importance for us is seen partly in the seriousness with which she sees the writer's dual, and perhaps contradictory, role of submerging herself in our age, and partly as well, in her struggle to achieve a transcendence of our time in her articulation of it. In Oates's most recent work one now discerns a movement, observable in her essays as well as her fiction, towards a fascination with Eastern renunciatory philosophical modes. It is as if the violence and egocentric destructiveness which have been such tragic outcomes of Western history and philosophy must somehow be transcended by embracing the opposite vision. Of course such a development in Oates's thinking is prefigured in Lawrence's own. Lawrence, too, came to despair at the cultivation of the uniqueness of the self which has been so fundamental to Western consciousness. His later vision is not unlike that of Oates in *The Assassins*, where we first see, in her novels, her espousal of something akin to Eastern renunciation, a growing interest which seems to be entering all her work in the mid-seventies. On the surface, such a development is strange in writers like Oates and Lawrence, so imbued with the possibilities of transcendence achieved through the flesh, and it may be that the next stage in her career will show her developing in surprising, even more experimental, directions.

Possibly more than any American novelist now writing, Oates has shown herself sensitive to the eddying feelings of living in the 1960s and 1970s. But of course we look to writers to respond to more than the intellectual or social fashions of their age. Oates sees the cultural roles of the artist as that of struggling with and articulating the underlying, ongoing movements of feeling, not merely its glittering surface. As readers and critics, we are, or should be, concerned continually with creating the necessary active relationship between art and our society's whole way of life at this fundamental, underlying level. In doing so, we may realize the crucial importance of art in our lives. Too often, we are tempted to take refuge—from our society, ultimately from ourselves—in an apparently autonomous aesthetic world; too often, too, as critics and scholars, we have constructed abstract and generalized world views and then tri-umphantly set an author within them. This equally is a kind of escapism. For a society's ongoing life is lived in individual men and women, within their spe-cific and changing lives—and it is the vocation of the artist to probe and capture that particularity in all its contradictions, tensions, confusions, or uncertainties.

As Oates presents us, we are a people between ages, living in a time of not yet. We are obsessed with what limits us most, and yet we believe passionately that it is through our obsessions that we will transcend them. She has been presenting our time of transition as one of a breathlessness and struggle, where obsession, not renunciation, has seemed the only authentic means to transcen-dence. It may be, as she has started to affirm, that our struggles for uniqueness will be transcended by a "new heaven, new earth" of egoless involvement and compassion, where struggle will not be destructive, where fulfillment wil come through self-transcendence not self-affirmation. Recently she has written, com-paring our age with Lawrence's, that "our own era is one in which prophetic eschatological art has as great a significance as it did in 1916; Lawrence's despairing conviction that civilization was in the latter days is one shared by a number of our most serious writers, even if there is little belief in the Apoc-alypse in its classical sense."[12] As with Lawrence, it is to the apparent impasse of our civilization that Oates's fiction offers its most radical challenge. What, it asks, are the possibilities that await us, and dare we meet them?

Notes

1. Ihab Hassan, *Paracriticisms: Seven Speculations of the Times* (Urbana: Univ. of Illinois Press, 1975), p. 105.

2. The works primarily under consideration here are as follows: *The Poisoned Kiss* (New York: Vanguard, 1975), *The Seduction* (Los Angeles: Black Sparrow Press, 1975), *The Assassins: a Book of Hours* (New York: Vanguard, 1975), *Crossing the Border* (New York: Vanguard, 1976), *Childwold* (New York: Vanguard, 1976), *The Triumph of the Spider Monkey* (Santa Barbara: Black Sparrow Press, 1976), *Night Side* (New York: Vanguard, 1977), *All the Good People I've Left Behind* (Santa Barbara: Black Sparrow, 1978), *Son of the Morning* (New York: Vanguard, 1978). In the text they are abbreviated as follows, in the order above: *PK, SD, ASS, CB, CW, TSM, NS, AGP, SOM*.

3. Wolfgang Iser, *The Implied Reader: Patterns of Communication in Prose Fiction from Bunyan to Beckett* (Baltimore: Johns Hopkins Press), p. 275.

4. Martin Heidegger, *Being and Time*, trans. J. Macquarrie and E. Robinson (New York: Harper, 1962), p. 67.

5. Paul Ricoeur, *Fallible Man*, trans. Charles Kelbley (Chicago: Regnery, 1965), p. 129; D. H. Lawrence, *Lady Chatterly's Lover* (Harmondsworth: Penguin Books, 1962), p. 104; Joyce Carol Oates, "Remarks by Joyce Carol Oates Accepting the National Book Aware for *them*," Vanguard Press Release, March 4, 1970, pp. 1–2.

6. Alfred Kazin, *Bright Book of Life: American Novelists and Storytellers from Hemingway to Mailer* (Boston: Little, Brown, 1973), p. 202; Joyce Carol Oates, *New Heaven New Earth* (New York: Vanguard, 1974), pp. 41–45; Joe David Bellamy, *The New Fiction: Interviews with Innova-tive American Writers* (Urbana: Univ. of Illinois Press, 1976), p. 26; D. H. Lawrence, *Women in Love* (New York: Viking Press, 1920), p. x.

7. Paul D. Zimmerman, "Stormy Passage," *Newsweek*, July 26, 1976, p. 74.

8. Joyce Carol Oates, "New Heaven and Earth," *Saturday Review*, 4 Nov., 1972, pp. 52, 54; *New Heaven New Earth*, pp. 114, 119.

9. D. H. Lawrence, "Art and Morality," *Phoenix*, ed. Edward D. McDonald (New York: Viking Press, 1972), p. 525; "Democracy," *Phoenix*, p. 707.

10. "Transformation of Self: An interview with Joyce Carol Oates," *Ohio Review*, 15 (1973), 52.

11. "Art" Therapy and Magic," *American Journal*, 1 (July 1973), 78; "Transformation of Self," p. 52.

12. Joyce Carol Oates, "Lawrence's Götterdämmerung: The Tragic Vision of *Women in Love*," *Critical Enquiry*, 5 (1978), 562.

INDEX

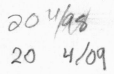
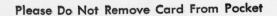

Please Do Not Remove Card From Pocket

YOUR LIBRARY CARD

may be used at all library agencies. You
are, of course, responsible for all materials
checked out on it. As a courtesy to others
please return materials promptly — before
overdue penalties are imposed.

The SAINT PAUL PUBLIC LIBRARY

DEMCO